International Perspectives on Education

Also available from Continuum

Comparative and International Education, David Phillips and Michele Schweisfurth
Introduction to the Philosophy of Education, Richard Bailey
Education Studies, Sue Warren
Exploring Key Issues in Education, Derek Kassem and Dean Garratt

International Perspectives on Education

Edited by

Chau Meng Huat
and
Trevor Kerry

continuum

Continuum International Publishing Group

The Tower Building   80 Maiden Lane, Suite 704
11 York Road   New York
London SE1 7NX   NY 10038

www.continuumbooks.com

© Chau Meng Huat, Trevor Kerry and Contributors 2008

© Howard Gardner, Harvard University, USA

British Library Cataloguing-in-Publication Data
A catalogue record for this book is available from the British Library.

ISBN: 9781847063878 (paperback)
       9781847063861 (hardcover)

Library of Congress Cataloging-in-Publication Data
International perspectives on education/edited by Meng Huat Chau
and Trevor Kerry.
    p. cm.
Includes bibliographical references and indexes.
ISBN-13: 978-1-84706-386-1 (hardcover)
ISBN-10: 1-84706-386-1 (hardcover)
ISBN-13: 978-1-84706-387-8 (pbk.)
ISBN-10: 1-84706-387-X (pbk.)

1. Comparative education. 2. Education–Cross-cultural studies.
   I. Chau, Meng Huat. II. Kerry, Trevor. III. Title.

LB43.I594 2008
370.9--dc22   2008018057

Typeset by Newgen Imaging Systems Pvt Ltd, Chennai, India
Printed in Great Britain by MPG Books, Cornwall

Contents

List of figures and tables

Figures

Tables

About the editors and contributors

Chau Meng Huat is head of an academic department at Batu Pahat MARA Junior Science College in Malaysia. His teaching experience has spanned a wide range of ages and interests, from kindergarten and primary school pupils, to secondary, high school and university students, to in-service teachers. With MARA, he writes, teaches and runs teacher development courses. He is also a member of the MARA committee that develops a national English language curriculum which focuses on increasing learners' confidence to use the language. At the international level, he is a founding member of the *International Society for Language Studies* and has published mainly on English language education.

Professor Trevor Kerry is Professor of Education Leadership at the Centre for Educational Research and Development at Lincoln University (UK) and the university's first Emeritus Professor. His career has spanned spells in primary, secondary, further and higher education, as well as teacher education. He has been a Senior General Advisor with a Local Authority and an Ofsted Inspector. He was Professor of Education at the College of Teachers (UK), and its Senior Vice-President and journal editor. He has written nearly 200 journal articles, and published education books with Macmillan, Routledge, Blackwell, Nelson Thornes and Pearson/Longman. He has also published an eco-history text.

Emeritus Professor Alan Bishop was Professor of Education at Monash University, Melbourne, Australia between 1992–2002. He edited (1978–90) the international research journal, *Educational Studies in Mathematics*, published by Kluwer, and has been an Advisory Editor since 1990. He is Managing Editor of the book series *Mathematics Education Library*, also published by Kluwer (1980–present). He is the author and editor of several influential books, reports, articles and chapters on mathematics education, and he is also the Chief Editor of the two *International Handbooks of Mathematics Education* (1996 and 2002) published by Kluwer (now Springer).

Howard Gardner is John and Elisabeth Hobbs Professor of Cognition and Education at the Harvard Graduate School of Education and Senior Director (and founding member) of Project Zero. Gardner, famous for his theory of multiple intelligences, has recently (with colleagues) been studying 'good work' – work that is at once excellent in quality, personally engaging and carried out in an ethical manner (see goodworkproject.org). He is the author of over 20 books in 26 languages. Gardner received a MacArthur Prize Fellowship in 1981. In 1990, he was the first American to receive the University of Louisville's Grawemeyer Award in Education, and in 2000 a fellowship from the John S. Guggenheim Memorial Foundation. In 2005, he was selected by *Foreign Policy* and *Prospect* magazines as one of the 100 most influential public intellectuals in the world.

George Jacobs Ph.D., works with schools and tertiary institutions in Singapore and elsewhere. For example, he teaches distance education courses for US teachers via Loyola Marymount University in Los Angeles. George has more than 75 publications on cooperative learning. His most-translated book is *Teachers' Sourcebook for Cooperative Learning* (Corwin) (www.georgejacobs. net). George serves on the Executive Board of the *International Association for the Study of Cooperation in Education*. He uses cooperative learning in his own teaching to teachers and students, and he attempts to apply the central cooperative learning principle and positive interdependence, in other areas of his life as well.

Kristján Kristjánsson received his Ph.D. from the University of St. Andrews, Scotland. He is Professor of Philosophy in the Faculty of Education, University of Akureyri, Iceland, and at the School of Education, University of Iceland. He is the author of *Social Freedom* (Cambridge University Press 1996), *Justifying Emotions* (Routledge 2002), *Justice and Desert-Based Emotions* (Ashgate 2006) and *Aristotle, Emotions and Education* (Ashgate 2007). He has also published a number of papers in international journals on issues in moral and political philosophy, philosophy of education, emotion theory and moral education.

Li Xishuang or Lisa (lisa20051972@126.com) graduated from Shanghai Teachers' University. She has taught English at the secondary level in Shanghai for 13 years. In 1999, she participated in a training course for English teachers at Lancaster University where she learnt about Communicative Language Teaching. From November 2006 to January 2007, she studied at the National Institute of Education, Nanyang Technological University in Singapore. Her areas of special interest include cooperative learning, communicative language teaching and reading methodology. Recently, she has started to implement cooperative learning in her classes. She wishes to continue to collaborate with colleagues in Shanghai, elsewhere in China and internationally via publications, conferences, workshops, email and face-to-face interaction.

John Loughran is Foundation Chair in Curriculum and Professional Practice in the Faculty of Education, Monash University, as well as Associate Dean. His research and teaching interests are based on the development of teachers' knowledge and how that is influenced and developed through teacher preparation, beginning teaching and professional development. His research has spanned both science education and the related fields of professional knowledge and reflective practice. John was Director of Teacher Education at Monash for five years. John is the co-editor of *Studying Teacher Education* and is a member of the editorial boards of *Research in Science Education, Teacher Education Quarterly* and the *International Journal of Reflective Practice*. He has a plethora of publications to his name.

John MacBeath, OBE is Professor Emeritus at the University of Cambridge and Director of Leadership for Learning the Cambridge Network. From 1997–2000 he was a member of Tony Blair's Task Force on Standards. He has been a consultant to numerous international bodies including the OECD, the European Commission and the Hong Kong Education Bureau. His recent books include *Schools on the Edge* (Sage), *School Inspection and Self Evaluation* (Routledge) and *Leadership for Learning: International Perspectives*, with YC Cheng (Sense Publishers). He is currently President of the *International Congress on School Effectiveness and Improvement*.

Colleen McLaughlin is a Senior Lecturer at the University of Cambridge Faculty of Education. She has taught in secondary schools and worked as an advisor in a local education authority (LEA). She teaches, writes, researches and consults on personal, social and emotional development. She edits the journal *Pastoral Care in Education*. She has been involved as an advisor to government and NGOs on the personal and social dimensions of schooling. She has researched care and counselling in schools, positive alternatives to school exclusion, bystander behaviour in bullying and how universities can work in partnership with schools to generate useful educational knowledge.

John (Jack) Miller has a BA from the University of Missouri, a MAT from Harvard University and a Ph.D. from the University of Toronto. He has been working in the field of holistic education for over 30 years. He is author/editor of more than a dozen books on holistic learning and contemplative practices in education which include *The Contemplative Practitioner, The Holistic*

Curriculum and *Educating for Wisdom and Compassion.* He also has written two books on curriculum theory: *The Educational Spectrum* and *Curriculum: Perspectives and Practices.* His writing has been translated into seven languages. Jack has worked extensively with holistic educators in Japan and Korea for the past decade and he has been visiting professor at two universities in Japan: Ritsumeikan University in Kyoto and Kobe Shinwa Women's College.

Wee Tiong Seah is a lecturer of mathematics education in the Faculty of Education, Monash University, Australia. He is also the Deputy Course Director of its primary education courses. His activities in the mathematics education research arena in Australia, and East and Southeast Asia have resulted in the conduct of collaborative research and consultancy activities in no less than eight countries in these regions over the last few years. Within Australia, Wee Tiong is member of the federal government's Expert Advisory and Research Group. Wee Tiong's research interests include the harnessing of socio-cultural factors in the teaching of mathematics, particularly values.

Wang Aili or Alice (teachinglearner@hotmail.com) teaches at a teacher education institution in Shanghai, China. She was a chemistry teacher and an English teacher in junior middle schools for 21 years. Her interests include second language teaching, teacher education, cooperative learning and reading methodology. Her interest in cooperative learning began with a meeting with Geroge Jacobs, but she was already employing Communicative Language Teaching (CLT) methods in her second language teaching. In CLT, the emphasis is on using the second language to communicate on matters related to students' lives and interests, while the focus on language as an object becomes secondary. Group activities feature prominently in CLT. Therefore, learning about cooperative learning was a natural next step for her.

Xie Yongye (Clark) has taught in secondary schools for 23 years. His students are from the 15–18 age group. Xie thinks highly of student-centred learning. He graduated from Anhui Institute of Education and had one year's training in East China Normal University and three months' training in the National Institute of Education, Nanyang Technological University in Singapore. His future plan is to increase his use of concepts derived from the theories of educational psychology (such as student-centred learning and cooperative learning) in his classes. He has already applied some of these concepts, with positive results. He thinks that arousing students' interest is paramount in providing them with opportunities to experience the learning process.

Dr. Michalinos Zembylas is Assistant Professor of Education at the Open University of Cyprus and Director of Curriculum Development for the Centre for the Advancement of Research and Development in Educational Technology (CARDET). His research interests lie in the area of exploring how discursive, political and cultural aspects define the experience of emotion and affect in education. He is particularly interested in how affective politics intersect with issues of social justice pedagogies, intercultural and peace education, and citizenship education. He has published articles in scholarly journals, and edited books and presented his research in national and international conferences around the world. He has also published the books *Teaching With Emotion: A Postmodern Enactment* (Information Age Publishing 2005) and *Five Pedagogies, a Thousand Possibilities: Struggling for Hope and Transformation in Education* (SensePublishers 2007).

Preface: the intentions of this book and how to use it

This book is intended for two main groups of educators. The first consists of all those who have an interest in education as an academic area or from the perspective of applied theory: undergraduate education students, trainers and university lecturers; higher degree students; and those involved in, or training for, the teaching profession. The second group consists of those who are concerned with the management and governance of education: those who formulate national and local policy, those charged with inspecting or advising the profession and those (such as head teachers and school governors) whose task is to guide others.

The chapters in this book are written by leading thinkers and practitioners in their respective fields. Each chapter can be accessed as a resource on the specific topic. But the chapters are also grouped into three sections: *Perspectives on education*, *Supporting the learning process* and *Teachers and professional development*. These three sections each provide an invaluable source of thinking and knowledge about the nominated area.

While the value of drawing on the knowledge and experience of a distinguished team of international educationists and publishing them in an edited collection is obvious, the individual papers should not be seen as 'right answers', but as a means of asking the 'right questions'. Thus, two important features forming part of the framework of each chapter should be highlighted here.

First, *Reflection* boxes are interspersed throughout each chapter. That is, each chapter pauses at several points in the argument to invite the reader to engage in a *Reflection*: to consider – and, by implication, to challenge and question – the argument so far.

Second, there is a *Further reading* section at the end of each chapter which selects some key texts that can be followed up by those who wish to take the chosen theme further, as well as providing a range of references on the theme.

Other features include a glossary at the end of the book that defines the key terms introduced in the text. These key terms are printed **bold** in the body of the text.

In these ways we hope the book remains true to the intentions expressed by the contributors about the interactive nature of education and learning.

Introduction
Chau Meng Huat and Trevor Kerry

An education that leaves young people alienated from the challenges and pleasures of learning, or places them in an environment of exclusion, rejection, violence and discrimination, cannot be an education of quality. Nor can an education that leaves young people bewildered, confused and perplexed in their attitudes and beliefs.

Koïchiro Matsuura, Director-General of UNESCO

As the quotation indicates, there is a need for the learning experience and environment to be not only stimulating and intellectually interesting, but also socially inclusive and fulfilling; there is also a need to develop learners' potential and personality around a set of good values and equip them with positive attitudes. All this lies essentially at the heart of quality education.

That is the prevailing view shared by a distinguished group of scholars who have contributed to this volume, *International Perspectives on Education*. With an emphasis on developing social and personal capacity in young people (among others), this collection of chapters reflects the development of education within an international context of trends, good practices and experience. A major concern in compiling and editing this volume has been to present and highlight debate, discussion and illustration of current issues in a variety of institutional, geographic and social contexts from different parts of the world.

International Perspectives on Education addresses contemporary issues in education by offering both conceptual foundations and practical strategies to the teaching profession for their critical review and exploration. Section 1, *Perspectives on education*, deals largely with how education is viewed. It raises some issues about education by examining the theoretical underpinnings of a number of recent approaches. In the first chapter, Gardner reviews his now familiar theory of multiple intelligences and suggests five kinds of minds that need to be cultivated in the future. They are the disciplined mind, the synthesizing mind, the creating mind, the respectful mind and the ethical mind. It is the latter two kinds of minds – which have to do with the human sphere – that Gardner seeks to privilege. In Gardner's words:

> Our challenge in the world is not in accumulating more knowledge – we are very good at that. Our challenge is to mobilize the knowledge that we have, in the service of ends that we can justify aloud to ourselves and to others; to follow principles even when they go against our self-interest; to take the risk of speaking out when we see injustices occurring; and, to the extent that we can, to create or join institutions that reflect our higher values, our better selves . . . That is why I seek to privilege the respectful mind and the ethical mind. (Chapter 1, p. 26)

This emphasis on personal and social development is shared by McLaughlin in her chapter that explores the personal, social and cognitive needs of young people. McLaughlin argues that these aspects are inextricably linked to, and influenced by, the learning processes in school, and that it is time to reform the connections between the three. This would involve a wider conception of the goals and pedagogies that we use in schools. In this respect, Kristjánsson's call in Chapter 3 for cultivating students' self-confidence is a welcome reminder of how young people approaching secondary-school age can be engaged with school life. Kristjánsson argues for the educational value of self-confidence by exploring two popular versions of individualized education – personalized learning and differentiated instruction. He concludes that self-confidence is an aspect of self-concept that needs to be seriously considered and retrieved.

The final chapter of this section, by Miller, explores the concept of the thinking heart and how it can be developed through holistic education. For Miller, holistic education focuses on interconnectedness. Some examples of connections that can be forged and established in the curriculum include those between various forms of thinking, connecting body and mind, and making connections between various subjects. It is argued that to develop the thinking heart both traditional forms of professional development that focus on theories and instructional strategies, and a range of contemplative and spiritual practices that lead to an awakening and development of the thinking heart need to be considered.

Section 2, *Supporting the learning process*, turns our attention to the classroom setting. It focuses on developing effective educational environments by showcasing a range of instructional practices that all teachers may apply or adapt locally to the needs of their student populations. The chapter by Kerry which opens this section aims to give the reader an overview of the range of intentions and purposes of education, and to draw from these an agenda of teaching skills required of an effective teacher. These skills are individually considered, with suggestions for further study that might help the teacher to develop professionally in the identified areas. The chapter concludes with a brief consideration of how personal growth might be supported by continuous professional development and by arguing that teaching is both a science and an art.

With group activities becoming increasingly common in education, the chapter by Jacobs, Wang, Li and Xie highlights the importance of cooperative learning. However, the authors also caution that groups of students can sit together and even produce a group product without cooperating at a high level. Nevertheless cooperation can be enhanced when students share their thinking with each other by telling and showing each other what is going on in their minds as they go about completing a task. The authors do exactly that: they remind us of the benefits of cooperation, they urge all teachers to persevere in the use of cooperative learning and they share with us cooperative learning principles and techniques. In this sharing – which is essentially an act of cooperation in and of itself – the authors make their thinking audible and visible to us, thereby setting an example for us to follow and bringing alive the central argument of this chapter.

The theme of developing effective educational environments as part of affective education is further pursued in Chapter 7 by Bishop and Seah who advocate teaching desirable values through mathematics education. However, this is, as the authors suggest, problematic at present because little is known about what happens with values teaching and learning in mathematics classrooms and how potentially controllable and effective such values teaching is. Bishop and Seah report three research projects that relate to 'values through mathematics' and make the case for researching teachers' values. They conclude by suggesting some teaching activities as well as teacher strategies to negotiate perceived value differences, all of which potentially foster and develop values in mathematics classrooms.

Section 3, *Teachers and professional development*, moves the debates on into the training process and into the realm of classroom teaching and continuing professional development. This section invites the reader to explore the complex and dynamic nature of teaching, and the need for a well-articulated teacher education. The opening chapter, by Loughran, offers an overview of some issues and ideas in developing and articulating a pedagogy of teacher education. Loughran suggests that the nature of teaching, and learning about teaching, is complex and that teaching requires skills, knowledge and ability that need to be recognized and acknowledged in the pursuit of quality in teacher education. He argues that making such knowledge public is a crucial element in creating deeper understandings of practice and in better valuing teaching and teacher education.

There is now a growing body of literature on caring teaching and Chapter 9 by Zembylas provides an overview of these conversations in education. The author draws implications from these particularly in terms of the emotional labour involved when an ethic of caring teaching is practised. This chapter puts forward the argument that it may be too deterministic to outline a number of principles and practices for caring teaching, given the competing perspectives of care in education. The goal is therefore not to create a list of principles and practices, but to outline a number of possibilities that are opened when school cultures are organized in ways that engage caring relationships. The chapter identifies some general ways with which practitioners may begin to formulate and sustain school cultures of care.

The final chapter, by MacBeath, reports on a study commissioned by the National Union of Teachers to assess the impact of government initiatives on the professional lives of teachers in secondary schools in England. It draws out some of the key themes and raises the questions of how these may be common or different in differing cultural contexts. While the chapter reveals a crucial conflict between the professional educator and government policy-makers, MacBeath makes the important point that 'from time to time, under the weight of government policies, we need to be reminded about the purposes and process of education, respect for the professionalism of teachers, and collaborative inquiry' and that 'strong leading edge schools . . . are characterized by a confident moral centre nurtured by critical inquiry, self evaluation, collaborative planning, peer observation and by moral leadership'.

The chapters in this book have been contributed by a group of international scholars from across a range of countries and disciplines upon the invitation of the first editor in October 2006 after a conference he chaired with the motto of 'Quality Education'. The contributors' brief contained few constraints on their choice of subject matter, and no close guidance on how their work should be packaged. Yet to read this text one could be forgiven for thinking the situation otherwise for, out of these collected works on what international educationists deem to be 'issues', have emerged a number of common themes. What characterized these themes is a move, for the most part, away from the political contexts in which the management of education is controlled at national levels.

So what are these themes?

What has struck the editors most forcefully as they have pored over the contributions is the number of times that individuals, working independently, have emphasized aspects of the importance of the affective domain. Here, the constant pressures in the daily lives of teachers to teach a specific set of materials, to assess every element of student outcomes from that teaching, to put didactic methods at the forefront of their work, to record and regulate everything that students do, to conform to government targets, to subject themselves to inspection based upon these political criteria – all of these pressures have been abandoned. Such abandonment is not in the cause of lowering standards and sacrificing quality, but in enhancing the learning experience of students, in making learning enjoyable, in providing content that is meaningful in real contexts and in the involvement of students in their own learning.

These themes, spontaneously selected by our authors, have been about developing positive values, about learning in groups, about paying more than ill-thought-through attention to individual learning, about creativity by students and by teachers, about caring as the root of student-teacher relations, about effectiveness in applied contexts, about the interdependence of types of subject matter, about giving meaning, about taking into account social contexts. They have been about matching the training of teachers to the kinds of pedagogies that achieve these desirable ends.

Over the last three decades education has lost its human face in an understandable, but misguided, attempt to tie its products and processes more closely, indeed too closely, to models generated in the world of commerce or of the market place. Now is the time for a new debate: not the de-humanization of education but the re-humanization of it.

While not sacrificing the quality that is demanded of learning and learners in an industrial and knowledge society, how can teachers and students make schools and colleges places that are vibrant, stimulating, intellectually interesting and socially cohesive? More importantly still, in a world where increasing levels of experience are at second hand (via a computer screen), where respect for others is diminishing because of the erosion of social skills, where the dogma of rights is replacing the doctrine of responsibility, where values are being eroded away and conflicts stirred up by instant media reporting, how then can students be nurtured in positive attitudes and productive skills?

It is an important question because clearly it is not happening universally at present. It is important because, unless an answer is found, the world will become a less pleasant place. It is important because the politicians who control education policy certainly do not have the answer. But here, in the themes of our authors, may be the germs of a solution that will lead to this new era.

These themes may herald a revolution, albeit a quiet revolution. There is much to be done, across the world, to persuade politicians that education is not mere rote learning and mindless regurgitation to whatever standard of excellence. The results will not be instant or the road without its turnings.

Yet it is a revolution worth striving for, worth waiting for, worth working for.

Most of us, parents, teachers, administrators, managers, even students, would rather that education was based on a sound and coherent blend of learning and teaching; that it was conveyed in cohesive surroundings and situations; that the process was creative, challenging and imaginative; and that the outcomes evinced acknowledged values and applications.

Most of us know that this is not what happens in many schools right now, though there are plenty that strive to those ends and many dedicated teachers.

Most of us are aware that no political decrees or legislation will bring about the revolution in education that we all need; that it is not a matter of structures or systems or procedures – it is a battle for the mind and the soul.

So we hope that this book will be, in a very real sense, futuristic: that in a decade or two decades of time, a reader will be able to recognize it as a prelude and prediction of 'a new time coming' and, hopefully by then, come.

If so, we will have fulfilled our intentions.

Section 1
Perspectives on education

Multiple lenses on the mind
Howard Gardner
Harvard University, United States

1

This chapter reviews three major lines of work: first, how the mind is organized; second, how various changes of mind take place; and third, five kinds of minds we will need to cultivate in the future. Three of these minds have to do with cognition: the disciplined mind, the synthesizing mind and the creating mind. The other two, equally important, have to do with the human sphere: the respectful mind and the ethical mind. The chapter concludes by arguing that we should mobilize the knowledge that we have, in the service of ends that we can justify aloud to ourselves and to others to follow principles even when they go against our self-interest; to take the risk of speaking out when we see injustices occurring; and, to the extent that we can, to create or join institutions that reflect our higher values, our better selves.

Some words about my background

Ever since I can remember, I've been interested in the mind. I remember the first time that I heard about the academic field of psychology. When I was a teenager, my uncle, Fred, the intellectual in the family, gave me a psychology textbook. I leafed through it until I saw a section on colour blindness. I happen to be colour blind, quite severely so. It was fascinating to read about this disorder and to know that scientists have deciphered some of the mechanisms of colour vision and devised tests for delineating various kinds of colour blindness.

I did not pursue the study of colour vision. Nor, indeed, did I take any psychology courses when I was in college. But I did become fascinated by the writings of Erik Erikson, a student of Freud's and an expert on human personality and human development. Erikson wrote more insightfully than anyone else about growing up in Soviet Russia, Nazi Germany and the United States of the first decades of the 20th century. Erikson became my tutor for two years and, through this privileged 'back door', I learned about human development, personality and psychoanalysis.

I thought that I would go on to graduate study in clinical psychology – the closest academic area to Erikson's own studies. But then one of those flukes occurred that alter one's life. I hitched a ride from Cambridge, Massachusetts to Ann Arbor, Michigan and learned that Jerome Bruner – a distinguished psychologist, a *real* psychologist – was looking for students to work on an interesting educational project. Bruner and colleagues were designing a social studies curriculum for fifth graders – 10-year-olds. The name of the curriculum was *Man: A Course of Study* (1965). It was designed to answer three questions: What makes human beings human? How did they get that way? How could they be made more human? I was mesmerized by Bruner's impressive intellect and magnetic personality, the intriguing questions raised in the course, the literally dozens of talented scholars whom Bruner had gathered around him and the challenge of teaching concepts of kinship, linguistics, myth and the human life cycle to 10-year-olds. Without fully realizing it, I was shifting my interest from personality and psychotherapy à la Erikson to cognitive studies and developmental psychology, à la Bruner. And within a year, I was enrolled in a doctoral program at Harvard, trying my best to understand how the mind develops and how it works in the mature, productive adult.

Let me provide a few contextual remarks. First of all, as a young person, the child of refugees from Nazi Germany, I had been a good student and a serious musician. When I began to study 'real' psychology, I was intrigued by the fact that the arts were rarely mentioned in serious psychology circles. To have a mind was to be a scientist, or at least to think scientifically; many psychologists were ex-engineers or suffered from physics envy; the last thing that they wanted to do was to be seen as artistic 'softies'. Early on, I decided that I wanted to illuminate the nature of artistic thinking. Also, I was particularly interested in issues of creativity – how does a person conjure up something new, whether it is a sonnet, a symphony, a sketch or a scientific theory?

The science of psychology and the Cognitive Revolution

For much of the 20th century, psychology was dominated by behaviourism – the science of the black box. The leading figure was B. F. Skinner. Skinner believed that the purpose of psychology was to predict and control behaviour, and controllers achieved their ends by varying rewards and punishment. Skinner was good at moulding behaviour – he could take pigeons from a Cambridge park and teach them to play ping-pong. But the limits of behaviourism were well illustrated by a famous joke. Two behaviourists make love: the first says to the second, 'Well, it was great for you – but how was it for me?'

As I was beginning my formal doctoral studies in the mid-1960s, an intellectual revolution was beginning. It was called the Cognitive Revolution and, later on, in my book *The Mind's New Science*, I became the first chronicler of the Cognitive Revolution (Gardner 1987). The Cognitive Revolution had a number of characteristics. For our purposes, the major goal of the Cognitive Revolution was to peer inside the behaviourist's black box – to figure out how the mind and, ultimately, the brain operate. Cognitive psychologists believe that the mind deals with various kinds of mental languages – which are called 'mental representations'. The job of cognitive scientists is to identify the key mental representations and to figure out how they work. Among the famous cognitive scientists are Jean Piaget (1953), the developmental psychologist; Noam Chomsky (1965), the linguist; and Herbert Simon (1997), the inventor of artificial intelligence. And nowadays, almost everyone would add that cognitive science has merged with the study of the brain, *in vivo*, as well as *in vitro*. We no longer talk much of cognitive science – we speak now of cognitive neuro-science.

My first studies

For the first 10 years of my professional career, I studied how the mind develops in children and how it breaks down under conditions of brain damage. As you may know, the single most important thing about a brain lesion is where the damage is. If one is right-handed, and suffers injury in the middle areas of the left hemisphere, one is likely to become aphasic – to have a major disturbance of one's language facilities. But if one suffers injury to the right hemisphere, one's language will be ostensibly fine, but, depending on the location and depth of the lesion, one is likely to be impaired in musical cognition, spatial cognition, and/or one's understanding of other people.

With normal and gifted children and with brain damaged adults, I studied how human beings deal with various kinds of symbols. As I've already mentioned, I had a particular interest in the arts. And so I studied the development and breakdown of musical abilities, graphic abilities, metaphoric and narrative capacities, and other abilities crucial in the arts. Of course, when one looks at these abilities, one necessarily encounters non-artistic capacities as well – mastery of ordinary language, calculation, understanding of other persons and the like.

At the time that my studies began, I had been a convinced Piagetian – I believed that logical-mathematical thought was the centre of all cognition. I believed that children passed through a series of qualitatively different stages, and that their mental world gets remade, whenever they enter the next stage. I believed that cognitive development is completed by the middle of adolescence, at the latest. And I never thought at all about intelligence tests.

I still think that Piaget is the greatest student of the development of the mind. Every student of cognitive development owes an incalculable debt to Piaget. And yet, with the benefit of hindsight, I can see that during that decade, I gradually lost my Piagetian religion. By 1980, I believed that there were a series of relatively independent cognitive capacities of which logical-mathematical thought was only one. I believed that stages were much looser than Piaget had envisioned, and, more importantly, that one's sophistication with one kind of mental representation did not predict one's sophistication with other mental representations. I believed that cognitive development continues well past adolescence, and that various cognitive capacities – like creativity, leadership and the ability to change the minds of other persons – remain to be illuminated, despite Piaget's remarkable achievements. Finally, I had become deeply estranged from standard intelligence (IQ) testing.

© Howard Gardner, Harvard University, United States

These opening remarks have identified the organization of the rest of this chapter, in which I want to review three major lines of work:

1. How the mind is organized – which introduces the theory of multiple intelligences.
2. How individuals – and particularly leaders – succeed or fail in changing the minds of other persons.
3. What kinds of minds we will need to cultivate in the future.

The organization of the mind

In the West, a certain view of mind has held sway for a century. Dating back a century to the time of the French psychologist Alfred Binet, psychologists believe that there is a single intelligence, often called 'g' for general intelligence (Binet 1916). We are born with that intelligence – our intelligence comes from our biological parents and, as a result, intelligence is not significantly alterable. We psychologists can tell you how smart you are – traditionally, by giving you an IQ test; more recently, by examining the shape of your brain waves; perhaps ultimately, by looking at a chip on which your genes are encoded.

My research in cognitive development and cognitive breakdown convinced me that this traditional view of intellect is not tenable. Individuals have different human faculties and their strength (or weakness) in one intellectual sphere simply does not predict whether a particular individual will be strong or weak in some other intellectual component. I developed a definition of intelligence – a bio-psychological information-processing capacity to solve problems or fashion products that are valued in at least one community and culture. I think of the intelligences as a set of relatively independent computers. One computer deals with language, a second with spatial information, a third with information about other people.

But how to figure out what is the right set of computers? I came up with a set of eight criteria of what counts as an intelligence. Unlike most approaches to intelligence, the criteria were not dependent on the results of a paper-and-pencil test. Rather I looked at criteria from neurology (which brain regions mediate particular skills), anthropology (which abilities have been valued in different cultures across history and pre-history), and special populations (such as prodigies, savants and individuals with learning disabilities). All these individuals have jagged intellectual profiles – ones not easily explained if one believes in a single 'general intelligence'.

Ultimately I came up with a list of eight, possibly nine intelligences. I will mention each, and then give examples of individuals or roles that stand out in that particular intelligence:

1. Linguistic intelligence: the intelligence of a writer, orator, journalist.
2. Logical mathematical intelligence: the intelligence of a logician, mathematician, scientist. Piaget thought that he was studying all of intelligence, but he was really focusing on this particular intelligence.

   Most tests of intelligence focus on logical and linguistic intelligence. They do a pretty good job at predicting success in school – but not nearly as good a job as last year's grades! My goal is not to denigrate these traditional *scholastic* intelligences, but rather to give equal attention to other intellectual faculties.
3. Musical intelligence: the capacity to create, perform and appreciate music. Some people call this a talent. That is fine, so long as you recognize that being good with words or with numbers is also a talent. What I cannot accept is that linguistic facility is deemed intelligence, while skill with music or with other persons is *merely* a talent.
4. Spatial intelligence: the capacity to form mental imagery of the world – the large world of the aviator or navigator, or the more local world of the chess player or the surgeon – and to manipulate those mental images.
5. Bodily kinaesthetic intelligence: the capacity to solve problems or fashion products using your whole body, or parts of your body, like your hands or mouth. This intelligence is exhibited by athletes, dancers, actors, craft people, and, again, surgeons.

   The next two intelligences have to do with the world of human beings.
6. Interpersonal intelligence: the understanding of other persons – how to interact with them, how to motivate them, how to understand their personalities etc. This skill is obviously important for people in business, teachers, clinicians and those involved in politics or religion.
7. Intrapersonal intelligence: the capacity to understand oneself – one's strengths, weaknesses, desires, fears. Access to one's emotional life is important for intrapersonal intelligence.

   Whether or not you have heard of the multiple intelligence theory, you have certainly heard of emotional intelligence. What Daniel Goleman (1998) means by emotional intelligence is similar to what I mean by the personal intelligences.
8. Naturalist intelligence: the capacity to make consequential distinctions in nature – between one plant and another, among animals, clouds, mountains and the like. Scientist Charles Darwin had naturalist intelligence in abundance. Most of us no longer use our naturalist intelligence to survive in the jungle or the forest. But it is likely that our entire consumer culture is based on our naturalist capacity to differentiate one car make from another, one sneaker from another and the like.
9. I have speculated that there may be a ninth or existential intelligence. I call this the 'intelligence of big questions'. When children ask about the size of the universe, when adults ponder on issues such as death, love, conflict or the future of the planet, they are engaging in existential issues. My hesitation in declaring a full-blown existential

© *Howard Gardner, Harvard University, United States*

intelligence stems from my uncertainty about whether certain regions of the brain are dedicated to the contemplation of issues that are too vast or too infinitesimal to be perceived. And so, recalling a famous Fellini movie, I speak of 8 ½ intelligences.

So there you have it, my list of the multiple intelligences. Even if my approach is correct, I am sure that I have not identified all of the intelligences and that I have not described them perfectly. I am equally confident that each intelligence itself has separable components. But I am not interested in proving the existence of 8 or 9 intelligences, or 40–50 sub-intelligences, in particular. I am trying to make the case that we have a multiplicity of intelligences, each relatively independent of the others.

From this claim – that we possess eight or nine relatively autonomous intellectual computers – three interesting claims follow:

a. All of us have these 8 or 9 intelligences, that is what makes us human beings, cognitively speaking. Rats might have more spatial intelligence, hummingbirds might have more musical intelligences, but we are the species that exhibits these particular intelligences. And that is important to know, whether you are a teacher, a businessman or a parent.
b. No two individuals have exactly the same profile of intelligences, not even identical twins. And so whether you are a teacher, business person or parent, you may assume that every person's profile differs from yours and from every other person, even clones of one another.
c. Having an intelligence does not mean that you will behave morally or intelligently. Intelligences are simply computers that can be put to work. But you can use your interpersonal intelligence for moral purposes – like Nelson Mandela – or for immoral purposes, like Slobodan Milosevic. By the same token, you might have a computer that works very well, and yet use it very stupidly. A mathematically talented person might prove an important new theorem, but she might also waste her time multiplying ever bigger figures in her head.

The theory of multiple intelligences has aroused enormous interest among educators and in many parts of the world. But that is a story for another occasion.

Reflection

Which of the intelligences described above do you often focus on in class and inculcate in your students? How would you change your practice to encourage the development of other intelligences in your students?

Changing minds

I turn now to the second of my three topics: how do we go about changing minds? Once one begins to think about mind changing, one becomes aware that it is a ubiquitous human activity. Political leaders try to affect the thoughts of a population; marketees try to affect our buying habits; teachers are attempting to introduce concepts and theories that are unfamiliar and that may violate common sense; parents and adolescents are constantly attempting to convince one another that a particular activity is okay, or not okay; and some of us pay a great deal of money to therapists or even psychoanalysts, in the hope that they will perform effective surgery on our mental states or motivate us to alter our mental representations.

Now it is possible that one would need a different theory of mind changing for each of these different arenas: one for the wide arena of the politician; another for the moderately sized arena of the business executive; still others for the intimate spheres of family, therapy or fellow employees. The challenge for me – as the theorist of mind changing – is to figure out whether a general analytic scheme can explain the range of mind-changing endeavours. I believe that it can.

First, though, a few words about the entities of mind changing. Put most simply, a mind is changed when one mental representation is converted or transformed into another. This can happen with a concept – for example, substituting one definition of intelligence for another. It can happen with a story; for example, a sympathetic portrait of Simon Bolivar for a less flattering picture of this leader. It can happen with a theory; as when Darwin's theory of evolution replaced earlier Lamarckian accounts. And it can happen with a skill; as when a person who used to write by longhand now composes on the computer. All of these are instances of mind changing.

Once one has determined which entity is to be changed, and in what way, it is possible to present the core of my theory of mind changing: what I call the seven levers of mind changing. I'll mention and define the levers briskly and then take an example drawn from the realm of politics. As it happens, each of these levers begins with the letter R in English.

1. *Reason*. Minds can be changed through logical argument.
2. *Research*. Minds can be changed through data, observations, case studies.
3. *Resonance*. Minds can be changed when the mind-to-be-changed resonates with the new content and with the presenter.
4. *Redescription*. Minds can be changed when the new content is presented in a number of different media and symbol systems.

5. *Rewards and resources*. Minds can be changed when sufficient rewards (or punishments) are invoked.
6. *Real world events*. Minds can be changed when there is a dramatic change in the conditions of the world.
7. *Resistances overcome*. Minds can be changed when the chief resistances to the desired mind change are neutralized.

As my example, I want to focus on what happened in Britain during the period of Margaret Thatcher's Prime Ministerial office. When I told my wife that I wanted to study Margaret Thatcher, she said, 'How can you study Thatcher? She is such a terrible person.' 'Well', I replied, 'Neither of us knows her personally so we can't really judge what kind of a person she is. But if you are interested in how leaders change minds, you can't just study people whom you like. For better or worse, we can learn a lot about mind changing by studying Mao Zedong, just as we can learn a lot by studying Mahatma Gandhi.'

First of all, what was the mind change that Margaret Thatcher sought to bring about? What was the story that she told, in an effort to change minds? In the late 1970s, Thatcher claimed, Britain was a society in retreat. Once a great empire, Britain had been content to play an increasingly minor role on the world scene. Since World War II, there had been a Conservative-Labour consensus: Britain should be moderately socialistic; unions should be treated gently; industries, education, health care should be nationalized; it sufficed for Britain to 'muddle through'. Thatcher wanted to change all this. She put forth a different story. In her words, 'Britain had lost its way.' She wanted to bring about a different society: one more entrepreneurial, more market driven. She wanted to privatize services and industries whenever possible; to weaken the unions, to unleash the power of individual Britons. As she once put it, memorably though perhaps unfortunately, 'There is no such thing as society.'

Now I do not necessarily approve of Thatcher's aims. Indeed, as an academic, I would probably have fought them tooth and nail had I lived in Britain. But Thatcher succeeded in her broad aim. She did reverse the direction of British society. The best proof of her effectiveness is that now, 15 years after the conclusion of her tenure, many issues that Margaret Thatcher brought to the table in Britain are still being debated.

I choose to focus on Margaret Thatcher because she actually exemplifies the seven levers of mind changing. To begin with, she was a lawyer who reasoned well and loved to argue. When she had to defend her policies in the House of Commons, she did so with great gusto and with powerful logical arguments. She also put forth copious data in support of her position. She commissioned studies, devoured their results, remembered the numbers and laced her presentations with research. Of course, like any embattled politician, she tended to cite the data that supported her position and to ignore or minimize those data that countered the story that she was trying to tell.

Moving to the third lever, Margaret Thatcher's person and her story resonated with large segments of the British population. By resonance, I mean that Margaret Thatcher sounded right and felt right to the British; she was on the same wave length as they were. Her countrymen felt that she had understood their situation and was talking directly to them. As she often put it, 'I am one of them.' Moreover, she was able to tell her story in a way that rang true to many British citizens.

As an aside, I'll suggest that resonance consists of two elements: likeability and trustworthiness. Margaret Thatcher may not have been lovable but she was sympathetic to the bulk of Britons, at least until the last few years of her lengthy tenure. And she was considered very trustworthy – when she said something, she meant it. As she once quipped, making reference to a famous English play, 'This lady's not for turning.' In the 2004 US election, the general population probably found George W Bush somewhat more likeable than John Kerry. But Bush probably won the election because he seemed more trustworthy. John Kerry's position was seen as changing unpredictably and thus people could not resonate to him. (Just in case you had not anticipated it, I must add that I certainly do *not* resonate to George W. Bush; after all, I am a Harvard Professor living in the blue state of Massachusetts).

The fourth lever is redescription – more technically, representational redescription. When you want to bring about a mind change, you need to make the same point over and over again. But it is a big mistake to make the same point in the same way – you lose people's attention very quickly. The challenge is to make the same point in as many different ways as possible. Margaret Thatcher was skilled at telling her story in many ways – in stories, in logical arguments, in jokes, in cartoons (she launched her first campaign with a poster of a long unemployment line bearing the caption 'Labour is not working' – a pun in English). Perhaps most important, she *embodied* the story that she told, – that is, her own life was the story of a woman who had risen from poverty, had earned two university degrees and had raised a family. She was not the member of a privileged élite – she was a hardworking, entrepreneurial person who had managed to become the first woman to hold many positions in the Conservative Party, and ultimately, the first woman Prime Minister in Britain's long history. As contemporary commentators put in, 'Margaret Thatcher walked the talk.' Almost everything that she said or did reinforced the story that she was trying to tell.

If you ask the man on the street how to change minds, he is likely to say 'Use rewards or punishments.' This lay theory, right out of behaviourism, is attractive to many persons. The problem with the reinforcement theory is that it is more likely to change behaviour than to change minds. If you reward me enough, I may do all kinds of things that you want me to do. But once the rewards or punishments cease, I am likely to revert to my former behaviours, because my mind has not actually changed. Nonetheless, I should mention that Margaret Thatcher was expert in rewarding those who agreed with her and who promoted her position, ruthless with those 'wets' whom she saw as in opposition. Of her ostensible comrades, she often asked 'Is he/she one of us?' Also it must be said that economic conditions in Britain improved during the 1980s, at least for most citizens. And these material rewards certainly contributed to Thatcher's (and her Conservative Party's) continuing ability to win elections.

A leader can control rewards and punishments, at least to some extent. By definition, however, real world events are those that occur outside of one's control. The challenge to any leader (or any of us, for that matter) is to monitor what is happening in the real world and to use the event in the service of the mind changes that are most important to you. Margaret Thatcher was brilliant at exploiting real world events. Consider: She did not cause the rise in oil prices in 1978–79, the election of Ronald Reagan in 1980, the rise of Mikhail Gorbachev in the Soviet Union, the invasion of the Falkland Islands or the bombing of the Conservative Party Congress in Brighton – but in each case she was able to seize upon this event and use it to help bring about the changes that she most desired. (One can say, equally, that George W Bush did not cause the attack on the Twin Towers on 9/11; but he, and certainly those in his inner circle, used that event as a justification for making war on Iraq one and a half years later.)

In my view the final lever of mind change is probably the most important: recognizing resistances and overcoming them. Most of us involved in mind changing spend too much time trying to marshal support in favour of our new position. We would be better advised to spend more time trying to understand why a person would *not* want to change his/her mind in a certain direction and then working on undoing this resistance.

Margaret Thatcher was a forceful proponent of her positions. She did not wallow in trying to understand and counter the resistances. But in looking back on her tenure, she paid tribute to the great strength of resistances:

> Orthodox finance, low levels of regulation and taxation, a minimal bureaucracy, strong defence, willingness to stand up for British interests wherever and whenever threatened – I did not believe that I had to open windows into men's souls on these matters. The arguments for them seemed to have been won. I now know that such arguments are never finally won. (1995, p. 416)

There are two concluding points to be made about my theory of mind change. First, while I have focussed here on how leaders change minds, the beauty of the theory is in its versatility. In my book *Changing Minds*, I show how these same levers are at work when a business leader like John Browne tries to bring about changes at British Petroleum, a teacher tries to present a novel scientific or political theory to her class, one colleague attempts to persuade another colleague about the best way to think about the workplace, two spouses are arguing about the best way to invest money or to raise children, or a person herself switches religious or political affiliation. At least within the United States, there is one topic that I avoid: no parent has ever been able to convince a teenager to clean his or her room!

Second, for better or worse, my theory of mind changing is amoral. That is, these levers are available for anyone to use: a saint, a sinner, an advertiser, a prophet. In the case of multiple intelligences, I prefer when people use their intelligences in benevolent way – I much prefer the poet Goethe's use of the German language to that of the Nazi propagandist Josef Goebbels. By the same token, in the case of mind changing, I much prefer the mind changes brought about by Pope John XXIII to those brought about by Benito Mussolini. But there is no way to ensure that a theory – like my theory of mind changing – will be used only by those of whom one approves or only in directions that one deems desirable. This topic will be revisited later in the chapter.

Reflection

What are some of the classroom implications that can be derived from a theory of mind change as discussed above? What kinds of changes could you make to your own teaching to make it more effective based on the theory? How would this theory relate to the leadership and management of schools?

Five minds for the future

So what are the implications of my theory for education: the five minds that we will need to cultivate in the future? I'll introduce the topic by telling you the story of how I came to address this topic.

In Spanish I have an excellent publisher named Paidos. I say that they, the Paidos group, are excellent because they have issued almost all of my books in Spanish; they keep them in print and when I came to Spain last year, they invited my son and his wife to have dinner at El Bulli (said to be the best restaurant in the world). What more could one ask from any publisher?

Last year the folks at Paidos told me about a new series that they have issued called *Asterisk*. As the name implies, these are very slim volumes: 50 to 100 pages. The dozen or so authors who have contributed to Paidos are a most impressive group: the novelist Günther Grass, the sociologist Pierre Bourdieu, the historian Eric Hobsbawm. My editors asked me whether I would like to contribute to the series. It took me about 10 seconds to say 'Si'. But then I did something no other author had done so far. Rather than offering some articles that had already been published in English (or French or German), I asked whether I could write an original manuscript. Not surprisingly, the editors at Paidos gave me an equally enthusiastic 'Si' – it is nearly always preferable to publish something new than it is to translate an already published manuscript. I said that I would like to use the *Asterisk* invitation to try out some ideas about education in the future. Now, many months later, we have 'Las Cinco Mentes del Futuro'. In April 2007, I published a longer version of these ideas, in a book called *Five Minds for the Future*.

So without further ado, here are the five minds for the future. Once again, I will mention them briefly and then say a few additional words about each. The first three kinds of minds are cognitive; they refer to the usual work of school:

- The disciplined mind masters bodies of knowledge and skill.
- The synthesizing mind decides what is most important and puts knowledge together in useful ways.
- The creative mind ventures regularly into new, unexplored territory.

The following two kinds of minds have to do with our treatment of the human sphere:

- The respectful mind prizes diversity and tries to work effectively with individuals of all background.

- The ethical mind proceeds from principles – it seeks to act in ways that serve the wider society.

To bring these five kinds of minds to life, let me describe how each kind of mind might be nurtured in a secondary school or college student. We'll call her Juanita.

In order to accomplish anything of significance in the world, Juanita must have a disciplined mind. The word 'discipline' has two complementary meanings. On the one hand, a disciplined mind is one that works regularly on a topic or skill, thereby bringing about steady improvement to a level of excellence. On the other hand, a disciplined mind is one that has mastered major disciplinary ways of thinking.

In school, at a minimum, we should expect Juanita to learn how to think scientifically, mathematically, historically and artistically. This goes well beyond learning rules and facts, as Kerry is at pains to emphasize in Chapter 5 of this volume. Juanita needs to be able to look at a piece of scientific reporting and decide whether it is credible: for example, should I use this medicine or does it have too many side effects? She needs to be able to examine a current event and determine the appropriate historical analogy. In general, it takes years to acquire a disciplined mind – one that actually thinks differently about scientific findings or historical events than does an unschooled mind, or one that does not think about them at all.

Unless one has acquired a certain amount of disciplinary thinking, one cannot integrate or synthesize knowledge. Murray Gell-Mann (2001), the Nobel laureate in physics, has suggested that the most valuable mind in the 21st century is the synthesizing mind – the mind that can surf the web, decide what is important, what is worth paying attention to and probing further and what should be ignored. Having decided what is important, Juanita needs then to put it together in a way that makes sense to her for she needs to be able to use it in the future. And, unless she is living as a hermit, she needs as well to be able to assemble syntheses which make sense to other persons: teachers, co-workers, readers, for example. Alas, we as psychologists know almost nothing systematic about how synthesizing occurs. I speculate that synthesizing always begins from a particular perspective or goal and that there are various formats which aid in synthesizing, for example, the various lists or, more technically, taxonomies that I have been presenting so far.

Disciplined knowledge is necessary for synthesizing; and synthesizing is necessary for creativity. In creating knowledge, the mind goes beyond what is given and what is known, into the unknown. The creating mind develops new ideas, concepts, stories, theories and skills, and seeks to demonstrate that they are desirable, needed and even indispensable. To use the current vernacular, the creating mind thinks 'outside the box'.

Clearly, knowledge and skill are indispensable for creativity. But my own studies suggest that the cognitive aspect is less important, and the personal aspects more important, than has been generally acknowledged. Put succinctly, if Juanita is to exhibit a creating mind, she must be comfortable in taking risks; she must enjoy going out on a limb, so to speak. Juanita must be willing to make mistakes, pick herself up, and try again. Indeed, she becomes bored or sceptical when her ideas are too readily accepted. If one wants to nurture a creative mind, it is less important to impart huge amounts of knowledge, more important to cultivate a questioning, even a challenging frame of mind – a theme picked up once more in Chapter 5. Of course, that iconoclastic stance does not guarantee that the 'out of the box' thinking will be any good. Only a group of knowledgeable others can make judgements about the quality of a novel idea; and sometimes it takes years, or even centuries, to separate out the quality innovations from those that are merely 'different'.

So far, my kinds of minds come out of the cognitive sphere, the one that I have probed for many years. But I think that two other kinds of minds are as important, and perhaps far more precious, at this particular moment in human history.

Human beings have always recognized differences among one another, and in particular, differences between one group or population and another. Indeed, even toddlers discriminate men from women. They immediately detect those with different skin colour, those who dress differently, talk differently or belong to different sects or tribes. Truth to tell, human beings are suspicious of those who look different from themselves; and they do not need formal training to treat 'others' as 'dangerous' or 'evil'. If the planet were big enough, or the populations separate enough from one another, this antipathy for 'the other' might not be so toxic.

Today, however, hardly any groups are isolated from one another. The cliché 'the global world' means that every group realizes that it is just one among many. And the term 'diversity' takes on a new and urgent meaning in any large city, where the once majority population is now, one among many groups, struggling to succeed. Indeed, whether one goes to Detroit, Delhi or Duesseldorf, the flow of migrants of different backgrounds, aspirations, religions and political beliefs is ubiquitous.

© *Howard Gardner, Harvard University, United States*

At the very least, Juanita needs to tolerate differences. As we observe in hot-spots like the Middle East, even barely perceptible differences are enough to launch warfare. However, we should not be satisfied with mere tolerance. Rather, I argue, it is far preferable if Juanita accepts and welcomes differences in appearance, background, aspirations and belief systems, so long as those differences are not actually threatening her physical well-being. Juanita's respectful mind gives the benefit of doubt to those who do not belong to her family or clan, seeks to understand them, to work with them, to weave a fabric which is actually stronger and more beautiful because of the different threads that constitute it.

'Loving one's neighbour' is as old as the Bible and as recent as the Commissions on Truth and Reconciliation that have sprung up in various corners of the world. And just what catalyzes tolerance and respect is an issue that has concerned people far wiser than me for millennia. At this point, it suffices to say that young persons learn from older persons to whom they look up. If Juanita lives in a respectful community, she is likely to respect others; if she lives in a community wracked by dislike and conflict, she is likely to grow up and join the ranks of the discontented. The challenge for wise persons is to figure out how to bring about more respectful communities and to sustain them.

The final 'kind of mind' is the ethical mind. While respect and morality are the realms of person-to-person relations, ethics entails a more abstract conceptualization. We think of ethics with reference to the *worker*, who seeks to fill her occupational mission with integrity; and with reference to the *citizen*, who seeks to work for the common or the wider good.

In a project which I have been associated with for over a decade, we seek to understand and cultivate 'good work' – work that is excellent, ethical and meaningful. Every profession has an ethical core: the doctor seeks to heal the ill, the lawyer to ensure that her client receives justice, the accountant to certify that the books are properly balanced and accurately reported to the management and to the public. The ethical worker seeks to honour that core commitment; she always asks, 'Am I proceeding in a way that, if others knew just what I was doing, I would be proud or embarrassed?'

The same kinds of questions arise with respect to the citizen. Citizens can shirk their responsibilities; they can support only those policies from which they personally benefit; or they can elect to think more universally, and act in such a way as to increase the welfare of others and of the community as a whole. Thomas Hobbes (1651) described the basic human condition as 'nasty, brutish, and short'. Jean-Jacques Rousseau (1911) said that humans were noble savages who were corrupted by society. I prefer the contemporary portrait introduced by the American philosopher John Rawls. Rawls (1980) said that we should seek to create a society in which we would want to live, if we did not know what particular hand we were dealt by fate.

It takes many years to build up an ethical core for a profession; and it takes equally long to develop a citizenry that is oriented towards the general welfare. Despite what some in contemporary Washington would like to believe, a democratic society cannot be imposed from without. And, alas, it is much easier to undermine a sense of professional calling or a selfless citizenry, than to create one from scratch.

Yet, if we want to live in a world that serves people other than those with plentiful financial resources, we have no choice but to work towards the creation of ethical minds. To put it more positively, we should strive to create ethical minds. Our studies suggest that Juanita is likely to develop an ethical mind if she comes from a family with a strong and positive value system, encounters persons and institutions that embody good work, has mentors and peers that model and seek good work, and can learn inspiring lessons from positive models and cautionary lessons from examples of bad or compromised work. If these conditions are absent, Juanita and those around her must attempt to create new institutions that embody ethical principles. I take inspiration from a famous line by the anthropologist Margaret Mead: 'Never doubt that a small group of committed people can change the world. Indeed, it's the only thing that ever has' (www.brainyquote.com/quotes/authors/m/margaret_mead.html).

Reflection

Reflect on your own classroom experience as an educator. Which kinds of minds have you been nurturing in the classroom? How do, or would, you go about encouraging especially the development of the respectful mind and the ethical mind?

Conclusion

We have covered a lot of ground in the last few pages – not too much ground, I hope, but a lot. I began by describing my own background, the reasons that

I was first attracted to the study of the mind, and my gradual disenchantment with the attractive but flawed vision of Jean Piaget. I then described the three principal lines of work in which I have been engaged:

- An effort to delineate the organization of the mind, as I best understand it. And that is the theory of multiple intelligences – a set of eight or nine separate computational capacities, that all of us have, but that no two of us have in identical profile.
- A theory of how various changes of mind occur. While the entities of mind change differ, and the size of the arenas varies as well, all mind changing can be described as involving one or more of seven levers: conveniently beginning in English with the letter R; they include *Reason, Research, Resonance, Redescription, Rewards and resources, Real world events* and *Resistances overcome.*
- A portrait of the five kinds of minds that are likely to be privileged in the future. Three of these minds have to do with cognition: the disciplined mind, the synthesizing mind and the creating mind. The latter two, equally important, have to do with the human sphere: the respectful mind and the ethical mind.

It may not have escaped your attention that my scholarship is of a certain sort. I don't spend a lot of time defining terms. I have carried out experiments, but much of my work is observational and descriptive. I see myself as a synthesizer, who tries to put ideas and findings in a way that makes sense to me, and, I hope to others. I use the intelligences in which I seem to be strong (linguistic, in particular) in a manner that is logical and that will be convincing to others – of course, that calls on interpersonal intelligence.

Finally, as a scholar, I have spent most of my life trying to understand and to explain. But in recent years, I have come to realize that understanding is not enough, at least for me. Unless knowledge that we have accumulated is used for good ends, we run the risk of being omniscient and yet destructive. Our challenge in the world is not in accumulating more knowledge – we are very good at that. Our challenge is to mobilize the knowledge that we have, in the service of ends that we can justify aloud to ourselves and to others; to follow principles even when they go against our self-interest; to take the risk of speaking out when we see injustices occurring; and, to the extent that we can, to create or join institutions that reflect our higher values, our better selves. The reader can compare this view with those of Jack Miller (Chapter 4) in what he calls education for wisdom and compassion, or with Zembylas in seeking an ethic of caring in teaching (Chapter 9). That is why I have been studying and trying to promote Good Work. That is why I seek to privilege the respectful mind and the ethical mind.

© *Howard Gardner, Harvard University, United States*

Further reading

Fischman, W., Solomon, B. M. A., Greenspan, D. and Gardner, H. (2005). *Making Good: How Young People Cope with Moral Dilemmas at Work.* Cambridge: Harvard University Press.

This text, drawn on the 'Good Work' project, explores the choices confronting young workers. It uncovers striking comparisons between these young professionals and the veterans in their fields, and suggests several factors that are likely to inspire young people to produce 'good work' – work that is both skilful and honourable.

Gardner, H. (2007). *Five Minds for the Future.* Boston: Harvard Business School Press.

This text describes the five minds that will be most important in the new millennium: disciplined, synthesizing, creating, respectful and ethical. It also details the ways in which these minds can be cultivated in young persons and selected for at the work place.

Gardner, H. (2004). *Changing Minds: The Art and Science of Changing Our Own and Other People's Minds.* Boston: Harvard Business School Press.

This text identifies seven levers that thwart the process of mind change. It also provides an original framework that shows how individuals can align these levers to bring about significant changes in perspective and behaviour.

References

Binet, A. (1916). New investigations upon the measure of intelligence level among school children (1911). In A. Binet and Th. Simon (eds), *The Development of Intelligence in Children* (pp. 274–329). Baltimore: Williams and Wilkins.

Bruner, J. (1960). *The Process of Education.* Cambridge, MA: Harvard University Press.

Bruner, J. (1965). Man: A Course of Study. Occasional Paper no. 3, The Social Studies Curriculum Programme, Educational Services.

Chomsky, N. (1965). *Current Issues in Linguistic Theory.* The Hague: Mouton & Co.

Gardner, H. (1987). *The Mind's New Science.* New York: Basic Books.

Gell-Mann, M. (2001). Simplicity and Complexity. In S. M. Fitzpatrick and J. T. Bruer (eds), *Carving Our Destiny: Scientific Research Faces a New Millennium* (pp. 305–11). Washington, DC: Joseph Henry Press.

Goleman, D. (1998). *Working with Emotional Intelligence.* New York: Bantam Books.

Hobbes, T. (1651). *The Leviathan* (now available as ebooks.adelaide.edu.au/h/hobbes/thomas/h68l).

Piaget, J. (1953). *The Origins of Intelligence in Children.* London: Routledge & Kegan Paul.

Rawls, J. (1980). *A Theory of Justice.* Cambridge, MA: Harvard University Press.

Rousseau, J. J. (1911). *Emile.* London: Dent.

Simon, H. (1997). *The Sciences of the Artificial.* (Third edn). Cambridge, MA: MIT Press.

Thatcher, M. (1995). *The Path to Power.* New York: HarperCollins. www.brainyquote.com/quotes/authors/m/margaret_mead.html. 21 June 2008.

Reforming the connections: the personal, social and cognitive in learning and young people's lives

Colleen McLaughlin

University of Cambridge, United Kingdom

Chapter Outline

This chapter explores the personal, social and emotional needs of young people and argues that these are inextricably linked to, and influenced by, the learning processes in school. It also explores the personal and social aspects of learning and argues that it is time to reform the connections between the personal, social and cognitive. This would involve a wider conception of the goals and pedagogies that we use in schools. Teachers' own learning about their practice is placed as central to this endeavour.

Introduction

For 34 years as an educator I have been fascinated by the complexity and rewards of teaching and learning. I have also been bewildered by the recent focus on the cognitive as the central business of classrooms and schools. My experience of teaching and learning is that it is deeply emotional, social and cognitive and that when teachers and students talk about their experiences in schools, it is not usually the cognitive aspects that engage them. It is the total complex blend that is the joy and challenge of education. As Gardner says in his opening paper, 'my own studies suggest that the cognitive aspect is less important, and the personal aspects more important, than has been generally acknowledged' (p. 23).

In this chapter I want to argue that learning is personal, social and cognitive and that in schools what young people are learning impacts profoundly upon their personal and social development. An examination of trends in the worlds of young people would also suggest the need to widen and change our views of education if we are to prepare them for a better future. We need to reconceptualize how young people learn and to see that how they learn impacts upon the deep challenges they face, such as those of emotional and social well-being. I argue that we must re-form the connections.

Trends and the context of schools

If we explore the thinking around the social context of education today we see some of the implications of the 'knowledge revolution' as it has been called. Research on helping students learn, student assessment and on developments in education emphasizes the role of the teacher as a learner (James et al. 2006) and shows how deeply connected to student learning it is. It demonstrates the need to explore our view of the knowledge needed in the 21st century. Also emphasized is the need for educators to work together and to collaborate. There is much talk of learning communities and teachers as enquirers. So first, the emphasis is on us as learners and we see that there is a deep connection to student learning. Second, there is an emphasis on how we work on knowledge together.

Engëstrom (2005) has done much in the world of work and looked at how our systems cope with the complexity of work and the knowledge needed to engage with that complexity. He argues that the knowledge we use is fragmented into different parts. For example, if you go to a hospital and are diabetic you will see different people for the blood levels, the diet and maybe even someone else to deal with your personal and social challenges. He calls this 'stability knowledge', that is, what we know and how we have always done things. He argues that this knowledge no longer suffices. It is not working to solve complex problems. What we need is what he calls 'probability knowledge'.

This is knowledge that is generated through negotiation in teams and has at its core the notion of joint responsibility and the sharing of knowledge for particular purposes. So, if we were working like this we would be working together with a team that included students: they would be given responsibility and engaged in joint problem-solving.

So it would seem that if we are to engage with the complex challenges of schooling and education then we need to reconceptualize how we work and we need to take on a learning role. This might include practitioner enquiry – it will definitely involve working together. It also suggests that we need to create 'probability knowledge' about (and with) students and their learning, that is, we need to break down the barriers we have set up between our different perspectives on students and how they learn. Just as in Engëstrom's work (2005) 'heartsink patients' (those who caused a sinking feeling in those working with them) were involved in shaping the treatment plan, so we would engage and consult 'heartsink pupils', for example, in the solving of problems. It also has implications for the young people we are educating. We need to educate them for a world where knowledge generation is central, collaboration may be a required way of working and where lifelong learning is on the cards for survival. What are the other trends that might inform what we do in schools? To answer this question we need to examine current thinking on the future personal and social needs of young people.

Young people's worlds

Today the concept of 'adolescence' and what it means to be an adolescent varies a great deal (Thomson and Holland 2002). There are big differences of class, culture, locality, identity and resources. However, some trends are detectable (Larson et al. 2002). These include increased urbanization and the accompanying growth of ecological issues, demographic changes with falling birth rates in many countries, and increased ethnic diversity. The ethnic mix within countries is changing and will continue to do so. This will entail changes in employment patterns and new patterns of migration. Increasing economic stratification, both globally and in the United Kingdom, threatens the developmental opportunities available to wealthier and poorer young people. The whole area of information and communication technology may reduce some disadvantages that adolescents experience based on their age, for it provides a new space of movement. However,

[c]ertainly one of the major findings of Western social science in the last 50 years is that economic prosperity and remarkable new technologies have not dramatically improved people's, including adolescents', well-being or liability to psychological problems. (Rutter and Smith 1995)

The demands placed on adolescents are increasing. Adult worlds are becoming more complex, rationalized and fast moving; with this increased complexity comes the need for adolescents to learn, navigate, create structures and make choices. A wide repertoire of interpersonal resources and skills will be needed and adolescents will spend longer periods achieving these fundamental competencies, since the period of adolescence has lengthened. The occupational worlds of young people will also become more complex. So the knowledge and skills needed will be different and we may need to develop our school learning to help with this.

The interpersonal landscape of adolescents

The landscape of important relationships that shape adolescents' personal and social development is changing dramatically across many nations. The family is central in this landscape but it has altered, as have non-family relationships. There will be a larger and more diverse portfolio of relationships and increased involvement with peers. Given this landscape young people will need *relationships* as well as competencies in relationships. Adolescents will need to master the ability *to form, manage and end relationships.* They will need to be adept at sizing up people, negotiating trust and seeking support. They will need skills for creating communities, managing conflict and repairing breaches. The social arenas in which adolescents learn these relationship skills are changing – peer arenas are more important. This experience of varied relationships' learning can provide more versatile skills for creating and managing connections to others. Education is an important arena for this learning to be developed.

The future will contain fewer hierarchical relationships. Parent figures are becoming less authoritarian and authority more based on reason, explanation and merit. There will be fewer opportunities for adolescents to develop *skills for hierarchical relationships.* So young people need to assimilate effective styles of authority – some may have negative models of authority. Boys in particular are getting few opportunities to learn parenting skills through childcare experiences (Maccoby 1998). The *skills for relationships with equals* will expand due to increased involvement with peers (Larson et al. 2002). The impact of this increased time on the development of cooperative patterns of relating is debatable. Greater peer interaction does not necessarily equate with cooperative and socially constructive behaviour. Adults matter; thus early experiences of trust in adults will be important as will cooperative learning in education.

There is a considerable debate about education and intimate relationships. In many countries there is great concern about teenage pregnancy rates, HIV/ AIDS and issues surrounding sexually transmitted diseases. One position is that the general approach to sexual and intimate relationships should be one of prohibition and restraint. Another argument is that we should accept that there has been a development in the landscape of adolescent relationships: we need to prepare young people for this world and should take a wider focus than we do currently.

Finally, the other key feature of this interpersonal landscape is its cultural difference. Young people will need the ability *to move between worlds*. The current complexity and sophistication of adolescents' personal and social worlds needs to be taken account of in education and schooling. What seems to be needed is the development of agency in young people so that they can move purposefully in their worlds. This theme holds good also for adolescent health and well-being.

Adolescent health and well-being

There are signs that issues related to emotional well-being are the biggest challenge facing many young people. For example, by 2020 depression is expected to be the second leading cause of disease burden (World Health Organisation 1998). The two key themes emerging from research on adolescent health are:

- That the most significant factors in adolescents' health are found in their environment and in the choice and opportunities for health-enhancing or health-compromising behaviours that these contexts present.
- That adolescence is a key time developmentally, for the foundations of later patterns are laid here. Supportive relationships and experiences of success foster the development of personal resources that in turn promote effective coping (Call et al. 2002).

These are helpful messages and ones that have great import for educators for they show the power of working with young people and of influencing future trends. Studies stress the importance of developing young people as active participants in their own health and argue against the tendency to see them as passive. The development of resilience – the quality of perseverance, feelings of self-efficacy and the interrelated success in learning – is key to later functioning as an adult. Rutter (1991) has shown that education plays a major role in developing protective factors, which are experiences and capacities that help us engage with life's difficulties and natural processes. There is increasing interest from researchers and practitioners in how we can shift the emphasis from a remediation or an illness-driven approach, where we use the language of diagnosis and treatment focusing on problems and antisocial behaviour, to a well-being framework, which focuses on developing young people who are equipped to live emotionally fulfilling lives and who have the qualities of problem-solving and forming constructive relationships with each other, adults and their communities. Education would be a central part of such a venture. The document *2020 Vision* (Department for Education and Skills, DfES 2007) is arguing that we must acknowledge these drivers and reconceptualize our teaching and learning in schools.

Reflection

How would you assess the social and personal needs of the young people whom you teach? What are their primary concerns about growing up in the modern world? How do you currently prepare them for the present world and the imminent future?

The implications

If we as educators were to take these studies seriously and use them to inform the planning of our learning intentions, then the curriculum would give much more emphasis to the personal and the social. We would use the multiple lenses that Gardner discusses in Chapter 1. We would not adopt a polarizing, one-dimensional view of the school-learning young people engage in. We would integrate the personal, social and cognitive elements of education. We would look at how they interconnect and inform each other. We would actively go out to develop these capabilities in young people by educating for social and interpersonal capability. We would address issues of gender and culture – focusing on dealing with diversity and the solving of conflict. We would aim to establish dialogue between peers and peers, adults and peers and we would listen to what young people in schools say about their concerns such as how they learn, school systems and specific issues such as bullying.

What would this new approach to education look like? It would involve a range of pedagogies in the classroom and a greater emphasis on group work and problem-solving. So in subject areas there would be a mix of teaching and learning strategies which would enable young people to develop interpersonal capabilities by experiencing working in groups and tackling problems together. This work would also be a focus of education, that is, students would be prepared for and reflect on their capacities in this area. Johnson and Johnson (2005) have developed a useful body of work, which exemplifies this. Other research has shown that using collaborative group learning strategies, in particular, programmes and projects aimed at developing cooperative skills are needed and effective (Maccoby 1998). It might involve engaging peers in helping each other with learning and personal and social education. We know that using peer-led education programmes can be effective in changing attitudes and that peers can be more effective than adults in some spheres (Mellanby et al. 2001), particularly in providing support for learning and social issues (Cowie 1998). We as teachers would be reflecting on and engaging students in reflecting on the experience that they have in class and whether we can work more effectively together. It might involve the systematic collection of data on this through observations or focus groups.

In the next section on learning I give further exemplifications of what this might imply for teaching and learning in the classroom. But before that let me summarize this section. I have argued that we need to focus on:

- teacher learning because it is deeply connected to student learning and to the creation of knowledge that is so necessary in this modern world;
- preparing young people to work collaboratively and creatively so that they can engage in the sort of probability knowledge creation;
- diversity, difference and inclusion; and
- the development of social, personal and interpersonal capability.

However, some would not accept that the relationship between the future and education is that simple or that schools should prepare young people in this way. For those who think that schools should only be about learning and knowledge, then I want to argue in what follows that the personal, social and cognitive are still deeply interconnected in learning and teaching.

Learning and myths about learning

There are some very strong and enduring myths that have permeated much of recent educational policy across the world.

Myth one

Myth one is that learning is an exclusively or very largely cognitive, passive activity, which is easily measured through tests and examinations. It is the 'pass the curriculum' idea that Kerry alludes to in Chapter 5 or the 'filling of empty minds' image that Charles Dickens wrote about through his character, Gradgrind in *Hard Times*. However, how people learn is understood very differently today. First is the notion that learning is constructed and that this requires that the learner has to make sense of what is new and fit it into what is already known (for more on this see Further reading). Learning comes from interacting with experience and they are inseparable:

> We learn by actions, by self-directed problem-solving aimed at trying to make sense of the world. (Learning How to Learn 2002)

We cannot have abstract thought without concrete experience and action. To memorize something without having an understanding of the deep connections is bound to fail.

> [E]ven comprehension of simple texts requires a process of inferring and thinking about what text means. Children who are drilled in number facts, algorithms, decoding skills or vocabulary lists without developing a basic conceptual model or seeing the meaning of what they are doing have a very difficult time retaining information (because all the bits are disconnected) and are unable to apply what they have memorized (because it makes no sense). (Shepard 1992, p. 303)

So this is clearly a cognitive process, that is, how we fit what is new into what we already know. But it is also a socially and psychologically demanding task. It requires us to adjust and alter ways of seeing the world that we have perhaps hung on to; it requires risk-taking and being able to deal with ambiguity; and it requires us to change or adjust our minds to new ways of seeing things. These are very complex emotional processes that require self-awareness and openness to new things. Jane Abercrombie, a lecturer in science at the University of Cambridge, was clear that this was central to good science. She was so convinced that the art of seeing and discovering in science was deeply connected to emotions, prejudices and other social influences in perception that she established Cambridge Group Work – a series of courses in which people in groups had experiences that involved them in examining their own ways of seeing the world (Abercrombie 1989).

Vygotsky's work on learning (1962) developed the emphasis on social processes and learning even further. He emphasized that learning occurs in the interaction between the teacher and the learner. The nature of the interaction and understandings of how these interactions occur are key. So the relationships and interactions between teachers and their students are significant, as are how children understand classrooms and learning. Other research studies have shown that those who progress better in learning turn out to have better self-awareness and better strategies for self-regulation than their slower learning peers (cf. Brown and Ferrara 1985). Claxton (2002) has developed the discussion of how these personal, social and emotional qualities are directly related to effective learning. So we see in these discussions on learning that the social, emotional and cognitive are inextricably connected and imply that students in classrooms should be assessing their learning but also themselves as learners and that teachers would be paying as much attention to *how* learning happens in the classroom as to *what* is learnt.

However, the work that illustrates these connections most clearly is the research by Dweck (1999). She has shown how our beliefs about learning and ability impact in an extraordinary way on how we learn, how we feel about ourselves as learners and people, and how adults affect these elements in children. She says that we grow with one of two mindsets, a *fixed* mindset or a *growth* mindset. If we have a fixed mindset we grow up believing that our abilities are

> carved in stone . . . [and this] creates an urgency to prove yourself over and over. If you have only a certain amount of intelligence, a certain personality, and a certain moral character – well then you'd better prove that you have a healthy dose of them. (Dweck 2006, p. 6)

Those who have a growth mindset believe that 'qualities are things that you can cultivate through your efforts' (Dweck 2006: 7). Such believers will be keen to acquire and develop new capacities and will risk doing so. What is very significant about Dweck's work is that these mindsets are learned through the feedback of and interaction with others – teachers are powerful here – and they have big implications for future learning and how we feel about ourselves as people. Dweck (1999) shows that if we are brought up in a performance orientation, that is, if ability is seen as limited and used as a framework for describing accomplishments and individuals (for example, comments like 'well she is bright so she would be able to solve that problem'), then we are less likely to engage in the sorts of behaviours necessary for learning. Many current educational systems are founded on the stones of performance and ability labelling. Children who have been brought up with these attitudes and internalized them are more likely to spend their time saving face (so as to avoid being shown up as failures), to take few risks and are quick to give up in the face of difficulties. If they are unable to perform a task or solve a problem they are likely to have negative thoughts about themselves, their identity and worth. This is the seedbed of depression. Not only does this mindset affect how students see a learning problem, it also impacts on their sense of their self-worth and their ability to engage in the personal and social problem-solving that we all have to engage with.

Children who have been brought up with and experienced a mastery orientation, that is, the *growth mindset* are more likely to be flexible in their approach to learning and problem-solving, increase their effort in the face of difficulty, be driven by learning goals and are willing to pursue goals with ambiguous outcomes. They will have good experiences of themselves and learning. As Dweck (1999) explains,

> [s]elf-esteem is not a thing you have or don't have – it is a way of experiencing yourself when you are using your resources well – to master challenges to learn to help others. (p. 128)

Here we see the deep connections between how we approach learning in our homes and schools and the profound implications on how we see ourselves. Here we see the connections between the concerns that we have for young people's health and social development and learning in schools. The myth that learning is a solely cognitive process is one that needs dispelling and we need to understand the deeply personal, social and emotional processes we are engaged in.

How do we see these processes in action in classrooms? Some examples of how we can influence the development of a *fixed mindset* or a performance orientation are as follows:

- We motivate students by telling them that passing the test is all or we give feedback that suggests their abilities are fixed. For example, 'Well, never mind, you aren't very good at these types of maths problems but you are good at art.'
- We develop a *growth mindset* by encouraging students to risk trying new strategies or by giving specific feedback on how to approach the task differently. For example, 'I noticed that you only used the one approach when you were trying to solve that problem. Before I have seen you try different strategies. Which one do you think works well in this situation?' or 'If you were to try again you might learn something new.' If we could change the way we give feedback, adopt a learning approach ourselves as teachers and enquire into the messages we are sending in our classrooms; we would

learn a great deal about what we inadvertently send as messages about ability, learning and worth.

- We would use pedagogies that encourage collaboration and teamwork and we would teach young people how to do this. So often I hear 'they aren't very good at working in groups' and when I enquire if they have had any specific developmental activities I am told no. Most young people have grown up with competitive individualistic pedagogies, which have a place, but we cannot blame them for not knowing how to do it differently when we have never shown them or educated them in these skills and processes.

Reflection

Think of the last challenging learning experience that you had. How did you feel? What did you do? What does this tell you about your own learning experiences and how they have shaped you? What does it tell you about your own beliefs about learning?

Myth two

The second myth is that personal and social development, learning and behaviour operate in separate compartments. The relationship between our self-image as learners and how this is developed through our pedagogical approaches (Dweck 1999) was discussed above. However, there are some other very strong connections of which we should be aware. There is an interesting body of evidence building up, mainly in the United States, that shows how engagement in school impacts on out-of-school behaviour such as risk-taking, future pathways as adults and our emotional well-being. Watkins (2005) has summarized research which shows the links between students' sense of belonging to the school as a community and their motivation and achievement. Students who had a strong sense of belonging were more likely to achieve higher grades and develop an internal locus of control (a sense that they were in control of their learning and their lives). This links to Dweck's concept of mastery. A sense of belonging was also related to motivation in that it correlated with engaged and persistent effort in the face of academically challenging work. This too connects to the work on resilience discussed earlier.

Another very interesting finding is that students' patterns of behaviour outside school were connected to the strength of their sense of belonging. Students who were highly engaged in the school as a community were less likely to engage in high-risk or delinquent behaviours. When students were asked what gave them a sense of belonging, their answers revealed that the school's supportiveness, sense of community and opportunities given to students to interact with teachers and their peers were key. What emerged from this research was that it was these processes in the classroom that really mattered. So, we see this virtuous circle – if as teachers we take the personal and social dimensions of the classroom seriously, if we respect and listen to students as well as give them an active role in their learning, then we are impacting on their academic achievement, their motivation to learn, as well as their personal and social development. This integrated approach is well illustrated in Kerry (2005), in a conversation about the culture of Brooke Weston College, Corby (UK). Resnick et al. (1993 and 1997) in a major review of research show the connections:

> We find consistent evidence that perceived caring and connectedness to others is important in understanding the health of young people today. (Resnick et al. 1997, p. 832)

Conclusions

I have argued that learning is a personal, social and cognitive process which engages all of our being and in our learning experiences at school we are learning deeply about ourselves as people as well as learners. If we are to serve our students well in the 21st century then we need to develop our goals and our pedagogies. We need to educate for social and interpersonal capability as these run on parallel tracks to the cognitive aspect of learning. Our pedagogies need to engage students in collaboration, for this is how they will learn about conflict and interpersonal negotiation capabilities that are central to effective local and global communities. Pedagogies that develop students' capacity to be effective agents in their worlds and that are inclusive and focused on social justice are central themes in the research and learning I have discussed. There are also implications for us as teachers. We need to be prepared to learn and enquire into our own practice. As Engëstrom (2005) has shown, this will involve teachers in collaborating to work on these challenges and it will involve engaging students in this collaboration. It will involve us in taking seriously our relationships and the messages we send to students about themselves and the learning process. We would be duty bound to examine the caring and connectedness, and realize that if we were to do these things we would be impacting on the lives of young people in very powerful and constructive ways. The time for re-form is here. Schools should be humanly attentive to all the aspects of the worlds of young people.

Reflection

How does what you have read here impact on your practice as an educator? What have you learned and how might you apply it in your practice tomorrow? What might be at risk? Have you talked to students recently about what they are learning in your classroom?

Further reading

Dweck, C. (1999). *Self-Theories: Their Role in Motivation, Personality and Development*. Philadelphia: Psychology Press Taylor and Francis.

This text reports in a very accessible style the major research undertaken on children's learning and development. The title does not fully do justice to this highly readable book.

On learning – The Economic and Social Research Council (ESRC) Teaching and Learning Programme (TLRP) (ESRC TLRP) has excellent materials on their website under the Learning to Learn project – www.learntolearn.ac.uk, 15 June 2008.

This website is for the Teaching and Learning Research Project in the United Kingdom and in particular the project on formative assessment and learning to learn. It has workshops and factsheets that will be very useful and can be downloaded free.

Watkins, C. (2005). *Classrooms as Learning Communities*. London: Routledge.

This book presents research on learning in classrooms and also has very useful developmental ideas pertinent to this chapter.

References

Abercrombie, J. (1989). *The Anatomy of Judgement*. London: Free Association Books.

Brown, A. L. and Ferrara, R. A. (1985). Diagnosing zones of proximal development. In J. V. Welsh (ed.), *Culture, Communication and Cognition: Vygotskian Perspectives* (pp. 273–305). Cambridge: Cambridge University Press.

Call, K. T., Reidel, A. A., Hein, K., McLoyd, V., Peterson, A. and Kipke, M. (2002). Adolescent health and well-being in the twenty-first century: a global perspective. In R. Larson, B. Bradford Brown and J. Mortimer (eds), *Adolescents' Preparation for the Future – Perils and Promises. A Report of the Study Group on Adolescence in the 21st Century* (pp. 69–99). Ann Arbor, MI: Society for Research on Adolescence.

Claxton, G. (2002). *Building Learning Power: How to Help Young People Become Better Real-life Learners*. Bristol: TLO Ltd. Also available at www.buildinglearning power.co.uk

Cowie, H. (1998). Perspectives of teachers and pupils on the experience of peer support against bullying. *Educational Research and Evaluation*, 4(2), 108–25.

DfES. (2007). *2020 Vision: Report of the Teaching and Learning in 2020 Review Group.* London/Nottingham: DfES Publications.

Dweck, C. (1999). *Self-Theories: Their Role in Motivation, Personality and Development.* Philadelphia: Psychology Press Taylor and Francis.

Dweck, C. (2006). *Mindset: The New Psychology of Success.* New York: Random House.

Engëstrom, Y. (2005). *Developmental Work Research: Expanding Activity Theory in Practice.* Berlin: Lehman's Media.

James, M., McCormick, B., Marshall, B., Black, P., Carmichael, P., Drummond M. J., Fox, A., Honour, L., MacBeath, J., Pedder, D., Procter, R., Conner, C., Swann, J. and Swaffield, S. (2006). Learning how to learn – in classrooms, schools and networks. *Teaching and Learning Research Briefing No 17,* July 2006. Retrieved 22 November 2006, from www.tlrp.org – www.learntolearn.ac.uk

Johnson, D. W. and Johnson, F. P. (2005). *Joining Together: Group Theory and Group Skills.* London: Allyn and Bacon.

Kerry, T. (2005). Beyond the cutting edge. *Managing Schools Today,* March/April 2005, pp. 48–51.

Larson, R., Bradford, B. and Mortimer, J. (eds). (2002). *Adolescents' Preparation for the Future – Perils and Promises. A Report of the Study Group on Adolescence in the 21ˢᵗ century.* Ann Arbor, MI: Society for Research on Adolescence.

Learning How to Learn. (2002). How do people learn? Facilitators guide. Retrieved 22 November 2006, from www.learntolearn.ac.uk

Maccoby, E. (1998). *The Two Sexes: Growing Up Apart, Coming Together.* Cambridge, MA: Harvard University.

Mellanby, A. R., Newcombe, R. G., Rees, J. and Tripp, J. H. (2001). A comparative study of peer-led and adult-led school sex education. *Health Education Research: Theory and practice* 16(4), 481–92.

Resnick, M. D., Harris, L. and Bloom, R. (1993). *The Impact of Caring and Connectedness on Adolescent Health and Well Being.* Minnesota, MN: University of Minnesota Child, Youth and Family Consortium.

Resnick, M. D., Blarman, P. F., Bloom. R. W., Bauman, K. E., Harris, K. M., Jones, J., Tabor, J., Beuhring, T., Cieving, R. E., Chew, M., Ireland, M., Bearinger, L. H. and Udry, J. R. (1997). Protecting adolescents from harm: findings from the National Longitudinal Study on Adolescent Health. *Journal of the American Medical Association,* 278(10), 823–32.

Rutter, M. (1991). Pathways from childhood to adult life. *Pastoral Care in Education,* 9(3), 3–10.

Rutter, M., and Smith, D. (1995). Time trends in psychosocial disorders of youth. In M. Rutter, and D. Smith (eds), *Psychological Disorder in Young People: Time Trends and their Causes* (pp. 763–82). New York: John Wiley.

Shepard, L. A. (1992). Commentary: what policy makers who mandate test should know about the new psychology of intellectual ability and learning. In B. R. Gifford and M. C. O'Connor (eds), *Changing Assessments: Alternative Views of Aptitude, Achievement and Instruction* (pp. 302–28). Boston and Dodrecht: Kluwer Academic Publishers.

Thomson, R. and Holland, J. (2002). *Inventing Adulthood: Young People's Strategies for Transition.* London: Economic and Social Science Research Council.

Vygotsky, L. S. (1962). *Thought and Language.* Cambridge, MA: The MIT Press.

Watkins, C. (2005). *Classrooms as Learning Communities.* London: Routledge.

World Health Organisation. (1998). *The World Health Report 1998: Life in the Twenty-First Century.* Geneva, Switzerland: WHO.

Self-esteem, self-confidence and individualized education

Kristján Kristjánsson

University of Akureyri and School of Education, University of Iceland

3

In this chapter, I rehearse the rise and fall of the self-esteem movement and ask what will happen in education once its worm-can has been fully opened. Some critics think that the self-esteem fallacy may have infected the ideas behind the concept of **individualized education** that was gathering speed during the halcyon days of global self-esteem. My exploration of individualized education – or at least two popular versions of it (personalized learning and differentiated instruction) – indicates that the thrust of this criticism cannot be sustained. The emphasis placed on students' self-concept in both versions can be more charitably interpreted as a call for cultivating students' self-confidence than for cultivating their self-esteem. I argue for the educational value of self-confidence, and conclude that it is an aspect of self-concept that needs to be considered and – after sloughing off global self-esteem – retrieved.

Introduction

When young children enter school for the first time, most of them do so with a healthy mixture of anticipation, excitement and enthusiasm. For many young people approaching secondary-school age, however, the excitement has ebbed and the enthusiasm has dwindled. For some students, adolescence becomes a time of educational underachievement and disengagement from school work; at worst it is a time of psychosocial alienation, culminating in risky delinquent behaviour. There is a wide array of possible contributing factors: *biological* (teenage hormones make mischief in many a young life), *personal* (many youngsters have already had their fair share of life's vicissitudes), *social* (self-conceptions and social expectations differ markedly among cultures) and *educational* (levels of educational attainment and student satisfaction seem to depend considerably upon individual schools and even upon individual teachers), as McLaughlin has pointed out in the previous chapter. Given this variety, it beggars belief that anyone would have thought that the 'teenage malaise' could be ascribed to a single cause. Yet in the 1980s and 1990s, the magic words 'lack of self-esteem' became an all-purpose explanation not only for that alleged malaise but for myriad other evils as well. Conversely, boosting self-esteem became the first business of teachers and pedagogues.

In the wake of harsh criticisms urged against the self-esteem movement in recent years, the pendulum has swung radically. Although some media pundits and populists continue to man the barricades of self-esteem – witness Oprah Winfrey, whose shows still contain copious references to people's destructive self-disesteem – the movement has, to all intents and purposes, struck its flag in academic circles. How long that news will take to percolate through to practitioners and the general public is another story. In any case, I review the *rise* and *demise* of the self-esteem movement within the fields of psychology and education in broad outline in the following section.

As 'this Titanic of educational fads' (Stout 2000, p. 274) sinks, some searching questions beckon educators. First, we should ask if and how the self-esteem myth has infiltrated general educational approaches of late; and, if it has, to what extent such approaches can be decontaminated and resuscitated. In response, I focus on the ideas behind *individualized education* from precisely that perspective. Second, we need to ask what should happen, after the implosion of self-esteem, to the powerful and pervasive intuition that students' *self-concept* has significant bearing on their educational achievement and general well-being. The most unyielding response would be to dispose of this intuition altogether. However, in shunning one kind of vice, we must be careful not to run to the opposite extreme. To hold fast to the belief that students' self-image – what they believe themselves to be worthy and capable of – is irrelevant to the school setting may be just as dogmatic and short-sighted as is the contention that it is the only thing that matters. Subsequently, I cast light on an aspect of students' self-concept that must, I argue, be given due consideration in any viable paradigm of good education: namely *self-confidence*, or what psychologists prefer to call 'perceived self-efficacy'.

All in all, this is an essay in retrieval. Both the rise and the fall of the self-esteem movement hit the educational world like an intellectual earthquake. Now it is time to take stock: What has really been damaged? What must be rebuilt? And of no less importance: What has actually been left untouched?

Reflection

Why did so many educators in the 1990s believe that most teenage problems were caused by a lack of self-esteem? Do you consider a lack of self-esteem to be a major problem among your students, and if so, how does it manifest itself?

The self-esteem fallacy

Questions of self and identity have fascinated philosophers since antiquity. This interest rubbed off on the precursors of modern psychology, most notably William James. It was James (1890/1950) who constructed what has come to be known as the social science conception of (global) self-esteem, as one's level of satisfaction with the general ratio of one's achievements to aspirations. The first operationalized notion of an aspect of a person's self was born, and with it the more general occupation with what psychologists would henceforth refer to as 'self-concept'.

Interest in the self, as in other 'internal constructs', waned considerably in psychological circles during the heyday of behaviourism – from the 1920s to the 1950s. It was rekindled with redoubled force in the 1960s, with the advent of humanistic psychology, which was, of course, all about 'finding', 'accepting' and 'actualizing' one's true self. It was during this time – spurred by humanistic psychology's view of education as self-therapy – that the mantra of the paramount importance of self-esteem spread to the school arena and became the rallying cry of progressive educators. By the early 1980s, self-esteem had become a household term in educational circles, especially in Britain and the United States; yet the general public had scarcely taken notice. A search of 300 UK newspapers in 1980 did not locate a single use of the term. That was all to change soon, however; and by the turn of the century, the popular media abounded in references to self-esteem (cf. Furedi 2004, p. 3).

As the fashion pundits would put it, the preoccupation with self-esteem was 'so much 1990s'. Old hat perhaps for insiders, but as noted in the Introduction, the emperor-is-naked disclosure has not yet fully filtered through to the public. Meanwhile, many educationists now preserve their own favourite snippet of the ferocious generalizations engaged in during the 1990s: the grandiose and extravagant claims made in the name of self-esteem that ultimately resulted in its ironic overkill.

At the most general level, the main claim of the self-esteem movement was that a lack of global self-esteem – a lack of satisfaction with one's general achievements-to-aspirations ratio – lies at the bottom of the cesspool of educational underachievement, juvenile delinquency and almost any other personal and social ills (ranging from excessive masturbation to serial killings!) one can think of (cf. Branden 1969). No one seemed to be immune from this malaise: girls' fragile self-esteem starts to plummet once they approach adolescence and realize that they are valued only for their looks, not for their brains; boys' self-image comes under attack at around the same time when they are expected to begin living up to the stereotyped image of the cool and rowdy male. Self-esteem needs to be injected into young people in the home and the school to vaccinate them against those ills and to carve out for them a safe path through school, work and life in general. The most notorious example of the smug and attitudinizing – although no doubt well-meaning – efforts of the self-esteem movement was the establishment of a state-funded 'Self-Esteem Task Force' in California, which was meant to concentrate on ways of improving self-esteem as a 'unifying concept to reframe American problem-solving' (Stout 2000, p. 13). Gradually, the self-esteem movement spawned its own cottage industry, making millions, offering everything from self-help manuals to jewellery specifically designed to help people soak up self-esteem.

The assumption of young people's vulnerable self, constantly in danger of a dearth of reflexive esteem if they experience any frustration, hardship or difficulty, had obvious educational ramifications (see Damon 1995; Stout 2000). Tough school work could be stifling, especially if introduced too early; the same applied to the teacher's criticisms, corrections and direct instructions. Any competition or grading was also looked upon with a beady eye. Everybody was supposed to feel good at school at all times, and self-affirming, sycophantic messages proliferated ('I am great; you are great, no matter what'), because students who feel good about themselves allegedly made better learners.

A backlash was long overdue, and it eventually crowded in from various quarters through a battery of criticisms. *Philosophical* critics complained that global self-esteem was a banal and artificial construct which obscured our rich ordinary-language repertoire of self-evaluation concepts and dislodged any reasonable criteria for distinguishing between truthful and untruthful feelings about oneself (Smith 2002; Cigman 2004). *Educational* critics argued that the self-esteem movement had wreaked havoc on educational standards and 'dumbed down' the curriculum. More specifically, self-esteem advocates were shown to have committed a number of mis-steps:

1. Transparently undeserved flattery is demotivating rather than motivating, condescending rather than uplifting. If students are rewarded for achievements that are fake and independent of effort, they quickly learn to enjoy self-esteem without making an effort (Damon 1995).
2. It is not true that what you lose on true attainment, you make back on an enhanced self. A diminution of educational standards may boost short-term positive feelings but it damages students' long-term self-image and well-being, as well as the interests of society at large (Damon 1995).
3. By trading substance for image, we have replaced the time-honoured educational ideal of a truth-seeking self with a narcissistic and ultimately cynical chimera-seeking self (Stout 2000).

Moral critics added their weight to the anti-self-esteem backlash:

1. Is the obsession with a subjective feel-good factor not symptomatic of a misguided morality that has abandoned self-respect in favour of hedonism (Kristjánsson 2006)?
2. Does the idea of external undernourishment of self-esteem as the root of personal failures not perpetuate the myth of all losers and malefactors as blameless victims (Lamb 1996)?
3. Does the empty praise bestowed up students as a result of the feel-good philosophy not teach them hypocrisy rather than a true valuing of oneself and others (Stout 2000)?

The potency of those criticisms notwithstanding, it was not until the publication of a number of comprehensive meta-analyses of the actual findings of *psychological* research into self-esteem and its various alleged correlates that the self-esteem movement finally gave up its academic ghost (see especially Emler 2001; Baumeister et al. 2003). Those results have been well-documented in the academic and popular literature (even making headlines in magazines such as *Newsweek*), and there is no need to review them in detail here. Let it suffice to say that the expected correlations between high self-esteem and salient, positively valenced factors, such as above-average school achievement and pro-social behaviour, failed to materialize in the empirical research. Null findings abounded, in fact, and, if any consistent correlation existed, it seemed to be a link between high self-esteem and various types of risky and antisocial behaviour. As difficult as it may have been to stomach for social scientists whose work had been hag-ridden for years by a self-esteem fallacy, the results did carry a positive message about psychology's ability to self-correct. Psychology could deconstruct its own constructs, should they fail to have grounding in real experiences; it was not required, as some critics had suggested, to adhere to its nasty tendency of producing sleight-of-hand stipulative concepts and self-fulfilling prophecies.

In hindsight, we may wonder if what collapsed was simply a particular fallacious view in psychology and education, or if this view was perhaps emblematic of a whole ideological current in contemporary Western thought: a current which considers people's selves to be essentially weak, disembedded and in need of reflexive discovery/retrieval – a current which has replaced a progressive view of human beings as active social agents with a regressive inward gaze, and which has psychologized and therapeutized the bulk of modern life (cf. Furedi 2004). We may, furthermore, ask whether this general current, of which the self-esteem movement was then a mere side-stream, constitutes a dangerous permutation of contemporary liberalism, as some critics seem to suggest (Stout 2000; Furedi 2004), or whether it is the natural outgrowth of liberalism's ultra-thin conception of the common human good and radical value-pluralism. If the latter were the case, we might need to do more than consign one particular fallacious view to the historical scrapheap; nothing less than a whole world view might be at stake.

This is not the place even to begin an exploration of such large philosophical questions. Let me simply note, at the end of this historical survey, some practical implications for schooling. The self-esteem movement placed students inside a cocoon of low expectations and abundant but hollow rewards. After its demise, we can safely return to a more classical conception of students as thriving on wholesome ambition and not being in danger of becoming overburdened, overstressed or overwhelmed if we expect them to achieve. As Damon correctly notes, young people progress most when they are given demanding challenges and chances to prove themselves (1995, pp. 22, 84). Our expectations are best pitched at a level slightly above the one which the students have currently mastered. Meeting new challenges of that sort helps students to cultivate a positive, while at the same time justified, image of themselves as learners, and that can hardly be a bad thing. In fact, it might well be the case that although *global* self-esteem proved to be barren, *domain-specific* self-esteem of oneself as a learner is related to educational achievement. I leave that suggestion for future empirical research.

Shedding one's belief in the industriously propagated legend of the value of global self-esteem hardly comes without cost. What has been objected to most strenuously in the case of global self-esteem as an educational ideal may well hit at other recent trends in education, powered by similar considerations. That much has been at least hinted at by some of the self-esteem critics. It is thus time to ask: After defusing the self-esteem fallacy, *quo vadis?*

Reflection

Do you think there is a marked difference between students' self-conceptions in Western and non-Western societies? If so, how would you characterize this difference? Some people say that the self-conceptions of upwardly mobile young people in Asia nowadays resemble more the self-conceptions of young people in the West than they resemble the self-conceptions of the older generation of Asians. Do you agree?

Individualized education

If global self-esteem is no longer to be touched with a barge-pole, what other educational ideals of late might be partners in crime? In this section, I concentrate on one possible culprit and a famous buzzword of our times: the concept of *individualized education.*

Individualized education is, despite its recent wide appeal in educational circles, not without its critics. Of those who dispute the method, most of them cavil at its *impracticalities.* It is unfeasible, they argue, to tailor education to the personal needs of 30 or more students working under one ceiling. Other detractors note the *inherent contradictions* in its philosophy of helping students master non-standardized, flexible aspirations at their own pace, in order to equip them for life in the real world of standardized tests, standardized working-sector demands and inflexible working hours! I sidestep those staple criticisms here – the followers of individualized education, after all, also have staple responses to them – to focus on a more specific objection that connects to my previous discussion. Smith (2006, p. 51) is concerned that the type of individualized education most touted in the United Kingdom – *personalized learning* – may have been infected by the self-esteem mantra. De Waal (2005) airs similar concerns about the *differentiation* version of individualized education that has been gaining ground in the United States. She believes that differentiation devotees have psychologized education in order to serve the unsavoury agenda of political correctness, and that they primarily pursue what should be education's secondary goal: student self-esteem. If ideas of individualized education are mere ripples in the same wave that drove the self-esteem movement, perhaps individualized education must reasonably fall by the wayside as well. This is a matter worthy of exploration.

Let me first note that 'individualized education' is a somewhat distended term, used to denote an array of educational strategies, ranging all the way from the 'Open School' to behaviourist systems of instruction based on individually tailored stimuli and responses. The term 'individualized education' yielded no less than 1,220,000 results in Google in November 2006. A quick look at the content of some of those websites indicates almost as much substantive and methodological divergence as convergence. In this section, I concentrate on 'personalized learning' and 'differentiation' (or '**differentiated instruction**') for two reasons: (1) They happen to be the versions directly referred to as possible victims of the self-esteem fallacy by the two critics mentioned above and (2) they are widely popular at the moment in different parts of the world. 'Differentiation' is, for instance, sweeping all before it in my corner of the world: Scandinavia. 'Personalized learning' already turns up 454,000 entries in Google (November 2006) and 'differentiated instruction' 606,000 (a staggering increase from the 41,100 websites found in a similar search conducted in September 2004). In the United Kingdom, *personalized learning* has the backing of the government, as the way forward in education. Smith (2006, p. 51) specifically mentions the UK-government-sponsored website on this method, and other Internet material linked from that site, as promulgating views in line with the self-esteem orthodoxy (students do not flourish at school when learning-tasks are pitched dauntingly high, for instance). A scrutinizing of this material may reveal if Smith's complaint is fair.

There is a great deal of political rhetoric on those web pages, especially long-winded speeches by the erstwhile minister responsible for school standards, David Miliband. Yet precisely those speeches enlighten us considerably about the philosophy behind personalized learning. It is said to be an integral part of the government's educational policy of high standards in education being available to all. According to the minister, personalized learning means 'building the organisation of schools around the needs, interests and aptitudes of individuals pupils; it means shaping teaching around the way different youngsters learn; it means taking the care to nurture the unique talents of every pupil'. Special emphasis is placed on the needs of the gifted learner, who – no longer ostracized as a smart alec – will thrive in a school celebrating individual success and challenging the culture of low aspirations. All in all, personalized education lays the foundation of an educational system moulded around the child, not of a child moulded around the system. Apart from the minister's lofty speeches, similar visions recur on page after page: In addition to the promise of having individual needs met, there is sharp focus on cultivating the autonomy of older students, by giving a voice to those at the secondary-school level, at least, and thereby motivating them to make decisions about their own education. So, youngsters at the age of 14–19 are promised significant curriculum choice. This is supposed to be part of the government's intention to place citizens at the heart of public services and to provide them with a say in the design and improvements of the systems that serve them (Personalised Learning Website 2006).

As pellucid as some of those promises are, it is not as clear where the centre of theoretical gravity lies in the philosophy of personalized learning. There is one reference to the 'multiple intelligences of pupils' *à la* Gardner, but no other educational approach or thinker is mentioned. The web pages in question are also singularly short on practical advice for precisely what is to be done in the classroom; indeed, a teacher with no other resources would starve on them. There is talk of greater collaboration with families, companies and the community at large; of diverse teaching strategies that need to be employed; and of schools being given greater flexibility for the allocation of their teaching resources, but there is little in the form of direct didactics. For present purposes, that is not a salient issue, however. My aim in delving through these pages was to gauge the extent to which they may have been contaminated by the self-esteem fallacy. *Pace* Smith, I find no indication on this website or in the linked material to suggest that personalized learning has any special truck with the self-esteem movement. There is no mention of the word 'self-esteem' or the danger of too daunting challenges. By contrast, there is a warning against allowing students to 'coast at their preferred pace of learning' and there are exhortations about giving students the 'confidence and skills to succeed' (Personalised Learning Website 2006). It may well be that the British government has a soft spot for self-esteem – I have noticed elsewhere that the government's advisory group on 'Education for Citizenship and the Teaching of Democracy in Schools' considers self-esteem to be an important 'core skill' (Furedi 2004, p. 62) – but any such preferences are happily absent from the material on personalized learning.

Let us now shift our scrutiny to the (originally US-based) educational approach of differentiated instruction. Its founder and current guru is Carol Ann Tomlinson, and I have studied two of her canonical works and two recent papers (Tomlinson, 1995, 1999, 2000; Tomlinson et al. 2003). One-size-for-all instruction will sag or pinch, she says (given student variances in readiness, interest and learning styles), exactly as single-size clothing would. In contrast, differentiating instruction means '"shaking up" what goes on in the classroom so that students have multiple options for taking in information, making sense of ideas, and expressing what they learn' (Tomlinson, 1995, pp. 2–3). Differentiation becomes a new way of thinking about teaching and learning: a 'philosophy' (Tomlinson 2000, p. 6). As an educational philosophy, differentiation is defined as 'an approach to teaching in which teachers proactively modify curricula, teaching methods, resources, learning activities, and student products to address the diverse needs of individual students and small groups of students to maximize the learning opportunities for each student in the classroom' (Tomlinson et al. 2003, p. 121).

As with 'personalized learning', Tomlinson's 'differentiation' is never clearly specified in a distinct theoretical background animating the project. The problem with differentiation is not so much a lack of reference to historical precedents, as was the case with personalized learning. The problem here is quite the opposite: We are offered a smorgasbord of quite diverse thinkers and ideals that have allegedly been synthesized into this new philosophy. There is learning-profile theory, recent brain research, Gardner's multiple intelligences, Csikzentmihalyi's 'flow' and last but not least, constructivism. However, none of these theories is explicated in detail; nor are we told the exact use that has been made of them. We already know that 'constructivism' can, for instance, mean a number of different things. It can refer to:

1. a *didactic* thesis about teaching being most effective when it connects to students' existing knowledge structures;
2. a *psychological* thesis about all learning necessarily taking place via students' own knowledge construction rather than through information provided to them by others;
3. an *epistemological* thesis about all knowledge being constructed knowledge; and
4. a *metaphysical* thesis, about there being no objective, knower-independent truth abroad in the world.

Those four theses tend to be loosely run together in much of the recent education literature. Yet they are far from being equivalent; one could, for example, subscribe wholeheartedly to (1) and perhaps tentatively to (2), while remaining agnostic on (3) and rejecting (4). Unfortunately, Tomlinson gives us few clues about the type of constructivism she espouses; her mention of 'building on the knowledge students bring to class' may indicate that she merely draws on the least radical and least controversial thesis (1).

Although Tomlinson is eager to characterize differentiation as a 'philosophy' rather than as an 'instructional strategy', her work is teeming with practical didactic advice. The most general tip is to use diverse instructional strategies that fit different students (or the same students at different times and in different subjects). Another overarching point of emphasis is to train students' critical thinking throughout their studies. More specifically, Tomlinson describes a variety of specific manoeuvres such as individual work folders, individual conferences with the teacher, small-group projects, writing-critique groups, tiered assignments and learning centres (see e.g., Tomlinson 1995, pp. 36 and Appendix). She is also concerned about underlining the significant degree to which teachers are, in fact, willing to respond to learner variance (Tomlinson et al. 2003).

Is Tomlinson's primary goal, as De Waal has suggested (2005), to boost students' self-esteem; and does that goal then carry the possibility of lowered standards and a curriculum pitched exactly at the students' current levels of aptitude in order not to hurt their feelings? I have tried but altogether failed to find either this goal or its implications in Tomlinson's work. She recommends that teachers create tasks that are a chunk more difficult that one believes students can accomplish. Thus students are encouraged to 'work up', not down (Tomlinson 1995, pp. 17, 45) – advice that also applies to the most gifted students (Tomlinson et al. 2003, p. 123). In sum, classrooms are supposed to be places of 'rigorous intellectual requirements', 'zones of proximal development', where simply 'reducing expectations' in order to achieve plain sailing is proscribed (Tomlinson et al. 2003, pp. 121, 123, 127). Moreover, educational content matters more than form or image: Tomlinson berates a teacher who taught students to write paragraphs in class simply to write paragraphs, without regard for meaning (Tomlinson 1999, pp. 40–41); and she thinks there is no inherent contradiction between differentiation and standards-based teaching (Tomlinson 2000). If this were not unambiguous enough, Tomlinson emphatically forswears self-esteem as a goal of teaching, but recommends self-efficacy instead: 'Self-esteem is fostered by being told that you are important, valued, or successful. Self-efficacy, by contrast, comes from stretching yourself to achieve a goal that you first believed was beyond your reach' (Tomlinson 1995, p. 15).

In summary, then, there is no freight heaped on students' self-esteem in the official UK material on personalized learning, and the 'guru of differentiation' goes out of her way to reject self-esteem as an educational goal. This does not mean that the self-esteem movement may not have had a pernicious influence on various strands in educational thought in the 1980s and 1990s – influence that now needs to be wound down. It simply means that the dismissal of one-size-fits-all instruction, implicit in the concept of individualized education, emerges unscathed from any encounter it may have once had with the now-discarded self-esteem fallacy.

Reflection

Are methods aimed at helping students master non-standardized, flexible aspiration at their own pace viable at the secondary-school level in modern competitive societies? Is class size a major practical hindrance here, or one that can easily be overcome by a resourceful teacher?

Self-confidence

Given how ill-suited global self-esteem turned out to be as a predictor of positively valenced outcomes such as school achievement – or any outcomes for that matter – one may start to wonder if there is any significant correlation between a person's self-concept and life success. Has psychology's obsession with the ramifications of self-concept simply been a wild-goose chase?

In my view, it strains credulity to think that people's image of themselves has no bearing on how well they do in their life tasks. As noted earlier, a person's self-concept comprises many different aspects. Showing that one of them – global self-esteem – fails as a predictor of achievement is not tantamount to showing that none of the aspects matter. I have already suggested that domain-specific self-esteem may be a worthy candidate for exploration. Rather than pursuing that line of inquiry here, let me focus on another aspect: *self-confidence*. Folk psychology teaches us that, given the same level of ability, people who firmly believe in their ability to accomplish a given task are more likely to be able to accomplish it than those who doubt their ability. Folk psychology must be taken with a grain of salt; its 'educated guesses' often turn out, on close inspection, to be half-truths or truths and a half. One of the callings of academic psychology is to subject such teachings to rigorous empirical investigation and either support or refute them. In this case, however, the folk-psychology hypothesis seems to be close to the truth. The recent psychology literature is replete with findings of a strong correlation between self-confidence and life success, including academic achievement (see e.g., Bandura 1997, Ch. 6; Valentine 2001).

We must be cautious not to smuggle in covertly through the side window considerations that have just been kicked out the main door: How can self-confidence be so vital to achievement if self-esteem matters so little? It requires only a minute's reflection, however, to realize that the contours and implications of self-confidence are radically different from those of self-esteem. Self-confidence is concerned with what one hopes to accomplish; self-esteem is concerned with what one believes oneself to have accomplished. Without prejudging the precise type of psychological entities that self-confidence and self-esteem are, the former is clearly related to optimism and pessimism; the latter to pride and shame. Having a low opinion of the present ratio of one's achievements to aspirations does not mean that one doubts one's ability to improve that ratio in due course; conversely, having high global self-esteem here and now does not mean that one judges oneself to be capable of maintaining one's present standing or improving it. Self-confidence is not a concept reared in the same abstract discursive tradition of self-worth or self-value as self-esteem is; at the same time it is less artificial, more earthbound. All teachers and sport coaches know what it means for their students and athletes to be brimming with or wanting in confidence; only those in the thralls of the self-esteem fallacy will care if these students and athletes have 'high self-esteem'.

It is no coincidence that the material on individualized education scanned here for possible allusions to self-esteem actually only contained references to student 'confidence' and 'self-efficacy', respectively. 'Self-efficacy' – or, more precisely, 'perceived self-efficacy' – is the typical psychological jargon of the day for self-confidence. (The claim that there is a correlation between self-efficacy and achievement would, of course, be a mere truism; the interesting claim is that there is a correlation between self-efficacy *beliefs* and achievement.) The social cognitivist, Albert Bandura (1997), is the father of perceived-self-efficacy research, which has already an extensive line of descent. I prefer to avoid unnecessary jargon and simply talk now about research on *self-confidence* – a term which has a comfortable home in common parlance. But before saying more about self-confidence, it is salutary to understand why Bandura and his colleagues prefer the cumbersome neologism 'perceived self-efficacy'. The first reason given is that 'self-confidence' is commonly run together with 'self-esteem'. That may well be true (Bandura 1997, p. 12; Furedi 2004, p. 159). However, it is usually more serviceable in conceptual analysis to try to clarify existing concepts rather than to create new ones. Although neologisms may be necessary to convey shades of meaning that simply do not exist in ordinary language (take the helpful, if controversial, construct of 'IQ'), Ockham's razor should be applied whenever possible. The second reason is that the type of self-confidence Bandura is interested in and takes to be a significant correlate of achievement is domain-specific or item-specific self-confidence. The term 'self-confidence', in ordinary language, is, by contrast, commonly understood globally, just as self-esteem is commonly understood in psychological research (cf. Bandura 1997, pp. 40, 50). Two things may be said in response:

1. Not all self-efficacy theorists follow Bandura in construing the term non-globally – witness, for instance, Schwarzer and Jerusalem's (1995) global self-efficacy scale, which is eerily reminiscent of typical self-esteem measures.
2. If what we are interested in is domain-specific self-confidence, then we can simply say 'domain-specific self-confidence'. It is no more cumbersome than 'perceived self-efficacy' and has the additional advantage of respecting ordinary language.

This is why I think it is wise to overrule Bandura's self-imposed division between 'perceived self-efficacy' and 'self-confidence' and simply rely on the latter, hereafter to be understood exclusively as *domain-specific* self-confidence.

Bandura's book (1997) is a tome, and I cannot do justice to all its subtleties here. What I would like to point out is that it contains a wealth of information that should be of interest to educators. Bandura understands self-confidence as a belief in one's capabilities to organize and execute the courses of action required to produce a given attainment. The book weaves together theoretical and empirical considerations to show that a person's (P) self-confidence *vis-à-vis* a task (T) – a student's self-confidence with respect to a given assignment, for instance – substantially influences the course of action P chooses to pursue, how much effort P puts forth, how long P perseveres in the face of obstacles and failures, the levels of stress P experiences in coping with T and, ultimately, the likelihood of P's accomplishing T (Bandura 1997, p. 3). Bandura argues that self-confidence is cultivated through 'enactive mastery experiences', 'vicarious experiences' provided by role models, 'verbal persuasion and allied types of social influences' and 'physiological and affective states'

(Bandura 1997, Ch. 3). Of those sources, the first and most essential one ('mastery experiences') turns out to resonate fully with the emphasis placed by various authors cited earlier in this chapter on the need to help students 'work up': learn to accomplish tasks that are slightly above their present level of attainment through perseverant effort, even when this means that they have to face temporary displeasing realities about gaps in their current knowledge and competencies.

Of special interest for readers of this volume is Bandura's discussion of the growth of self-confidence through the transitional experiences of adolescence – the time when many secondary-school students have lost their early eagerness to try their luck at every suggested school project, believing instead that they are useless at this and that – and what teachers can do to guide them through this make-or-break period (1997, pp. 177–84). Furthermore, Bandura is keenly aware of the extent to which teachers are able to stimulate self-confidence in students only if they possess enough of it themselves (1997, pp. 240–43).

Reflection

What can we do to revive the shrunken self-confidence of many secondary-school students? What practical tips would you give a novice teacher about this issue?

Concluding remarks

Let me finally recapitulate the principal points of my discussion and relate them more directly to school practice.

I rehearsed the rise and fall of the self-esteem movement. It seems that self-esteem, as understood by psychologists, is not a good indicator of school achievement. Indeed, one could go as far as to claim that (global) self-esteem is more or less irrelevant to school practice.

Some critics of the self-esteem movement think that it may have infected the ideas behind the concept of individualized education that was gathering pace during the halcyon days of global self-esteem. My exploration of individualized education – or at least the two popular versions of it canvassed here: **personalized learning** and differentiated instruction – indicated that the thrust of this criticism could not be sustained. The emphasis placed on students' **self-concept** in both versions can be more charitably interpreted as a call for cultivating a student's self-confidence than for cultivating a student's self-esteem. Teachers thus do not need to worry that because the self-esteem movement has been disarmed, the rug has somehow been pulled from under the idea of individualized education also. Quite the contrary, I strongly encourage teachers to make themselves acquainted with instructional strategies such as those described in Tomlinson's books on differentiation. Whatever our views may be on the educational philosophies that Tomlinson enlists as background support, much of her didactic advice is sound. Indeed, her advice is so eminently sensible that it deserves some discussion space here.

Let us first consider briefly some guidelines she and her colleague offer in a recently published resource book for teachers when they discuss differentiated instruction as 'a systematic approach to planning curriculum and instruction for academically diverse learners' (Tomlinson and Eidson 2003, p. 3).

Tomlinson and Eidson suggest that there are five classroom elements that the teacher can differentiate or modify in order to increase the likelihood of each student learning as much as possible and as efficiently as possible:

Content: This refers to what we teach and how we go about giving students access to the information and ideas that they need.
Process: This, in Tomlinson and Eidson's words, refers to 'how students come to understand and "own" the knowledge, understanding, and skills essential to a topic'.
Products: Here we are concerned with how students display what they have come to know, understand and be able to do as a result of a segment of study.
Affect: This has to do with how students link thought and feeling in the classroom.
Learning environment: This includes such considerations as space, time and materials used as well as the rules and procedures that govern a flexible learning environment.

Tomlinson and Eidson (2003, pp. 3–4) have further encouraged teachers to actively respond to three student characteristics (i.e., readiness, interest and learning profile) as an attempt to realize a differentiated instructional approach:

Readiness: The current knowledge, understanding, and skill level a student has related to a particular sequence of learning. Readiness is not a synonym for ability; rather, it reflects what a student knows, understands and can do today in light of what the teacher is planning to teach today. The goal of readiness differentiation is first to make the work a little too difficult for students at a given point in their growth – and then to provide the support they need to succeed at the new level of challenge.
Interest: What a student enjoys learning about, thinking about and doing. Interest is a great motivator. A wise teacher links required content to student interests in order to

hook the learner. The goal of interest differentiation is to help students connect with new information, understanding and skills by revealing connections with things they already find appealing, intriguing, relevant and worthwhile.

Learning profile: A student's preferred mode of learning. Individual learning profile is influenced by learning style, intelligence preference (see Gardner 1993, 1997; Sternberg 1988, 1997), gender and culture. There is neither economy nor efficiency in teaching in ways that are awkward for learners when we can teach in ways that make learning more natural. The goal of learning profile differentiation is to help students learn in the ways they learn best – and to extend the ways in which they can learn effectively.

Tomlinson and Eidson have also suggested six principles that 'typify a defensibly differentiated classroom' (2003, p. 13). Given space constraints, however, I will not discuss them here; interested readers are encouraged to consult the resource book for details.

As indicated above, Tomlinson's suggestion to make a task 'a little too difficult' for students and then help them to master it is meant to nurture (item-specific) **self-confidence**, not (global) **self-esteem**. In my earlier exploration of the nature and value of self-confidence, I concluded that self-confidence is, indeed, an aspect of self-concept that needs to be considered and – after sloughing off global self-esteem – retrieved. This conclusion has crucial implications for classroom practice that go beyond Tomlinson's specific message. Here are some general suggestions that, I believe, will help promote and inspire self-confidence in students:

- Students should be guided through 'mastery experiences' and also given the chance to emulate moral and educational exemplars.
- Tasks must be individually tailored to the needs of each particular student.
- More attention should be given to the emotional aspects of students' learning experiences.
- The construction of students' self-concept must be seen as an integral element, rather than as a happy by-product, of the school curriculum.
- Teachers must learn to build their own self-confidence so that it can positively affect students' self-confidence through emotional contagion.

Other aspects of self-concept than self-confidence, such as *domain-specific self-esteem* and (perhaps even more importantly) *self-respect*, may be equally important for educational achievement and also stand in need of retrieval. For those of us who agree with Howard Gardner's point, in his contribution to the present volume, about the primacy of the 'respectful mind' and the 'ethical mind', self-respect will indeed be a crucial aspect of self-concept. But students' self-respect must remain a topic for another day.

> ## Reflection
>
> What is the relative salience of self-esteem, self-confidence and self-respect for a positive self-concept? Should the enhancement of self-concept be addressed in the school curriculum?

Further reading

Dweck, C. (1999). *Self-Theories: Their Role in Motivation, Personality, and Development.* Philadelphia: Psychology Press Taylor and Francis.

This book develops an interesting paradigm with which to examine educational self-concept, achievement and motivation.

Pajeres, F. (2002). www.des.emory.edu/mfp/self-efficacy.html

This web page contains a wealth of information on Bandura's work and on perceived self-efficacy in general.

Roland, C. E. and Foxx, R. M. (2003). Self-respect: a neglected concept. *Philosophical Psychology*, 16(2), 247–88.

This article explores self-respect as an important aspect of self-concept, but one typically neglected by psychologists and educators.

References

Bandura, A. (1997). *Self-Efficacy: The Exercise of Control.* New York: W. H. Freeman & Co.

Baumeister, R. F., Campbell, J. D., Krueger, J. I. and Vohs, K. D. (2003). Does high self-esteem cause better performance, interpersonal success, happiness, or healthier lifestyles? *Psychological Science in the Public Interest*, 4(1), 1–44.

Branden, N. (1969). *The Psychology of Self-Esteem: A New Concept of Man's Nature.* Los Angeles: Nash Publishing.

Cigman, R. (2004). Situated self-esteem. *Journal of Philosophy of Education*, 38(1), 91–105.

Damon, W. (1995). *Greater Expectations: Overcoming the Culture of Indulgence in Our Homes and Schools.* New York: Free Press.

De Waal, A. (2005). When kindness kills standards. Retrieved 10 October 2006, from www.civitas.org. uk/blog/2005/03/when_kindness_kills_standards.html

Emler, N. (2001). *Self-Esteem: The Costs and Causes of Low Self-Worth.* York: Joseph Rowntree Foundation.

Furedi, F. (2004). *Therapy Culture. Cultivating Vulnerability in an Uncertain Age.* London: Routledge.

Gardner, H. (1993). *Multiple Intelligences: The Theory in Practice.* New York: Basis Books.

Gardner, H. (1997). Reflections on multiple intelligences: the theory in practice. *Phi Delta Kappan,* 78(5), 200–07.

James, W. (1890/1950). *The Principles of Psychology,* vol. 1. New York: Henry Holt & Co.

Kristjánsson, K. (2006). Emotional intelligence in the classroom: an Aristotelian critique. *Educational Theory,* 56(1), 39–56.

Lamb, S. (1996). *The Trouble with Blame. Victims, Perpetrators, and Responsibility.* Cambridge, MA: Harvard University Press.

Personalised Learning Website. (2006). Retrieved 10 October 2006, from www.teachernet.gov. uk/management/newrelationship/personalisedlearning

Schwarzer, R. and Jerusalem, M. (1995). Generalized self-efficacy scale. In J. Weinman, S. Wright and M. Johnston (eds), *Measures in Health Psychology. A User's Portfolio* (pp. 35–37). Windsor: NFER-Nelson.

Smith, R. (2002). Self-esteem: the kindly apocalypse. *Journal of Philosophy of Education,* 36(1), 87–100.

Smith, R. (2006). On diffidence: the moral psychology of self-belief. *Journal of Philosophy of Education,* 40(1), 51–62.

Stout, M. (2000). *The Feel-Good Curriculum: The Dumbing Down of America's Kids in the Name of Self-Esteem.* Cambridge, MA: Da Capo Press.

Sternberg, R. (1988). *The Triarchic Mind: A New Theory of Human Intelligence.* New York: Viking Press.

Sternberg, R. (1997). What does it mean to be smart? *Educational Leadership,* 54(6), 20–24.

Tomlinson C. A. (1995). *How to Differentiate Instruction in Mixed-Ability Classrooms.* Alexandria, Virginia: Association for Supervision and Curriculum Development.

Tomlinson, C. A. (1999). *The Differentiated Classroom. Responding to the Needs of All Learners.* Alexandria, Virginia: Association for Supervision and Curriculum Development.

Tomlinson, C. A. (2000). Reconcilable differences? Standards-based teaching and differentiation. *Educational Leadership,* 58(1), 6–11.

Tomlinson, C. A., Brighton, C., Hertberg, H., Callahan, C. M., Moon, T. R., Brimijoin, K., Conover, L. A. and Reynolds, T. (2003). Differentiating instruction in response to student readiness, interest and learning profile in academically diverse classrooms: a review of literature. *Journal for the Education of the Gifted,* 27(2/3), 119–45.

Tomlinson, C. A. and Eidson, C. C. (2003). *Differentiation in Practice: A Resource Guide for Differentiating Curriculum, Grades 5–9.* Alexandria, Virginia, United States: Association for Supervision and Curriculum Development.

Valentine, J. C. (2001). The relation between self-concept and achievement: a meta-analytic review. Doctoral dissertation, University of Missouri-Columbia.

The thinking heart: educating for wisdom and compassion

4

John (Jack) P. Miller

University of Toronto, Canada

Chapter Outline

This chapter explores the concept of the thinking heart and how it can be developed through holistic education. Holistic education focuses on interconnectedness and thus various connections in the curriculum are discussed. These include making connections between various forms of thinking, between body and mind, and between various subjects. Finally, the role of the teacher and the importance of contemplative practices are discussed.

The modern world needs to regain the ancient way of thinking with the heart, in which the whole creation appears sacred, every event appears meaningful and death is just a door into a vaster reality.

Lex Hixon

Introduction

I came across this quotation about 15 years ago and over the years I have revisited it. It is the part of the quote concerning 'the thinking heart' that I want to explore here: the meaning of this term and how the thinking heart can be nurtured in educational settings.

The *thinking heart* is the source of wisdom. Wisdom is intelligence that is rooted in our entire being; it is deeply integrated in our body, emotions and spirit. The thinking heart sees the interconnectedness of all things and, through this insight, compassion arises.

I recently finished reading Thackeray's *Vanity Fair*. The three main characters of the novel represent different aspects of the thinking heart. Becky Sharp, is extremely clever but lacking in compassion. She uses her intelligence to climb the social ladder at the expense of others. The novel suggests that she murders her lover to obtain insurance money. Becky occasionally shows compassion but less often than manipulative behaviour. Amelia Sedley, has a big heart but not a thinking heart and, lacking discrimination, is often manipulated by Becky. Will Dobbin is the one who possesses the thinking heart.

John Carey, in his introduction to the novel writes that 'It is Dobbin that makes *Vanity Fair* great' (p. xii). He embodies a deeper wisdom. Dobbin is not perfect; Thackery paints him as a human being with flaws. Still, he has a huge heart as well as the insight to see through Becky's manipulations which Amelia cannot.

People with the thinking heart can be found in real life, too: Martin Luther King, Gandhi, Mandela and the Dalai Lama. The Dalai Lama has written extensively about how education should nurture wisdom and compassion in students. The Dalai Lama (1995) draws the connection between how the loving teacher can connect and nurture the mind of the student:

> Similarly with education, it is my experience that those lessons which we learn from teachers who are not just good, but who also show affection for the student, go deep into our minds. (p. 60)

> Of course in the field of education, there is no doubt that compassionate motivation is important and relevant . . . With that motivation, I think your students will remember you for the whole of their lives. (p. 72)

Holistic education attempts to nurture the thinking heart. Gandhi (1980) has given one of the best definitions of holistic education when he wrote:

> . . . true education of the intellect can only come through a proper exercise and training of the bodily organs, e.g. hands, feet, eyes, ears, nose, etc. In other words an intelligent use of the bodily organs in a child provides the best and quickest way of developing his intellect. But unless the development of the mind and body goes hand-in-hand with a corresponding awakening of the soul, the former alone

would prove to be a poor lopsided affair. By spiritual training I mean education of the heart. A proper and all-round development of the mind, therefore, can take place only when it proceeds *pari passu* with the education of the physical and spiritual faculties of the child. They constitute an indivisible whole . . . it would be a gross fallacy to suppose that they can be developed piecemeal or independently of one another. (p. 138)

Ministries and departments of education around the world, of course, have committed the gross fallacy that Gandhi refers to education by focusing almost solely on the intellect. The hands and the heart have been ignored.

Reflection

Describe examples of the thinking heart that you have encountered in your own life.

Holistic education and the thinking heart

I believe that we can nurture the thinking heart through holistic education (Miller 2006a; Miller 2007). As Gandhi states, the aim of holistic education is to educate the whole person: body, mind and spirit. It also seeks to connect the person to the whole, or the cosmos. Aurelius (1997) makes this connection in his *Meditations:*

I am part of the whole that is governed by nature; next, that I stand in some intimate connection with the kindred parts . . . By remembering, then, that I am part of such a whole . . . I shall turn all my effort to the common interest . . . a happy citizen is one who continues a course of action that is advantageous to his fellow citizens and is content with whatever the state may assign to him. (p. 77)

Aurelius's vision is at the heart of holistic perspective which has roots that go back to the ancients and indigenous peoples (Miller 2006b).

Holistic education is about connections. It moves away from the fragmented curriculum that is predominant today; the Batesons (1987) have described this fragmentation:

The truth that the aborigine and the [medieval] peasant share is the truth of integration. By contrast, we must be concerned today because, although we can persuade our children to learn a long list of facts about the world, they don't seem to have the capacity to put them together in a single unified understanding – there is no 'pattern which connects.' (p. 196)

Today we are not able to see our relation to the whole that Aurelius and our ancestors saw. Holistic Education, then, focuses on students and teachers making connections. These connections include but are not limited to:

- various forms of thinking (e.g. Gardner's intelligences, Chapter 1);
- body-mind;
- integrating subject areas;
- community;
- earth;
- soul.

Thinking connections

Gardner's work has been important in broadening our conception of intelligence beyond what he calls logical mathematical intelligence and linguistic intelligence and includes six other forms. Unfortunately policies such as *No Child Left Behind* have tended to focus primarily on developing linguistic intelligence to the exclusion of the others. Holistic education attempts to incorporate all the intelligences and to link them.

Johnson (2006) refers to Gardner's work and also develops the concept of holistic intelligence (HI) which is the ability to solve problems in a ways that nurture self, others and the environment. Johnson suggests that holistic intelligence can be developed in classrooms through introducing real-life problems that are 'mediated by values such as kindness, compassion, honesty, cooperation, integrity or fortitude' (p. 44). Clearly, this approach is a way of developing the thinking heart.

Body-mind

A fragmentation in modern life is the separation of body and mind: there is a tendency to live in our heads with little connection to body and soul. Abrams (1996) points to Descartes' work as contributing to our alienation from the body. He believes this has led to our disconnection from the environment instead of recognizing that the body and the earth are intimately connected. Abrams describes how the native peoples of Australia would walk the routes of their ancestors and in this process the body and the land would become one. Abrams states: 'he virtually *becomes* the journeying Ancestor, and thus the storied earth is born afresh' (p. 170). Abrams, referring to the French philosopher Merleau-Ponty's concept of language, writes:

> The complex interchange that we call 'language' is rooted in the non-verbal exchange always already going on between our own flesh and the flesh of the world . . . Experientially considered, language is no more the special property of the human organism than it is an expression of the animate earth that enfolds us. (p. 90)

Holistic education seeks to restore the connection between body and mind; for example, Waldorf education uses eurythmy to maintain this connection. Eurythmy is a unique form of movement education that is usually taught by a teacher trained in the field, but the classroom teacher is encouraged to take part in the lesson. Harwood (1958) suggests: 'When the eurythmy teacher is as much interested in what the children are learning in their main lessons, as the class teacher in what they are doing in movement, the children thrive in a harmony of mind and will' (p. 154). In secondary school eurythmy can be combined with drama, 'perhaps in a play when there are nature spirits, as in Milton's *Comus*, or *A Midsummer Night's Dream*' (p. 155). Harwood concludes by emphasizing the importance of eurythmy in Waldorf:

> Of all elements in modern life it is the rhythmical side which is most deficient – a deficiency only too apparent in the arts today. The whole of a Waldorf education is based on rhythm, and may therefore be called curative for an age. (p. 155)

An ancient practice for connecting body and mind is yoga which is being used more frequently in schools. One of my students, Zigrovic (2005), teaches at a secondary school in Oakville, Ontario and uses both meditation and yoga with her students. She describes her experience with one class of Grade 10 non-college bound students (14 out of 20 being boys):

> Many of these students provide the quintessential example of discouraged learners – they are adolescents who often find the traditional classroom a very difficult place to be. They find it hard to focus and listen attentively, and are often described by teachers as 'behavioural problems'. However, from the first time that we tried both meditation and yoga together, they were receptive and open to new approaches. In our meditation, we began with short exercises in breathing and focus. They seemed at first reluctant to close their eyes in the presence of their

peers; I explained that they could simply gaze downwards in front of them. When they could see that I felt comfortable in the classroom and had closed my eyes, all began to follow what I was modeling. Even in our first debriefing, they talked about how they liked being still for a few moments.

During my next and subsequent visits with the History class, we moved into a more physical form of hatha yoga, incorporating what we had already learned about breathing and focus. One of the initial responses from a boy in the class included, 'I thought that this yoga was pretty good. If we did it a little longer, it would probably be better. And once we get past the stage of laughing it would be good.' We did work at sustaining our practice for longer periods of time and the students became more comfortable with the various asanas as well as with making space for silence . . . I have been meeting with this particular class two times per week during the past two months, and some of their comments include:

> At first when we were doing it, I didn't think it would really work, but after doing the exercises, I felt really relaxed and good. My favourite one would be the Namaste. It really makes me stretch and relieve stress. Thank you for doing it with us.

> I like the yoga because it helps me concentrate a lot better because usually I can't concentrate very well. It also helps me calm down and focus on what I am doing. (pp. 9–10)

Movement education, eurymthy and yoga are just some of the ways to connect body and mind. The goal of these methods to assist in the embodiment of learning so that learning does not remain a disconnected fact or an abstract concept in the head but is integrated through our entire being. This integration is essential to the thinking heart.

Subject connections

Holistic education facilitates connections betweens subjects so that the student may see what John Dewey called the unity of all knowledge. Connections among subjects are also referred to as integrated curriculum. This can occur on a number of levels. The first level is the *multi-disciplinary*. Here the curriculum retains separate subjects, but establishes linkages between the separate subjects. For example, the history teacher might reference the literature and art of a specific historical period and explore how the art was representative of that period. At the *interdisciplinary* level, two or three subjects are integrated around a theme or problem. For example, in examining the problem of city traffic and other problems of urban planning, subjects such as economics, political science, design technology and mathematics can be brought together and integrated. At the *trans-disciplinary* level, several subjects are integrated around a broad theme. Issues such as poverty and violence in society lend themselves to this broadly integrative approach. At each level, connections between subjects and concepts become more numerous and complex.

Beane (1997) is an advocate of interdisciplinary integrated curriculum. For Beane, the central features of integrated curriculum include:

> First, the curriculum is organized around problems and issues that are of personal and social significance in the real world. Second, learning experiences in relation to the organizing center are planned so as to integrate pertinent knowledge in the context of the organizing centers. Third, knowledge is developed and used to address the organizing center currently under study rather than to prepare for some later test or grade level. Finally, emphasis is placed on substantive projects and other activities that involve real application of knowledge. (p. 9)

The final key feature of Beane's approach is the participation of students in curriculum planning. He suggests that students participate by identifying questions related to personal issues and those that are oriented towards society and culture. The former could include questions such as 'What kind of job will I have when I become an adult?' and 'Will I get married?' Societal oriented questions might include 'Why do people hate each other?' and 'Will racism ever end?' After all the questions have been put up on the board or chart paper the teacher negotiates with the students – themes or organizing centers based on the questions. These themes are usually broad and include 'conflict and violence', 'living in the future' and 'money'. Beane suggests using a concept web with the central theme in the middle and with a number of sub-themes surrounding the main theme. The students research the theme and sub-themes and then can present their conclusions through some kind of activity or performance. Through these projects students see how knowledge and subjects are connected to problems in real life. They also call upon the student to approach this work with the 'thinking heart' as the projects arise from their deeper concerns (heart) and ask the student to apply their thinking to these issues.

Community connections

Community is essential to the development of the thinking heart. Students should study and work in an environment of caring and love. Martin Luther

King talked of the 'beloved community' and classrooms should strive for this form of community. Lin (2006) provides a powerful vision of schools that are beloved communities:

> The culture permeating the school for love is one of harmony. When there is suffering from a loss in the family, willing hands will be there to wipe away the tears: whoever has a disturbing question in the heart, safety is provided for the child to open up and carry on a dialogue in a supportive environment. People who have made mistakes are not looked down upon; rather sincere support, understanding and forgiveness are offered, along with a holistic analysis of the causes leading to the acts. Students are immersed in the air of love; where they go, they breathe it in and feel it. (p. 34)

Noddings (1992) has written extensively about how caring can be a central value and practice in our schools. Community must start with the teacher so that students feel safe and cared for in the classrooms and schools. But students should also experience community outside the school. This can occur through service learning where they are engaged in community activities. Engaged service is the term that John Donnelly (2002) uses to describe the work he does with at-risk adolescents. The goal of this work is the development of compassion in students or the ability to see that another person's suffering is not separate from ourselves. In short, this form of service develops the thinking heart. Engaged service is a process of attempting to heal the suffering in others and ourselves. Donnelly likes to use field trips in nature to engage his students.

> On one occasion during a field trip, ten of my students helped one student who was confined to a wheelchair gain mobility around a mountain camp that had not been adapted for children with specific physical needs. They assisted him off the bus, folded his wheelchair, set out his silverware at the table, and by splitting into three different teams, helped him hike on trails that were inaccessible to children with special needs. They finished a full day of these activities by helping him get ready and go to bed . . . I doubt if any more love or concern could be shown by a group of students. (Donnelly 2002, p. 310)

Many of the students in this program come from extremely challenging backgrounds. One of his students was shot on the streets of LA. Yet Donnelly, with this love and commitment, has been able to bring hope to many of his students. He remains hopeful that we can offer an education that is truly life affirming.

> ### Reflection
>
> What connections in the holistic curriculum could you bring into your teaching?

Earth connections

Holistic education and the ecology movement are closely linked through the concept of interdependence. Both share the principle that interconnectedness is a fundamental reality of nature and should guide our awareness and actions. The ecology movement can be traced to Thoreau, Muir and others but many feel it was the picture of the earth taken from the moon in 1968 that led to a deeper ecological awakening. We saw the beauty and mystery of the planet in space. For many people this photograph led to a deeper love and reverence for the earth and concern for how it is being threatened by modern life.

Due to industrialization, competitiveness and consumerism, we are no longer able to feel or sense the world around us. Berry (1988) comments:

> We are not even seeing what we are looking at. We are not even smelling the odors that are around us. Our senses are becoming deadened. Such diminishment of our sensitivities kills off our religious sensitivities and diminishes our understanding. It dulls our imagination. I sometimes say, 'Don't go to sleep, stay awake, stay awake!' (p. 95)

In 1837, Emerson began his first book, *Nature*, by expressing a concern that we still share today. He felt that people could not see the world around them and said, 'Why should not we enjoy an original relation to the universe? . . . The sun shines today also. There is more wool and flax in the field' (1966, p. 27). If Emerson felt that his fellow citizens had lost an original relation to the universe, what would he think of a world where consumerism, the media, technology and industrialization have deadened our relationship to the natural world?

Earth connections, then, can reawaken us to the natural processes of life. As much as possible, students should have direct experiences with the earth through such activities as gardening, caring for animals and outdoor education. They can also read indigenous peoples literature and others who have written so passionately about their relationship to earth. Ecological education should arise from a love and reverence for the earth rather from a sense of guilt. This love and reverence nourish the thinking heart.

Reflection

What are the barriers to implementing holistic education and nurturing the thinking heart? How can they be addressed?

Soul

Finally, holistic education connects us to the deepest part of ourselves, our soul. The work of Moore (1992) has done much to reawaken us to the language and experience of soul. He writes, '"Soul" is not a thing, but a quality or dimension of experiencing life and ourselves. It has to do with depth, value, relatedness, heart, and personal substance' (p. 6). Moore does not use the word in a religious sense and this is important when we think about nourishing the student's soul in public education. I have discussed this aspect of holistic education in my book *Education and the Soul* (2000) and have suggested a 'curriculum for the inner life' that includes journal writing, narrative, imagery work and story telling. In some situations contemplative practices such as meditation can be incorporated and Levete (1995) in the United Kingdom has made a strong case for this work.

The teacher and the thinking heart

It is essential that teachers nurture their own thinking heart if students are to develop theirs. Contemplative practices are one vehicle for doing this. And I use them in my graduate courses for teachers. The essence of meditation has also been summarized in a Buddhist quotation:

> The thought manifests as the word,
> The word manifests as the deed,
> The deed develops into habit,
> And the habit hardens into character.
> So watch the thought
> And its ways with care,
> And let it spring from love
> Born out of respect for all beings.
>
> (Source unknown)

This quotation is good example of the thinking heart. In the ancient Buddhist texts there was only one word for both heart and mind. The Korean

Buddhist scholar Won Hyo (617–86) developed the concept of One Heart Mind (OHM) which is another metaphor for the thinking heart. Park and Song (2004) write about OHM: 'All people are equal with respect to OHM, which is the source of compassion, wisdom, peace and loving kindness' (p. 11).

In my classes on holistic education I present students with a range of choices with regard to meditation practice (e.g. breath, visualization, mantra, walking, etc.) and ask them to do it every day for six weeks. They find the practice has many physiological and psychological benefits which are congruent with the research on meditation (Walsh 1999). It also strengthens the thinking heart. Below is one teacher's report on the impact of the practice.

Claire. Claire first took the course in 1993 and had been practising walking meditation for seven years when she was interviewed for a study by (Miller & Nozawa 2002). Claire is a special education teacher at the intermediate level. Below are some excerpts from her journal. She starts by focusing on the breath and counting the breath. Like most beginners, the first weeks were sometimes frustrating for Claire.

> Distracted! I don't get this . . . my environment is certainly cooperating, a silent house, my dog curled at my feet. I try to maintain focus, finding the counting to be a comforting anchor but after a few breaths I find myself fidgeting.

For the rest of the course she practised visualization and some walking meditation which is the meditation that she does today. In a later entry she notes: 'It feels like whatever I do I am doing it bigger, or more, or deeper or something – especially walking . . . it is strong and rhythmic with my movement and my breathing synchronizing.'

Now Claire walks almost every day for 45 minutes. When she begins the walk, she often prays for 10 minutes or so. After that she settles into a rhythm for the rest of the walk:

> I get a pace with my walking that matches my breath so that it's just a comfortable, familiar place that I know. I know when I've hit it. It's just the way the breath goes in and comes out is at peace with the way that I walk. And when I get to that place, I feel that's the part where I feel myself becoming still . . . I just feel the process brings me to a place of gratitude, brings me to a place of peacefulness, and calm and stillness.

The walking meditation has become part of Claire's life. She says: 'It carries its own momentum. When you practice it becomes easier to practice.'

> Claire works with kids that have behavioural difficulties who are often angry. She notes: 'I feel a patience with them and tenderness towards them . . .

The kid is being rude – driving me crazy. Instead, I see the kid is hurting and I care for him differently. I think I see the student as myself.'

Claire's reflections are not unusual as countless other teachers have commented on how contemplative practices have made such a difference in their personal and professional lives.

Reflection

How can you work on developing the thinking heart in your own life?

Conclusion

To develop the thinking heart we cannot just rely on traditional forms of professional development that focus on theories and instructional strategies. We need to offer a wide range of contemplative and spiritual practices that lead to an awakening and development of the thinking heart.

Further reading

Gallegos Nava, R. (2001). *Holistic Education: Pedagogy of Universal Love*. Brandon, Vermont: Foundations for Educational Renewal.

> This is an excellent introduction to holistic education from Professor Gallegos Nava who has organized annual conferences on holistic learning in Guadalajara, Mexico.

Lin, J. (2006). *Love, Peace and Wisdom in Education: A Vision for Education in the 21ˢᵗ Century*. Toronto: Rowan & Littlefield Education.

> Professor Lin has written a powerful text on the importance of love, peace and wisdom in education. She uses a wide range of sources to develop her ideas.

Miller, J. (2006). *Educating for Wisdom and Compassion: Creating Conditions for Timeless Learning*. Thousand Oaks, CA: Corwin.

> This book develops the concept of timeless learning and how it can be developed through contemplative practices.

Miller, J. (2007). *The Holistic Curriculum*. Toronto: University of Toronto Press.

> Originally published in 1988, this is the second revision. It focuses on how educators can develop a curriculum of connections. This book has been translated into four languages.

Nakagawa, Y. (2000). *Education for Awakening: An Eastern Approach to Holistic Education*. Brandon, Vermont: Foundation for Educational Renewal.

> A synthesis of a wide and diverse literature in holistic education, this scholarly work provides a theoretical framework for holistic education.

References

Abrams, D. (1996). *The Spell of the Sensuous.* New York: Vintage.

Aurelius, M. (1997). *Meditations.* Mineola, New York: Dover.

Bateson, G. and Bateson, M. C. (1987). *Angels Fear: Toward an Epistemology of the Sacred.* New York: Macmillan.

Beane, J. A. (1997). *Curriculum Integration: Designing the Core of Democratic Education.* New York: Teachers College Press.

Berry T. (1988). *The Dream of Earth.* San Francisco, CA: Sierra Club Books.

Donnelly, J. (2002). Educating for a deeper sense of self: understanding, compassion and engage service. In J. P. Miller and Y. Nakagawa (eds), *Nurturing Our Wholeness: Perspectives on Spirituality in Education.* Brandon, Vermont: Foundation for Educational Renewal.

Emerson, R. W. (1966). In H. M. Jones (ed.), *Emerson on Education.* New York: Teachers College Press.

Golden, S. (1991). Lex Hixon: profile. *Yoga Journal,* January/February, 26–27.

Harwood, A. C. (1958). *The Recovery of Man in Childhood: A Study in the Educational Work of Rudolf Steiner.* Spring Valley, New York: Anthroposophic Press.

Johnson, A. (2007). Becoming fully intelligent. *Encounter: Education for Meaning and Social Justice* 19, 40–46.

Levete G. (1995). *Presenting the Case for Meditation in Primary and Secondary Schools.* London: Interlink Trust.

Lin, J. (2006). *Love, Peace and Wisdom in Education: A Vision for Education in the 21ˢᵗ Century.* Toronto: Rowan & Littlefield Education.

Miller, J. (2000). *Education and the Soul: Toward a Spiritual Curriculum.* Albany, New York: State University of New York Press.

Miller, J. (2006a). *Educating for Wisdom and Compassion: Creating Conditions for Timeless Learning.* Thousand Oaks, CA: Corwin.

Miller, J. (2006b). Ancient roots of holistic education. *Encounter: Education for Meaning and Social Justice,* 19, 55–59.

Miller, J. (2007). *The Holistic Curriculum.* Toronto: University of Toronto Press.

Moore, T. (1992). *Care of the Soul: A Guide for Cultivating Depth and Sacredness in Everyday Life.* New York: Walker.

Noddings, N. (1992). *The Challenge to Care in Schools: An Alternative Approach to Education.* New York: Teachers College Press.

Park, Y. and Song, M. W. (2004). Hyo's one heart-mind and mediation on one heart-mind as part of holistic education. In J. P. Miller, S. Karsten, D. Denton, D. Orr and I. Colalillo-Kates (eds), *Holistic Learning and Spirituality in Education: Breaking New Ground.* Albany, New York: SUNY Press.

The Dalai Lama. (1995). *The Power of Compassion.* San Francisco, CA: Thorsons.

Walsh, R. (1999). Asian contemplative disciplines: common practices, clinical applications and research findings. *Journal of Transpersonal Psychology,* 31, 83–108.

Zigrovic, N. (2005). *Journey Towards Spirituality.* Unpublished manuscript.

Section 2
Supporting the learning process

The art and science of effective teaching

Trevor Kerry

University of Lincoln, United Kingdom

5

Chapter Outline

This chapter aims to give the reader an overview of the range of intentions and purposes of education, and to draw from these an agenda of teaching skills required of an effective teacher. These skills are individually considered, with suggestions for further study that might help the teacher to develop professionally in the identified areas. The chapter concludes with a brief consideration of how personal growth might be supported by continuous professional development. The chapter rejects the notion of teaching as a 'craft', and argues that it is both a science and an art.

Introduction

This chapter has three purposes: to define the intentions and outcomes of classroom teaching as a context for identifying and rehearsing the teaching skills required to deliver them (this is done through a series of models); to outline a specific agenda of teaching skills that fits the preferred model; to consider some parameters of how those skills might be acquired by practitioners and trainees.

Defining effective teaching

It is impossible to define effective teaching, and the skills that constitute it, until one has identified the intentions and desired outcomes of that teaching as perceived by the actors in the classroom drama: students, teachers, parents, politicians and society. Recently, debate has raged about the nature of these intentions and who should have ultimate control of them. In this short chapter, discussion can only be indicative rather than exhaustive; but it is nonetheless essential to provide a view before attempting to describe any practical approaches to the art and science of teaching. So the following paragraphs summarize some of the prevalent views of what schooling should deliver, examining five common models.

The models considered here are exemplified in Table 5.1 and consist of: knowledge models, target-driven models, fiscal models, utilitarian/social models and intrinsic value models. This discussion will be limited to some key points; readers will need to follow up the references cited in the text. The models are constructed from a blend of teaching/learning theory, curriculum theory, philosophy and sociology of education and psychology, and are thus more complicated in reality than can be presented in a short chapter.

Some models of teaching

Knowledge models

In England and elsewhere, the predominant (almost unquestioned) model of teaching rests on the assumption that the task of the teacher is to move the content of a body of information from a syllabus into the head of the student (Middlewood and Burton 2001, p. 23). The corollary of this is the view that a successful student is one who will be able to reproduce accurately that body of prescribed information (Elliott 1998, p. 25). In schools, formal, written examinations are the vehicles for measuring teaching effectiveness (such exams are even referred to as 'the gold standard' – Crace and Smithers 2006). That the British government connives at these assumptions is evidenced from the fact that lesson notes for teachers about the **National Curriculum** are now widely

Table 5.1 Models of teaching: some key characteristics

Model	Key characteristics	Key driver(s)	Strengths	Drawbacks
Knowledge models	Teaching is construed as imparting facts, information, data about discrete 'disciplines' The content of syllabi is stressed rather than its implications or applications These models are more about schooling than about education in any wider sense	Politicians, in the cause of 'measuring success' and having 'evidence' of 'tangible achievements' or 'standards' Teachers in so far that their role is sharply defined and their achievements can be clearly perceived Parents if the outcomes produce 'rewards' such as places in higher education institutions or prestigious employment for students	'Information about' is clearly a pre-requisite of more advanced thinking	The place of knowledge itself is threatened by technological advance: people no longer need to store information in their heads, they need to know how to access it, sift it, evaluate it, order it, apply it and use it These models lead to an examinations' culture which ignores other human abilities Compartmentalized knowledge is less useful than integrated knowledge found to underpin the intrinsic value models

(Continued)

Table 5.1—Cont'd

Model	Key characteristics	Key driver(s)	Strengths	Drawbacks
Target-driven models	An extreme form of knowledge models and emergent from them: targets form the agenda for political success, and reaching them the compulsion for teachers and students	Politicians, who are then able (if the targets are achieved) to claim 'educational success' and thus gain votes during democratic elections	Targets may be about more than just knowledge, but any implicit skills are quite simple and set minimum standards	Targets are a useful way of monitoring school progress in a very generalized way, but are usually insensitive to important issues such as social context
	These models require increased/ frequent testing, often limited to factual recall (as in the knowledge models) rather than understanding	Government agencies such as inspection and monitoring bodies, whose work is facilitated by having clear and unambiguous (albeit limited) criteria against which to evaluate teachers, students and institutions		Where they are set up so as to provide comparative data between schools and the public 'naming and shaming' of poor performance they fall short because of their inability to factor in contextual issues, can cause serious damage to all participants
	Norms of achievement are established, sometimes capriciously, and these become the marker posts of success			In general the outcomes from targets have little educational meaning, and are useful only as a means for politicians to try to prove their effectiveness

Fiscal models	Are based on the premise that since society foots the bill for education, teachers, students and others must deliver 'good value' in return for the public investment These models may appear to be value-free in terms of teaching content and method, but usually need to be contextualized within another model in order to give them 'reality'	Politicians, who can claim that they are using the tax-payers' money wisely Government financial agencies, whose job is to monitor public expenditure and comment on 'value for money'	Society has a right to know that its money is being invested wisely It is a proper aspiration of citizens and governments to avoid waste and promote efficiency	Fiscal models cannot exist in a vacuum, and need some 'educational measurement' to weigh against public expenditure Since the 'measurement' chosen is usually in the range of one of the 'target' models, it suffers the same educational drawbacks as the model selected
Utilitarian/social models	A wide range of models embracing broadly social purposes for education At one level they may highlight vocational aspects of learning, for example, the need to provide enough/sufficiently well-qualified plumbers/engineers/teachers etc. At another level they may echo the Callaghan view that people have to be educated to 'fit their place in society'	The key beneficiary is 'society' – the individual's needs, aspirations and ambitions being sometimes subjugated to some kind of (often ill-defined) social need or social good These models are highly pragmatic	Vocational education is essential to society, to public and individual economic success	These models fail when they try to 'pigeon-hole' people or when they depress the learner's potential They often assume that children of specific social strata should remain within those strata, being educated to that end

(Continued)

Table 5.1—Cont'd

Model	Key characteristics	Key driver(s)	Strengths	Drawbacks
Intrinsic value models	These models stress education rather than schooling; see education as 'satisfying curiosities'; place the student at the heart of the learning process; adopt integrationist views about subject-matter; and stress education as fitness for life in a broad sense	The key beneficiaries of these approaches are students	These models value the potential of every human being	These models are harder to deliver – teaching is a more demanding occupation
			These models leave open the possibility for social advancement of the individual	Criteria for judging success by students and teachers have to be more flexible
			Intrinsic value models promote life-long learning	Teachers themselves have to be better educated than in, for example, the knowledge and target-based models
			They cross the boundaries of 'disciplines' and promote integrated approaches to learning	Some would say that, by producing more critical and evaluative citizens, they have a potential to be more disruptive on society
			They encourage higher order thinking in all students, along with questioning, problem-solving and 'discovery' approaches	

available via the Internet (e.g. www.teachernet.com), thus requiring little if any imagination, forethought or individualization from the teacher in presentation. Among curriculum theorists, Ross (2000) describes this controlled approach as 'the imposed curriculum', while the late Lawrence Stenhouse (1975, p. 2) joked as if he were asking for the salt-pot: 'pass the curriculum'. At its worst, the resultant approach to teaching rests on behaviourist psychology, where training replaces education (Harris 2002, p. 86). It accords with a modern trend to turn teachers from professionals into technicians, and teaching from an art or a science into a craft (Maclure 1993). Teachers are not always happy with these trends (Husbands et al. 2003, pp. 12–14, 135), and Jarvis's (2005, p. 14) attempt to diminish the negative associations of 'craft' and 'technicianship' by re-defining them is unconvincing. If the National Curriculum supported by a narrow testing régime can be viewed as 'learning by numbers', then the new **National Standards for Qualified Teacher Status** (QTS) (**Teacher Training Agency** (TTA) 2001, 2002) are equally 'teaching by numbers' – they are a hotchpotch of subject knowledge and craft skills based on no coherent conceptualizations of teaching and learning (Mahony 1999) and which rely on teacher competencies rather than teaching skills. Teaching within this knowledge model, it is argued, results in 'surface' learning as described by Watkins (2002, p. 63). To compound the situation, knowledge-led learning is substantially associated in many cultures (cf. Rasmussen 2002) with education for the more able, and is often deemed unsuitable for other kinds of students even though they are forced to endure it (Collings 1999, p. 64).

Target-driven models

If the first genre of models of teaching – knowledge models – is a constraining one, the second is more so: target-driven models. Target-driven models begin where knowledge models leave off, adding to the mix a concoction of regular assessment, target levels of achievement, (national) standards of attainment, value-added measures and the publication of school outcomes in public '**league tables**'. All of these are, almost inevitably, based on a knowledge approach overlaid by heavy emphasis on measurement. Targets (typically, that nationally x per cent of a specific age-cohort should reach a specified examination level) are set by government, transmitted to **Local Education Authorities** (LEAs) for implementation in their areas, and passed on by them to individual schools as specific intentions for that school. If this sounds bizarre, it is because it is (Porter 2000, p. 23). Government-generated training materials that facilitate teachers using these models are unbelievably mechanistic – even for young students (DfES 2004).

Assessment/targets are designed to establish a set of benchmarks that log where students are, and which then track their progression (Farrell 2001). Targets are established so that minimum achievements are defined (**Department for Education and Employment**, DfEE 1998), and the buzzword in England is 'standards' (DfEE 1997). But recent government emphasis on targets have not been successful because the approach 'seemed to imply that it is possible to achieve equality of outcomes without addressing the impediments to equality of opportunity' (Whitty 2000, p. 119). Even the government itself admits failures to take proper account of schools' diversity (House of Commons 2003: conclusion 10). In English primary schools, students have frequently failed to reach the required national targets in **Standard Attainment Tests** (SATs) (Guardian 2003). In secondary schools, while standards have appeared to rise year-on-year in terms of the number of students achieving grades A*–C in **General Certificate of Secondary Education** (GCSE) exams (taken at age 16 – see, e.g., www.jcq.org.uk), there has been a loss of faith in the validity of the results. Boys perform less well than girls overall and there are issues of inconsistent performance across ethnic communities – all factors which defy the intentions of target-setting (Docking 2000, p. 18). Even the alleged lowering of standards in **General Certificate of Education** (GCE) advanced level public exams (usually taken at age 18) has questioned their importance (Stubbs 2002).

In the same way, value-added measures are meant to track how much 'value' has been added by schools to students' learning over time and this can be deduced by tracking performance data such as public examination results. But while the measures are interesting, and despite the valiant work of Jesson (2000), and Jesson and Crossley (2005), controversy rages around whether the measures are true representations and Preedy et al. (2003, p. 275) have been cautious about claiming any degree of insight from studies in this area about causes of value-add or lack of it. Further, the government's determination to reject all attempts to contextualize results by taking into account social factors means that many believe the playing field is not a level one (Porter 2000, p. 23). The best that can be said about these measures is that they form one tool in the teacher's armoury by which to keep a watching brief on one's own and the students' performance (Kerry and Wilding 2004, p. 139).

But many critics see a major drawback of these approaches in the fact that they encourage testing which is essentially knowledge-bound and confined to tightly demarcated syllabi that may be less than relevant to the students involved, and based on no defined teaching philosophy (Kirby 2001, p. 12). Kinchin's (2001) research in science, for example, identifies that students are presented with 'ideas' but not with the links between them. When the results from public examinations are required to be exhibited in the form of league tables (as they are), the outcomes are more punitive than helpful to schools and teachers (Rudduck 1999). Add to this a dose of inspection against a *Framework* document described as reducing 'a very complex and tentative business to ringing assertions of certainty' (Bowring-Carr 1996, p. 42) by an unpopular inspectorate (Secondary Heads Association 1996), and there is bound to be resentment and rejection of a system whose flaws are only too obvious (Alino-Wilkcockson and Falconer 1999, p. 22). Thus one is led to conclude that models of teaching predicated on targets are not persuasive and are not unfairly described as straight-jacketed. To illustrate this point, let us end the outline of this model of teaching with a quotation of singular bleakness from a guru of the genre:

> The operational key is for the school's managers and teaching staff to translate their expectations, expressed as *levels, grades or points*, first, into what the pupils will have to know, understand or be able to do, and, second, into the teaching plan . . . that will deliver those expectations. (Blanchard 2000, p. 70; my italics)

Fiscal models

The third set of models – fiscal models – need detain us but briefly. Soucek (1994, p. 46) describes these as 'articulating educational outcomes in terms of national economic priorities'. Fiscal models of teaching depend upon the previous two genres because there have to be clear elements to be taught and measurable levels of achievement in order that relative 'value for money' between schools can be assessed. Once some measure of 'teaching efficiency' is applied, it can be weighed against investment in time and resource in order to assess cost effectiveness. The equation is simple: quantity taught plus levels reached, divided by overall teaching cost, equals value. These models presuppose views of education as a market economy, with its overtones of 'individualism, competition, performativity and differentiation' (Ball 1994). Porter (2000, p. 21) calls this approach 'deeply flawed'. Though cost effectiveness is measured (not unreasonably) by Ofsted during school inspections, it surfaces in the public consciousness usually as a result of some oblique controversy. One recent example has been in **public/private funding initiatives** (PPIs), where commerce (as opposed to LEAs) has been encouraged to build and run schools (Kerry 2001; 2006a), but among the many drawbacks are dangers about the control of curriculum and teaching by minority groups and the fact that huge private profits can be made on the back of public investment. Another debate has been about the (alleged) use of non-qualified support personnel to undertake some teaching duties, previously the domain of qualified teachers – teaching on the cheap (Kerry and Kerry 2003). Menter et al. (1997) seem to make two points in the primary sector that probably apply equally to the secondary realm: first, that schools have suffered from lack of resources which drives them to greater competition (p. 51) and second, that the energy consumed by this phenomenon of schools chasing 'quasi-markets' as if they were commercial businesses has wasted significant amounts of energy that might have been expended on education (p. 80).

Utilitarian and social models

In considering the fourth cluster of models, the utilitarian and social models, it is immediately possible to be more positive. Pragmatically, one of the functions of education in society is to equip people for living – both in life in general and employment. Bimrose's (2006) excellent paper summarizes both the present position and the challenges for vocational education. Ross (2000) labels the vocational approach 'objectives-driven' since learning is applied substantially in the contexts of specific careers. Teaching usually includes not only applied knowledge that will be useful in the practice of some occupation, but 'life-skills' which may be as diverse as budgeting, safe sex or citizenship (Jerome 2001). These models are often seen as useful mainly for those students below the top academic strata; the putative university degrees will see the latter on their, rather different, career paths. Vocational education has been eroded in England over recent decades following its popularity between World War II and the 1960s, and there are now strong moves afoot to re-establish this approach in schools (Tomlinson 2003). Two factors exemplify this trend: the infiltration of **National Vocational Qualifications** (NVQs) and similar courses alongside (academic) qualifications such as the GCE (Docking 2000, pp. 126–27); and in the current emphasis on involving local businesses in the life and governance of schools (Analysis 2005). The downside currently is that the government, probably because of its fixation with other forms of teaching, seems unable to decide how to implement vocational education for the 21st century despite a continuing claim to be committed to it (DfEE 2000; Curtis 2005;

Kerry 2006b). Even if not currently well-implemented, however, vocational approaches to teaching and learning have obvious attractions for individuals and society and have intentions to promote and liberate individuals giving them knowledge, skills and understandings of immense value.

It is, then, disappointing to find that some exponents of this model espouse a form of extremism that is highly controlling but which fits all too readily with the English social class system (Whitty 2002, p. 114). Such a view might have a pedigree that stretches back as far as Plato's men of gold, silver and bronze, but it has evolved modern formats, most notably Callaghan's Ruskin College speech (Chitty and Dunford 1999, p. 10) where education becomes a vehicle of state control and of stratifying citizens. Even where this philosophy is not overtly espoused, and when students are able to access public examinations at age 16, pressures (social, educational and of expectation) militate against such students maximizing benefit from their school achievements, as Eggleston (2000) and Plummer (2000) ably exemplify in different ways.

In so far as vocational approaches to teaching have value, they are values that espouse the application of knowledge and its contextualization in the practical world of employment and personal development; the more socially divisive models are, in our view, inappropriate.

Intrinsic value models

And so, accepting that the pragmatism and experiential elements of vocational education at its best are a worthwhile element in forming an approach to teaching, we move to the final – and preferred models: intrinsic value models. Here the reader must consult the sources closely and define his/her own synthesis of them. These models accept two complementary approaches to learning by students: that valuable learning is 'deep learning' (Bowring-Carr and West-Burnham 1997), and that part of the teaching process is to move learners through the low orders of thinking into the higher (Bloom 1956). These views resonate with the concept of the 'learning school' described by Dimmock (2000) and McGilchrist et al. (1999). The view of the learner which these models espouse traces its routes back to the **Plowden Report** (1967). These models accept the value of discovery (with a pedigree back to John Dewey), and integration of subject matter (Kerry 2007). The learner is motivated by creativity (Blishen 1969, p. 90) and as one student put it: 'we should work to satisfy our curiosities' (Blishen 1969, p. 115). The flip side of that coin is the need for teachers to engage students in active learning (Ratcliffe and Grace 2003, p. 160) and in learning that embraces the kinds of emotional intelligences identified by Gardner (1993). Further, teaching itself should be 'reflective' (Pollard and Tann 1997; Schon 1983). Writers like Hopkins (2001) have attempted to identify the school-level and leadership agendas for achieving some of these intentions.

Summary

The intention of this first part of the chapter has been to examine models of education/teaching widely adopted in schools (in the United Kingdom and elsewhere) and touted by government, and to discriminate between them. Time spent on this has been worthwhile, because it has enabled a reasoned acceptance of the intrinsic value models and the more socially integrative elements of the utilitarian models, and has provided an argued rejection of the alternatives which so often hinder effective teaching. The second part of the chapter builds on the preferred models to suggest the key skills needed by teachers to teach effectively. In doing this, the material will draw on three texts (Kerry 2002a; 2002b; Kerry and Wilding 2004). No further reference will be made specifically to these; however, the reader might wish to consult them in detail. In such a limited space, it will not be possible to do more than hint at good practice.

Reflection

Which of the features of the models illustrated above most accurately describe your own teaching? How would you change your practice to accord with your preferred model if you were free to do so? What barriers prevent change in the desired directions?

Effective teaching skills

A skills' model

It is relatively easy to define the core skills of teaching; acquiring them is a lifetime's work. Definition of core skills begins from a skills' model that makes these assumptions:

- Practical teaching consists of skills
- Skills can be isolated and identified

- Skills can be broken down into their component parts
- Skills can be studied and taught
- Skills can be learned
- Skills can be reflected upon and refined
- Skills can be evaluated and assessed.

Class management

So what are the necessary skills? First, and paramount, is the skill of class management. It would be bizarre to suggest that teaching can be effective until order and discipline are established. Class management embraces two basic components: attention to the organizational details of classroom life (being punctual, being prepared, keeping proper records, maintaining the learning environment, paying attention to safety, marking work diligently and on time), and affective activities (negotiating rules, being fair and just, knowing names, establishing good relations with students, setting a learning tone, encouraging achievement, rewarding creativity and progress, reinforcing good behaviour, insisting on equality of treatment, etc.). It is entirely possible to define the good habits of classroom organization and invent checklists for particular circumstances. However, within the affective domain there is more latitude, since the exact 'psychological mix' of students within a class, their personalities and that of the teacher, will have an effect on the way that a group functions. Hard and fast rules cannot be defined down to the last detail. One teacher will operate with a degree of noise and movement, another will have a quiet and purposeful approach, and both may produce flourishing, well-motivated classes. These differences are sometimes called 'teaching style'. In reality, style also includes many of the other factors concerning how teachers teach that are discussed below. An individual teacher's style is also conditioned by the blend of classroom activities which they use (Table 5.2), and the evidence suggests that the more varied the approach, the more amenable the learners are to learn.

It must be emphasized, however, that class management must be mastered, and discipline established, before teachers can teach and learners can learn. Common errors in this area indicate the minefields that lurk here for the unwary: turning up late and setting a bad example for students, casual or over-friendly relations with students that lead them to take advantage, working practices (e.g. in practical classes) that put students at risk, failure to record progress so that proper accountability to parents, students or senior staff cannot be maintained – these are examples of management in jeopardy. Poor discipline leads to distraction from the learning task. Equally, learning and

Table 5.2 Some possible teaching techniques to make lessons varied, and their advantages

Exposition/explaining by the teacher	Some teachers use this (didactic) method to excess
Questioning by the teacher	Is most effective when questions seek higher order responses
Experimental work by students	Helps to promote many understandings and skills
Problem-solving by students	Adds interest and realism
Devising problems	Much more demanding on students' intellects than problem-solving
Role play	Encourages understanding and empathy
Debate – formal or informal	A preparation for democracy and life
Self-study or individual 'research' by students	Properly used, can develop critical faculties
Written exercise	Useful for assessment purposes
Project work	Encourages extended interest and sustained concentration
Drama	Encourages insight and empathy
Creative writing or other composition (art, music)	Requires higher order skills
Peer critique of drafts/finished work	Affective learning is combined with academic
IT-based activity	Crucial skill but one where students need to develop judgement and a critical approach
Use of film, video and other visual media	Especially useful for students who find expression in writing difficult
Examination	Provides summative assessment
Interviewing of external experts	Promotes confidence
Building models	Requires imagination and reasoning
Marking of one's own work by students	Self-appraisal is an important life-skill
Class quiz	Fun, and a productive activity for using spare moments of time effectively

teaching can take place only in a climate of psychological and intellectual security where thinking and debate are valued and there is room for error and speculation: creating such a climate is part of a teacher's fundamental skill. The following list suggests just a few of the skills that are needed by a good class manager, though it merely provides a few examples and is far from exhaustive:

Vigilance: eyes that absorb all of what is happening in the classroom and can interpret signals, read pupils' thoughts from their expressions, understand when someone is struggling with a difficult piece of work, and so on.

Aural awareness: hearing what is happening, which may be poor behaviour or inattention that is out of sight, or the semantics of a student contribution that suggests he or she is not understanding the lesson; being a listening ear when students are troubled; hearing what is not said.

Sensitivity to individuals' needs: knowing one's students well enough to read from the body language when an individual is unhappy or unwell; knowing when to draw attention to this and when not.

A sense of humour: being able to share a joke or laugh at a sardonic piece of work without allowing merely silly behaviour to take over.

Judgement: knowing when to act, when to wait for a better opportunity and when to turn a blind eye to a piece of student behaviour; understanding that sometimes teachers can be the catalyst in a student's discontent; not operating rules mindlessly.

Hopefully, enough has been said on this inexhaustible topic to exemplify its importance and provoke further reflection. So, once class management is established, what other skills do teachers need? These seem, from research and experience, to be the main areas to consider:

- Preparing the learning objectives for the lesson
- Setting effective tasks
- Differentiating work
- Explaining effectively
- Questioning effectively

Formulating learning objectives

If good preparation is part of the need to engage students in learning, then how that preparation is carried through is critical. Learning objectives (for individual lessons or larger schemes of work) should fall into five areas or domains. These are: the domains of knowledge, understanding, skills, attitudes, and the affective domain. The domains are best exemplified by imagining a teacher asking pertinent questions about his/her teaching, notably: at the end of this session what do I want my students to know that they didn't know before, understand that they didn't understand before, be able to do that they could not do before? How can I have moved their attitudes on so that they are more empathetic towards the topic and enjoy it more? How can I encourage them to work successfully and (where appropriate) collaboratively? Let us suppose a teacher is preparing a lesson/course on a segment of ancient Greek history such as the battle of Thermopylae – the lesson objectives might include that at the end students should:

- know the basic facts about the geography, history and social conditions in Greece at the time;
- understand how the geography of the Pass of Thermopylae dictated the tactics and strategy of the battle;

- have built a 3-dimensional model of Thermopylae from a relief map of the area to simulate the geological conditions;
- empathize with the heroism of the soldiers who attempted to hold the Pass and with the various contemporary accounts of the battle from their different perspectives; and
- work effectively in small groups to produce a class 'newspaper' containing accounts of incidents leading up to and during the battle.

Over time, such an approach will become increasingly sophisticated, and will help to reinforce the learning ethos of the school through the establishment of sound intellectual patterns of thinking in the students. Some of the objectives imply that the teacher will set tasks to the students (building a model, finding out about the geology of the area, writing newspaper articles). It is on the skill of task-setting that we now focus attention.

Task-setting

Just as learning objectives apply to the preparation of lessons, so each task which the teacher sets needs to be defined by its learning objectives, and these should be shared with the students and will form the criteria for successful completion of the task. Further, tasks have an intellectual value: some demand higher order thinking – on a Bloomian (1956) model – and others are merely low-level events. Higher order tasks include the following:

Imaginative tasks: writing a piece of poetry or putting one's self in another's shoes; characteristic verbs that define the task are 'suppose' or 'imagine'.
Deductive tasks: sifting through evidence to come to a conclusion; characteristic verbs might be 'compare', 'contrast', or 'provide evidence'.
Application tasks: answering 'how?' questions.
Analytical tasks: answering 'why?' questions.
Synthesis tasks: requiring the simultaneous viewing of a number of insights from different perspectives or disciplines and building them into a coherent whole; characteristic verbs might include 'discuss' or 'debate'.
Evaluative tasks: asking for reasoned judgement; characteristic verbs might include 'assess' or 'consider the advantages/disadvantages of'.

A diet of higher order tasks with carefully defined learning objectives contributes more to students' cognition and intellectual development than a stew of low order, manual and repetitive activities in which students lack interest and commitment. Tasks contribute to building intellectual climate in the classroom. Research shows that tasks which are too easy or too difficult have the same basic outcome: disengagement from learning. Pitching tasks at the right level for the target group is crucial. Higher order tasks can be used with students of all abilities; however, to make a judgement about each individual's progress the teacher needs a means to differentiate performance on tasks and to make assessments about students' achievements.

Differentiation

Differentiation is the process whereby the levels of tasks set to students in class or for homework are matched to the known levels of performance and potential of the individual students involved. It is common to see, at least in the United Kingdom, a single task being set to all the students in a class. As a result, differentiation can only be by outcome, that is, each student performs the task on his/her own level. But this approach is that it is a blunt instrument: the task is – inevitably – too easy or too difficult (or couched in the wrong language) – for many. A more professional solution is to set either a range of tasks, or else individual tasks. Teachers sometimes complain that this is too time-consuming but again, in the United Kingdom, teachers have never had so much in-school time for preparation nor so many resources on which to draw. One very successful secondary school insists that tasks are differentiated at four levels in every lesson (you can read about this in Campbell and Kerry 2004). Forgive a personal comment: I once taught in a class of mixed ages spanning four years and all abilities and wide differences of maturity. In these circumstances differentiation had to be even more fine-grained; and it is entirely possible for a teacher to plan around this kind of individualization.

Differentiation can come, then, in a variety of guises: by outcome, by enriching the task for some students, by setting a range of different tasks with different cognitive levels of demand or by rate of response (quicker tasks for slower workers and vice versa). It can involve changes to task content, the extent to which students need to consult sources, and by the levels of support offered (help for those who struggle, independence for those who don't). Sometimes what is needed is to set a similar task to a range of students, but to invite groups to respond in different media (extended writing, pictorial work, an oral presentation).

There are important reasons why differentiation by more than just outcome is a critical teaching skill. Differentiation can encourage a variety of teaching approaches, thus undermining boredom. It can stretch students intellectually by linking their work to higher order skills. It can be used, in this way, to extend students' own boundaries of performance. Differentiation promotes interest in students who feel their individualism counts. It avoids time-wasting caused by overeasy or too difficult tasks and thus uses time more effectively. It promotes a steady growth in independence in learning such as is required for more advanced education or in lifelong learning. Differentiation is about individual challenge; it implies increasing knowledge, understanding and skills; it is part of a process in which the students take some control of their own learning and progress through personal study skills.

A final word is in order about the three skills discussed above: setting learning objectives, task-setting and differentiation. The word is: assessment. Though assessment has become a major goal in education in some parts of the world it is often carried out ineffectually, especially when assessors rely on tests and examinations. But the delineation of proper learning objectives, the setting of differentiated and demanding tasks, and the sharing with students of the intentions of these tasks and criteria for good performance in them, imply that teachers can make excellent and informed judgements about students' abilities and progress. That is the real target of assessment, and what has been said here strengthens the assessment process; it does not diminish it. For this reason, the skill of assessment (and of the need to keep proper records of student performance and progress) is assumed to be a teaching skill embedded in good practice as outlined above and in what follows.

Explaining effectively

Teachers talk extensively, typically for about two-thirds of class time. Much talk is in the form of exposition or explanation. It is crucial, then, that all this teacher-dominated talk is effective in bringing about learning!

Explanations can be pitched at low orders of thinking (rehearsing facts or revising known material; or even dealing with administrative or disciplinary matters). Preferably, they can be aimed at provoking or leading to higher levels of thought. Explanations need to be well prepared, delivered in a logical order, and without hesitations or the undue use of mannerisms (like 'err . . .', 'well'). They will usually demonstrate specific skills on the part of the teacher. These are some explaining skills along with a short commentary about each:

> *Think of a dynamic introduction:* an ear-catching phrase, illustration, idea or problem that engages students' interest.
> *Ensure that any new ideas, concepts and technical language are clarified:* otherwise the flow of the explanation will be interrupted and meaning impaired.
> *Link the explanation to concrete experience if possible:* indicate to students how the matter relates to the real world.

Use examples: these can be positive or negative or both – 'it works like this, but not like this'. Examples might include models, videos or other visual or aural aids.
Begin to develop the principles, rules or laws that underpin the explanation: for example, whenever you do x, y follows as a consequence.
Think about the language of explanations: though explanations of this kind are oral, they still need words like 'therefore', 'however', 'nevertheless' and so on to give them light and shade.
Remember that linguistic ploys are useful: 'Listen to this next bit very carefully', or 'This is the main issue'; such ploys focus the listener's mind.
In the same way, one might number the key points: 'In telling you how this works I am going to describe three important parts to the process. The first one is . . .'
Pace your explanation: provide variety by covering some elements more slowly, and more familiar elements more quickly; don't be afraid to pause or recap.
Link the content of the explanation: to other knowledge that the students already own.
Finish the explanation by getting feedback on students' understanding: you can also do this as the explanation proceeds by pausing to ask or receive questions.

Explanations are the keys that unlock understanding in hearers. The principles of clear explanation must be transferred to worksheets or other written, audio/visual or IT materials that a teacher might prepare. Explanations can be made more interesting and varied if the explainer remembers other basic skills such as the use of appropriate humour, skilful voice control and vigilance to ensure that learners' attention is still focused on the topic. Explaining can be interspersed with questioning.

Questioning effectively

Let us be clear: it is impossible even to give a brief overview of the skills of questioning in a short chapter like the present one, but the reader should consult Kerry (2002b) and the many references there for a fuller picture. Instead, one can give only a few pointers.

Questions can be constructed to demand higher or lower order thinking from students. Research in schools suggests that less than 10 per cent of all teacher questions ask students for higher order responses. Clearly, it is preferable for learning that this proportion is increased. Questions may relate to matters of order and discipline, of factual recall or revision – these are usually lower order questions. Alternatively they can invite students to imagine, analyze, deduce, apply, synthesize and evaluate – these are higher order functions. The major purposes of questioning are to stimulate students' curiosity, to put learning into a problem-solving mode and to encourage what is called the 'intuitive leap'. Effective questioning works only in a secure psychological climate where students feel free to speculate, experiment and even to get things wrong.

Just a single example must suffice of how questions can raise the cognitive stakes of lessons. Consider this sequence as part of a lesson about the Roman war machine:

1. Who can remember when the Romans landed in Britain for the second time?
2. What sort of weaponry did they wear or use?
3. How do we know this?
4. Can you think of ways in which the Roman legionary shields could have been used in battle apart from self-defence?
5. What might have motivated the invasion?
6. How might you have felt as a Roman legionary landing on British soil?
7. Suppose you were the general in charge, what kinds of logistics would be needed to support your army?
8. Look at what actually happened in your textbook: how do you think you could have done better?
9. What do these episodes tell us about the morality of war?

We move from recall or revision (1), through simple comprehension in following a text (2), to possible deduction drawing on evidence (3). (4) asks the students to apply and analyze their knowledge, and (5) to bring together disparate bits of knowledge, perhaps, into a theory or synthesis. Empathy and imagination apply in (6); deduction and imagination in (7); and evaluation at various levels in (8) and (9). Less than 25 per cent of questions (1, 2) are of low order; most at a higher order – so a good balance. Too often lessons remain at the low end of the cognitive spectrum, despite the fact that students generally enjoy challenge.

With this brief look at questioning we draw our sketch map of major teaching skills to a close, and consider briefly the processes of acquiring such skills.

Reflection

In which of the skills areas discussed above do you feel you perform effectively on a daily basis? On which do you fall short? What kinds of changes could you make to your own teaching to make it more effective?

Learning teaching skills

Anyone who has read the foregoing sections of this chapter will, hopefully, have acquired two things: first, an ability to justify the model(s) of teaching which they deem the most effective and second, a ground plan of what effective teaching might look like, including the skills that comprise it. But what can be said about the process of learning to teach?

Though an indicative answer only to this question can be given in the limited space available here, its importance should not be doubted. Teaching skills are learned initially in specialist institutions; but even the nomenclature of these last carries important messages. Thus, as we have seen above, to call them teacher *training* colleges carries a whole different set of meanings from calling them teacher *education* colleges. For, our preferred view of teacher *education* implies an enhanced professionalism, and lifelong progression and improvement in teaching skills based on growing wisdom and reflection. Training implies a once-for-all exposure to competencies acquired by example and imitation (Aspland and Brown 1993). In our view, teacher education is not just about 'hoop-jumping' but about judgement and attitudes. Leeferink and Klaasen (2002) argue from a Dutch perspective (and the United Kingdom is similar) that recent emphasis on school improvement, with its narrowed definitions of effectiveness, militates against the development of teachers as rounded professionals. Thus, to be an effective teacher, it is argued here, one needs to follow a road to reflective and reflexive practice (Pollard and Tann 1997).

In a sense, the wheel has turned full circle in this chapter, for one is forced back to where we began and to confirm the view of McGilchrist et al. (1999) that teacher effectiveness involves three dimensions: the content of teaching, a knowledge of how students learn and an ability to manage the processes of teaching and learning. Collins et al. (2001) go on to examine three further bases of effective teaching: social-constructivist models of education, active learning and the centrality of the student to the process. Given these considerations, it is small wonder that teachers now prefer to abandon the label 'in-service training' in favour of 'continuous professional development' (CPD). One of the failings of current UK teacher education is a failure to define how teaching is to be conceptualized or of what teachers' professionalism is composed (Docking 2000, pp. 145–52).

Bowring-Carr and West-Burnham (1997, p. 149) are right to insist that teacher development is 'facilitated, mentored, encouraged' rather than being the result of teaching, still less of training. There are different models of such supportive development (cf. the labels *mentor, appraiser, coach, performance manager*). Research carried out in initial teacher education identified some criteria for successful mentoring (putting time aside, listening effectively, analyzing practice with insight, being supportive, being organized and recording the mentee's progress systematically). But the research also drew attention to potential shortfalls in mentoring practice on the part of mentees: especially, failure to listen to advice or act on it (Kerry and Farrow 1996). Research from the same stable (Kerry and Farrow 1995) also identified factors inherent in school placements or in the students' colleges which might diminish the effectiveness of mentoring and support, such as poor selection and preparation of appropriate mentors, poor institutional organization, lack of communication between the parties and mentor sessions which lack structure. It was discovered that where mentoring worked well it was highly valued by mentees, but when it failed it tended to fail spectacularly; as mentees progressed in skill they also tended to become more discerning about the quality of the mentoring they were offered.

Nevertheless, some form of mentoring is a valuable tool in CPD; and in the United Kingdom both appraisal and performance management are endemic to the education system. Other forms of in-service work (courses, lectures, conferences and even higher degrees) have lost their potency at present. There is a tendency for most CPD to be conducted within schools by the school's own personnel. While there are exceptional schools where this might work, on a longer-term view shortened horizons, blinkered visions and complacency are real dangers with this option. In Kerry (1993) some quality criteria for judging the worth of CPD activities were established. But the real key to effective CPD lies in one's philosophies of teaching, of teachers and of professionalism. Teaching, it is argued, should be seen in a sociological context, one broader than mere targets and league tables, as a science and as an art.

Reflection

Think back over your own experience as an adult learner and as a professional engaged in professional development activities. What do you value among your learning experiences? What was less valuable? Do you, or how do you, convey professional knowledge to those in your care?

Conclusion

This chapter has put the case for the place of teaching skills and for the teacher as a 'rounded educator', and implicit in all this is a view of professionalism (Hargreaves 1997). This chapter has been about giving teachers pride in their distinctive skills, in the value of their work to society, and in the calibre of the job that they do in promoting the learning of young people in their care. Done well, no job can be more satisfying.

Further reading

Jarvis, M. (2005). *The Psychology of Effective Teaching and Learning*. Cheltenham: Nelson Thornes.

A good, modern approach to the application of psychology to classroom teaching.

Kerry, T. and Wilding, M. (2004). *Effective Classroom Teacher*. London: Pearson/Longman.

This book provides teachers with the skills of being a 'master teacher' and puts these skills in a context of research and grounded theory.

Kyriacou, C. (1997). *Effective Teaching in Schools: Theory and Practice*. Cheltenham: Nelson Thornes.

Kyriacou's work is characterized by readability and sound advice aimed at helping teachers improve their performance.

References

Alino-Wilcockson, D. and Falconer, A. (1999). Assessing the performance of Ofsted inspection in primary schools. *Education Today*, 49(4), 18–23.

Analysis. (2005). Tomlinson unpicked, part 2. *Managing Schools Today*, 14(4), 13–16.

Aspland, R. and Brown, G. (1993). Keeping teaching professional. In D. Bridges and T. Kerry (eds), *Developing Teachers Professionally* (pp. 6–22). London: Routledge.

Ball, S. (1994). *Education Reform: A Critical and Post-Structural Approach*. Buckingham: Open University Press.

Bimrose, J. (2006). *The Changing Context of Career Practice: Guidance, Counselling or Coaching?* Occasional Paper. Derby: University of Derby, Centre for Guidance Studies.

Blanchard, J. (2000). *Teaching and Targets: Self-Evaluation and School Improvement*. London: Routledge/Falmer.

Blishen, E. (1969). *The School That I'd Like*. Harmondsworth: Penguin.

Bloom, B. (1956). *Taxonomy of Educational Objectives*. London: Longman.

Bowring-Carr, C. (1996). Inspections by the book. In J. Ouston, P. Earley and B. Fidler (eds), *Inspections: The Early Experience* (pp. 42–51). London: David Fulton.

Bowring-Carr, C. and West-Burnham, J. (1997). *Effective Learning in Schools*. London: Pitman.

Campbell, A. and Kerry, T. (2004). Constructing a new Key Stage 3 curriculum at Brooke Weston CTC: a review and commentary. *Educational Studies*, 30, 391–407.

Chitty, C. and Dunford, J. (eds). (1999). *State Schools: New Labour and the Conservative Legacy*. London: Woburn Press.

Collins, P., Insley, K. and Soler, J. (2001). *Developing Pedagogy: Researching Practice*. Maidenhead: Open University Press.

Collings, P. (1999). Schools in deprived areas. In C. Chitty and J. Dunford (eds), *State Schools: New Labour and the Conservative Legacy* (pp. 60–72). London: Woburn Press.

Crace, J. and Smithers, R. (2006). Is the gold standard looking tarnished? *Guardian Newspaper*, 15 August 2006.

Curtis, P. (2005). Blair to expand vocational education. *Guardian Newspaper*, 11 February 2005.

Department for Education and Employment. (1997). *Excellence for All*. London: Stationery Office.

Department for Education and Employment. (1998). *Target Setting in Schools*. (Circular 11/98). London: DfEE.

Department for Education and Employment. (2000). *Vocational Education and Training: A Framework for the Future*. London: DfEE.

Department for Education and Skills. (2004). *Excellence and Enjoyment: Learning and Teaching in the Primary Years*. London: DfES.

Dimmock, C. (2000). *Designing the Learning-Centred School*. London: Routledge/Falmer.

Docking, J. (2000). *New Labour's Policies for Schools: Raising the Standard?* London: David Fulton.

Eggleston, J. (2000). *Staying on at School: The Hidden Curriculum of Selection*. Warwick Papers on Education Policy no. 9. Stoke-on-Trent: Trentham Books.

Elliott, J. (1998). *The Curriculum Experiment: Meeting the Challenge of Social Change*. Buckingham: Open University Press.

Farrell, M. (2001). *Key Issues for Secondary Schools*. London: Routledge/Falmer.

Gardner, H. (1993). *Frames of Mind*. New York: Harper Collins.

Guardian. (2003). Government misses SATs targets. *Guardian Newspaper*, 19 August 2003.

Hargreaves, A. (1997). The four ages of professionalism and professional learning. *Unicorn – Journal of the Australian College of Education*, 23(2), 86–114.

Harris, A. (2002). *School Improvement: What's in It For Schools?* London: Routledge/Falmer.

Hopkins, D. (2001). *School Improvement for Real*. London: Routledge/Falmer.

House of Commons. (2003). *Secondary Education: Diversity of Provision*. London: Stationery Office.

Husbands, C., Kitson, A. and Pendry, A. (2003). *Understanding History Teaching*. Maidenhead: Open University/McGraw-Hill.

Jarvis, M. (2005). *The Psychology of Effective Learning and Teaching*. Cheltenham: Nelson Thornes.

Jerome, L. (2001). Teaching citizenship: from rhetoric to reality. *Education Today*, 51(1), 8–12.

Jesson, D. (2000). *The Comparative Evaluation of GCSE Value-added Performance by Type of School and LEA*. Discussion Paper 2000/52, University of York, York.

Jesson, D. and Crossley, D. (2005). *Specialist Schools Outperform Non-Specialist in all Areas and Academies top Value-added Chart*. Specialist Schools and Academies Trust. Retrieved 22 November 2006, from www.specialistschools.org.uk/article.aspa?PageId=806&NodeId=1

Kerry, C. and Kerry, T. (2003). Government policy and the effective employment and deployment of support staff in UK schools. *International Studies in Educational Administration*, 31, 65–81.

Kerry, T. (1993). Evaluating INSET: the search for quality. In D. Bridges and T. Kerry (eds), *Developing Teachers Professionally* (pp. 165–77). London: Routledge.

Kerry, T. (2001). *PPPs: An Apple for Teachers and Pupils?* SourceUK.net. Retrieved 22 November 2006, from www.sourceuk.net/article/1/1621/ppps_an_apple_for_teachers_and_pupils.html

Kerry, T. (2002a). *Learning Objectives, Task Setting and Differentiation.* Cheltenham: Nelson Thornes.

Kerry, T. (2002b). *Explaining and Questioning.* Cheltenham: Nelson Thornes.

Kerry, T. (2006a). *PFI – Public Funding Initiative or Plums for Investors?* SourceUK.net. Retrieved 22 November 2006, from www.sourceuk.net/article/8/8354/pfi_public_funding_initiative_or_plums_for_investors.html

Kerry, T. (2006b). *The Murky World of Policy and Diploma.* SourceUK.net. Retrieved 22 November 2006, from www.sourceuk.net/article/8/8220/the_murky_world_of_policy_and_diploma.html

Kerry, T. (2007). Integration: dirty word or golden key? *Forum for Promoting 3–19 Comprehensive Education*, 49(1, 2), 77–92.

Kerry, T. and Farrow, J. (1995). Reflections on a mentoring programme in a school-based PGCE programme. *Education Today*, 45(4), 45–53.

Kerry, T. and Farrow, J. (1996). Changes in initial teacher training students' perceptions of the effectiveness of school-based mentoring over time. *Educational Studies*, 22, 99–110.

Kerry, T. and Wilding, M. (2004). *Effective Classroom Teacher.* London: Pearson/Longman.

Kinchin, I. (2001). Concept mapping and progression in the National Curriculum. *Education Today*, 51(3), 3–7.

Kirby, P. (2001). The national literacy strategy and the literacy hour. *Education Today*, 51(3), 8–14.

Leeferink, H. and Klaasen, C. (2002). An investigation into the pedagogical identity of the teacher. In C. Sugrue and C. Day (eds), *Developing Teachers and Teaching Practice* (pp. 26–40). London: RoutledgeFalmer.

Maclure, S. (1993). Fight this tooth and nail. *Times Educational Supplement*, 18 June 1993.

Mahony, P. (1999). Teacher education policy and gender. In J. Salisbury and S. Riddell (eds), *Gender Policy and Educational Change* (pp. 229–42). London: Routledge.

McGilchrist, B., Myers, K. and Reed, J. (1999). *The Intelligent School.* London: PCP.

Menter, I., Muschamp, Y., Nicholls, P., Ozga, J. and Pollard, A. (1997). *Work and Identity in the Primary School.* Buckingham: Open University Press.

Middlewood, D. and Burton, N. (eds). (2001). *Managing the Curriculum.* London: PCP.

Plowden Report. (1967). *Children and Their Primary Schools: A Report of the Central Advisory Council for Education (England).* London: HMSO.

Plummer, G. (2000). *Failing Working Class Girls.* Stoke-on-Trent: Trentham Books.

Pollard, A. and Tann, S. (1997). *Reflective Teaching in the Primary School.* London: Cassell.

Porter, J. (2000). Schools, teachers and the democratic imperative. *Education Today*, 50(1), 21–26.

Preedy, M., Glatter, R. and Wise, C. (2003). *Strategic Leadership and Educational Improvement.* London: PCP.

Rasmussen, P. (2002). Education for everyone: secondary education and social inclusion in Denmark. *Journal of Education Policy*, 17, 627–42.

Ratcliffe, M. and Grace, M. (2003). *Science Education for Citizenship*. Maidenhead: Open University/McGraw-Hill.

Ross, A. (2000). *Curriculum: Construction and Critique*. London: Falmer.

Rudduck, J. (1999). 'Education for all', 'achievement for all' and pupils who are 'too good to drift'. *Education Today*, 49(2), 3–11.

Schon, D. (1983). *The Reflective Practitioner*. London: Temple Smith.

Secondary Heads Association. (1996). *Towards More Effective Schools: Secondary School Inspections Beyond 1997*. Leicester: SHA.

Soucek, V. (1994). Flexible education and new standards of communicating competence. In J. Kenway (ed.), *Economising Education: Post-Fordist Directions* (pp. 43–103). Australia: Deakin University Press.

Stenhouse, L. (1975). *An Introduction to Curriculum Research and Development*. London: Heinemann.

Stubbs, Sir William. (2002). Gold standards and A-levels. *Education Today*, 52(4), 3–8.

Teacher Training Agency. (2001). *Standards for the Award of Qualified Teacher Status*. London: TTA.

Teacher Training Agency. (2002). *Qualifying to Teach*. London: TTA.

Tomlinson, M. (2003). *Working Group on 14–19 Reform Progress Report*. Key Skills Support Programme. Retrieved 23 November 2006, from www.keyskillssupport.net/organising/policy/workinggroup

Watkins, D. (2002). Learning and teaching. In A. Walker and C. Dimmock (eds), *School Leadership and Administration* (pp. 61–76). London: Routledge/Falmer.

Whitty, G. (2000). *Making Sense of Education Policy*. London: PCP.

Making thinking audible and visible via cooperative learning

George Jacobs

JF New Paradigm Education, Singapore

Wang Aili, Li Xishuang, Xie Yongye

Ministry of Education, China

6

Chapter Outline

Group activities are common in education. However, groups of students can sit together and even produce a group product without cooperating at a high level. Cooperation can be enhanced when students share their thinking with each other by telling and showing each other what is going on in their minds as they go about a task. Cooperative learning principles and techniques can help teachers encourage such enhanced cooperation among students.

Introduction

This chapter is designed to share a learning technique the authors value, and to set anyone unfamiliar with it on the path to using it. It begins with a section that describes cooperative learning and explains eight cooperative learning principles. The second section looks briefly at *why*, in the process, making thinking audible and visible enriches students' thinking. Section three shows *how* cooperative learning techniques can be used to make thinking audible and visible. As cooperative learning is a generic methodology, it can be used in any content area, with any age of student and at any stage in a unit of learning. Cooperative learning fits well with other modes of instruction, such as teacher talk and individual work. Thus, in any one lesson students can usefully listen to the teacher, work cooperatively with peers and study alone. The study resonates with the study by McLaughlin in Chapter 2.

Cooperative learning

This section begins by surveying cooperative learning in terms of its history, research, theoretical support and definition. Eight cooperative learning principles are described, noting each principle's possible role in encouraging thinking.

What is cooperative learning? Cooperative or collaborative learning is a body of concepts and techniques for helping to maximize the benefits of cooperation among students. A wide range of theoretical perspectives on learning – including behaviourism, socio-cultural theory, humanist psychology, cognitive psychology, social psychology and Piagetian developmental psychology – have been used to develop and justify different approaches to cooperative learning. Similarly, various principles have been put forward in the cooperative learning literature (Baloche 1998; Jacobs, Power and Loh 2002; Johnson and Johnson 1999; Kagan 1994; Slavin 1995).

Cooperative learning is certainly not a new concept for educators in Malaysia or elsewhere. For thousands of years, humans have utilized the power of cooperation in a broad range of endeavours, including education. The term *cooperative learning* dates back at least to the 1970s when a great deal of research and practical work began on discovering how best to harness the power of cooperation to promote learning. Many hundreds of studies – perhaps thousands – have been conducted across a wide range of subject areas and age groups (for reviews see Cohen 1994b; Johnson, Johnson and Stanne 2000; Slavin 1995).

The overall findings of these studies suggest that group activities structured along cooperative learning lines are associated with gains on a host of key variables: achievement, higher level thinking, self-esteem, liking for the subject matter and for school and inter-group (e.g. inter-ethnic) relations. Indeed, at a conference on cooperative learning in Penang, David Johnson claimed that cooperative learning is one of the best-researched approaches in education and that, when the public asks what we know that works in education, cooperative learning is one of our surest answers.

Jacobs initially came upon cooperative learning in the mid-1980s. We believe that his main attraction to the use of cooperation as a way of learning comes from his positive experiences with cooperation (whether in sports teams, in his family and with friends or in classrooms) and from his negative experiences when cooperation was lacking. He used group activities because they were consistent with the communicative pedagogy that was prevalent in language teaching in the 1980s and still is today.

Whatever the reasons, he was using group activities in English classes at Chiang Mai University. However, he faced problems, problems that we are sure the readers of this chapter have also faced, such as students who did not want to share with their groupmates and students for whom a disagreement was not an opportunity to discuss and learn but a call to confrontation. In the hope of addressing these problems, he searched the University's library and came upon his first article on cooperative learning, by David and Roger Johnson, whose works are cited in this chapter.

In the more than 20 years since that fortuitous encounter in the University Library, Jacobs has used cooperative learning in almost every class he has taught including ones attended by the co-authors. What we are sharing with you in this chapter is what he has learned since his days in Chiang Mai and what we four have learned from further reading, from interacting with colleagues and observing students. Thus, almost none of the ideas in this chapter are 'our own' ideas. We include them because we believe they are important.

Cooperative learning principles

In what follows we discuss eight cooperative learning principles and how they can shape teaching practice.

Heterogeneous grouping

This principle means that, in cooperative learning groups, students are assigned groups by one or more of a number of variables: gender, ethnicity, social class, religion, personality, age, language proficiency and diligence. Table 6.1 contrasts heterogeneous with homogeneous grouping.

To achieve heterogeneous groups, teachers often make conscious decisions about which students should work together, rather than leaving the matter to chance or students' choice. The latter option often results in groups with low levels of heterogeneity. When students work in heterogeneous groups, they may want to spend some time on ice-breaking (or teambuilding) activities because, as Slavin (1995) notes, the combination of students that results from teacher-selected groups is likely to be one that would not have been created

Table 6.1 Differences between heterogeneous grouping and homogeneous grouping

Heterogeneous grouping	Homogeneous grouping
• More peer tutoring, as groups contain members of past achievement levels.	• Less peer tutoring, as students tend to be fairly close in terms of past achievement levels.
• Students see more perspectives, as they interact with group mates different from themselves.	• Students see fewer perspectives, as they interact with those similar to themselves.
• Thus, the value of diversity is on display for students to appreciate.	• Students have fewer opportunities to appreciate the value of diversity.
• Students have more opportunities to learn about people different from themselves and how to collaborate with them.	• Students have fewer opportunities to learn about people different from themselves and how to collaborate with them.
• Students come to know a larger number of their classmates.	• Students stay with the same classmates who they already know.
• Students may come to feel more confident that they can work with anyone.	• Students feel less confident about working with new people because they have less experience doing so.
• Initial difficulties in group cohesion are more likely, as group mates may not feel comfortable working together, making teambuilding activities even more important.	• Initially, groups may work together better because students already know each other or, at least, have many similarities.

otherwise. The hope: by interacting with a wide variety of classmates, students' thinking will be stretched, as they encounter different perspectives.

Other ideas for helping heterogeneous groups cooperate effectively are:

1. Students can select a group leader; many teachers report finding that this and other rotating roles (see below) can be useful.
2. The teacher can ask one group to demonstrate for the class how to proceed, not just on the task itself but how to interact with groupmates.
3. Groups that finish ahead of others can assist those groups that are struggling.

Cooperative skills

Cooperative skills are needed to work effectively with others. Students often lack these skills. Teachers need to consciously teach them. Which cooperative skill to teach will depend on the particular students and the particular task they are undertaking. Some examples of skills important to successful collaboration are: checking that others understand, asking for and giving reasons, disagreeing politely and responding politely to disagreement, and encouraging others to participate and responding to encouragement to participate.

Group autonomy

This principle encourages students to look to *themselves* for help instead of relying only on the teacher. When student groups are having difficulty, it is very tempting for teachers to intervene either in a particular group or with the entire class. Sometimes teachers cannot resist this temptation, but as Roger Johnson writes, 'Teachers must trust the peer interaction to do many of the things they have felt responsible for themselves' (www.clcrc.com/pages/qanda. html). Group autonomy encourages students to become more independent thinkers.

Maximum peer interaction

In classrooms in which group activities are not used, the normal way that people interact is for one person at a time – usually the teacher – to speak. For example, in didactic teaching, the teacher stops, asks a question to check students' comprehension, calls on a student to answer and evaluates that student's response. In contrast, when group activities are used, one student per group is, hopefully, speaking; for example, in a class of forty divided into groups of four, ten students are speaking simultaneously. The hope is that greater participation leads to greater thinking.

Even when teachers use groups, it is common for each to report individually to the class and the teacher. When this takes place, we are back to one-at-a-time interaction. Instead, we want maximum peer interaction because interaction promotes thinking and learning. To maximize peer interaction, many alternatives exist: for example, one person from each group can go to another group to explain (not just show or tell) their group's ideas.

The principle of Maximum Peer Interaction also refers to the *quality* of the interaction, not just to the quantity. While there may be benefits in students practising rote learning tasks with partners, more benefits may accrue when students engage in deeper and broader thinking. Cooperative learning offers many ways to maximize peer interaction by deepening and broadening student thinking.

Equal opportunity to participate

A frequent problem is that one or two group members dominate the group and make it difficult for other members to take part in the activity. If students are not participating, there is less chance that they are thinking. Cooperative learning offers many ways of providing everyone with an equal opportunity to participate. Two of these are: the use of rotating roles in a group, such as facilitator, checker (who checks to see that everyone understands what the group is doing or has done), questioner, praiser, encourager and paraphraser; and the use of multiple ability tasks (Cohen 1994a; Gardner 2006), that is, tasks that require a range of abilities, such as drawing, singing, acting and categorizing, not just language abilities.

Individual accountability

Individual accountability is, in some ways, the flip side of equal opportunity to participate. Everyone must feel they have opportunities to take part in the group. By encouraging individual accountability in groups, we hope that no one will attempt to avoid using those opportunities. In other words, we want to prevent students letting their groupmates do the thinking for them. These techniques overlap with those for encouraging equal opportunity to participate: including giving each group member a designated turn to participate, keeping group size small, calling on students at random to share their group's ideas and assigning tasks to be done individually after the group activity is finished.

Positive interdependence

This principle is the most important one. When positive interdependence exists among group members, they all feel that what helps one member of the group helps the other members and that what hurts one member hurts other members. It is the factor that leads group members to want to support each other in realizing the common goal. That goal is for everyone in the group to learn. The group is not finished just because they have finished a task, such as completing an assignment. The work is not finished until everyone in the group has gained the ability to do that assignment and until everyone can explain what the group has done and why they did it. Positive interdependence provides students with peer support to do the thinking necessary so that all group members reach that level.

To support these intentions Johnson and Johnson (1999) outline nine ways to promote positive interdependence:

1. Goal positive interdependence: The group has a common goal that they collaborate to achieve.
2. Environmental positive interdependence: Group members sit close together so that all can easily see each other's work and hear each other without using loud voices.
3. Role positive interdependence: In addition to the roles mentioned above, for example, checker and questioner, there are also housekeeping types of roles, such as timekeeper who reminds the group of time limits and 'sound hound' who tells the group if they are being too loud in their deliberations. Roles should rotate.
4. Resource positive interdependence: Each group member has unique resources which can be information or equipment, such as readings or a computer.
5. External challenge positive interdependence: Students collaborate within their cooperative learning groups to do better than an external guage of quality, for example, their own past achievement or another group's achievement.
6. Reward or celebration positive interdependence: If groups meet a pre-set goal, they receive some kind of reward. If extrinsic rewards are used, Lynda Baloche (personal communication, 14 May 2001) recommends that teachers never begin an extrinsic reward programme without having a plan for how to end it.
7. Fantasy positive interdependence: Students imagine that they are a group of people in another place, time or situation, for example, they could imagine that they are a group of sharks preparing a report for humans on the eating of shark-fin soup.
8. Identity positive interdependence: Groupmates form a common identity such as a group name, motto, poem or handshake.
9. Task positive interdependence: Each group member has a separate task to perform, for example, in a science experiment.

Cooperation as a value

This principle means that cooperation is not only a way to learn, that is, the *how* of learning. Cooperation also becomes part of the content to be learned, that is, the *what* of learning. This flows from the central cooperative learning principle, positive interdependence. Cooperation as a value takes the feeling of 'All for one, one for all' and expands it beyond the small classroom group to encompass the whole class, the whole school and far beyond. In this way, increasingly greater numbers of people and other beings are welcomed into students' circle of cooperation. Cooperation as a value encourages students to think beyond their classrooms and to explore further applications of their learning.

Reflection

What problems have you encountered when your students were engaged in group activities? Do you think that applying cooperative learning principles might address some of those problems? When your students work in groups, how can you encourage equal opportunity to participate? In what ways could you foster positive interdependence among students?

Making thinking audible and visible

The Merriam-Webster Online Dictionary defines the verb *think* as 'to form or have in mind'. Thus, thinking is seen as an internal process, which others can only access based on what the thinker does or says. Such internal thinking is insufficient in education. Instead, teachers and students need to externalize their thinking. When teachers externalize their thinking, they provide students with a model of how an expert goes about a task. This modelling invites students to join the community of practice (Wenger 1999). Wenger defines communities of practice as '[G]roups of people who share a concern or a passion for something they do and learn how to do it better as they interact regularly' (Wenger, no date).

For example, physics teachers think aloud and show the steps as they tackle a physics problem, thereby inviting their students to think and act like physicists and join the international community of practice of physicists. Of course, students are not likely to drop all their other studies and do cutting edge research in physics. That is not the point. The point is that when students think like physicists, learning comes alive; students gain much greater insight into what they are doing and why they are doing it. (Cf. Marzano's first dimension of thinking: students' attitudes towards and perceptions of learning.)

This externalized thinking fits with the process approach to education (Jacobs and Farrell 2003). The approach represents a contrast with the formerly dominant product approach, in which teachers focus on what students produce, such as their answers on a test, rather than on how they go about arriving at those answers. The process approach still values student products, but the emphasis is now on helping students on the paths they set for themselves as they create those products. (Cf. Marzano's fifth dimension of learning: developing habits of mind, such as being clear and seeking clarity.)

Now that we have looked at why teachers should make their thinking audible and visible, let us next look at why students should externalize their thinking. First, by making their own thinking audible and visible, students encourage meta-cognitive thinking, in which they can assess their own strengths and weaknesses, and plan how to improve. Second, when teachers hear and see what students are doing as they go about a task, teachers are better able to assess their own teaching and to figure out how best to help their students. Third, and of most relevance to cooperative learning, when students' thinking is audible and visible, their peers are better able to help and to learn from them.

How can thinking be made audible and visible? As identified above, thinking aloud allows teachers and students to make their thinking audible (Ericsson and Simon 1993). Originally developed as a research tool, thinking aloud is now used in classrooms. In thinking aloud, the thinkers say what is going through their minds as they go about a task. Most students are not accustomed to thinking aloud. As a result, teachers need to model the process and even provide students with think-aloud scripts or guidelines. Questions (see Kerry's Chapter 5) can be very effective in making thinking audible: for example, asking 'Why do you say that?', 'How did you arrive at that answer?' or 'Could you please explain your thinking?' pushes students to externalize their thinking.

Similarly, many ways exist to make thinking visible: for example, in mathematics, teachers and students can show the steps they take as they solve a problem. Another means of making thinking visible is via graphic organizers such as mind maps, tables, Venn Diagrams and flow charts. Furthermore, thinking can be made audible and visible simultaneously. All of the ways of making thinking audible and visible fit well with cooperative learning. Examples of the system at work will be provided in the third part of this paper.

Cooperative learning techniques for making thinking audible and visible

Well over 100 techniques for use within cooperative learning have been developed, and each technique has a range of variations. In this section we explain the steps in several exemplar cooperative learning techniques and highlight how each technique can help students externalize their thinking. But first, we set out four ways in which to get started on using the collaborative learning technique.

Pointers for getting started with cooperative learning

1. *Play to success:* Research suggests that cooperative learning is a powerful pedagogy, but it is not magic. Before students begin a cooperative learning task, teachers should ask themselves if students are intellectually ready to tackle that task: initial failures may sour students on cooperative learning. One route to success is for the teacher or experienced students to demonstrate how to make learning audible and visible. Once groups have started their task, the teacher might usefully draw attention to good practice in progress.

2. *Teachers need to start with success for themselves:* Just as students need to experience successful collaboration, so do teachers new to cooperative learning need to see it succeeding. Therefore, teachers are advised to begin with simple cooperative learning techniques (Sharan, Gobel and Sim 2006) and to first implement cooperative learning in those classes where it is most likely to thrive, for example, for highly motivated, high achieving students. But, with practice, the technique works equally well with students who have experienced mostly failure in their academic careers, and with special education students.

3. *Cooperating about what?:* We need to ask about the nature of the task. Is it a task that encourages deeper thinking, or simply a rote learning task?

4. *Remember cooperative learning principles:* The first section of this chapter explained eight cooperative learning principles. These principles should be kept in mind by teachers as their students collaborate.

Reflection

How do you make your own thinking audible and visible to students? What do your students already do to make their thinking audible and visible to you and their peers? What thinking skills do you teach? How does making thinking audible and visible connect with teaching effective habits of mind?

What follows are some examples of cooperative learning techniques for externalizing thinking:

Everyone can explain
Steps:
- Each member has a number: 1, 2, 3, 4, depending on the number of group members.
- The teacher asks a question or gives a task.
- Each student tries alone, then takes a turn to share with their groupmates.
- The group tries to reach a consensus.
- Everyone prepares to present and explain their group's ideas.
- The teacher calls a number at random; students with that number give and explain their group's answer.

Pointers:
- Note that instead of calling on a group and letting the ablest student in that group answer, teachers call a number at random. This encourages everyone to be ready and to help their groupmates.
- Students need to do more than just give an answer. Everyone must be ready to *explain* their group's answer.
- One way to help everyone to be ready to explain is for group members to rehearse answers with groupmates.
- To highlight the point that students are representing their group, not themselves as individuals, any feedback on an answer or explanation goes to the group, not to the respondent.

SUMMER
(A technique slightly adapted from one developed by Donald Dansereau and colleagues at Texas Christian University.)

Steps:
Set the mood:
A group of two engage in discussion and make sure they are clear on the procedure to follow.

Understand by reading silently:
A reading passage (or a section from a textbook) has been divided into sections. Both students read the first section silently.

Mention key ideas:
Without looking at the text, one of the pair acts as Recaller, summarizing the key ideas of the section.

Monitor:

The other group member looks at the text and acts as Monitor, pointing out any errors, omissions or unnecessary information in the Recaller's summary and praising the Recaller for a job well done. The roles of Recaller and Monitor rotate for the next section.

Elaborate:

Both students elaborate on the ideas in the section. Types of elaborations include:

- connections with other things the students have studied
- links between the section and students' lives
- additions of relevant information not included in the section
- agreements or disagreements with views expressed
- reactions to the section such as surprise, gladness or anger
- applications of the ideas and information
- questions, either for comprehension or from curiosity

Not all types of elaborations are relevant to every section. Pairs repeat the Understand, Recall, Mention and Elaborate steps for all the sections of the passage.

Review:

The pair combines their thoughts to summarize the entire text.

Pointers:
- Research suggests that after doing SUMMER in groups, when students read alone, they continue to do the types of thinking encouraged by the SUMMER script.
- This highlights why the teaching of thinking skills prepares students to be lifelong learners.

Exchange-a-question
Steps:
- Students work alone to write one or more questions or problems.
- They write answers, with explanations and perhaps illustrations, to their questions on another paper.
- Students exchange questions but not answers.
- After students have answered their partner's questions, they compare answers.

Pointers:
- Teachers need to demonstrate how to write thinking questions.
- Before exchanging questions with a groupmate, students can check their questions and answers with a different groupmate.

Group mind-mapping

Steps:

- The group begins with the central concept written as a word and/or image in the middle of the page.
- Each group member takes a turn to identify and draw the main ideas related to the central image. Every time someone adds to the group's map, they explain what they are adding and why it is being added in that particular place in the map.
- Group members continue taking turns to add other ideas that spring from and connect to the main ideas. In addition to words and images, different colours and sizes of letters are also used to make the Group Mind Map more understandable and memorable.
- Students display and perhaps explain their Group Mind Map to another group and/or the entire class.

Pointers:

- A similar taking of turns can be used to construct any other type of graphic organizer.
- Ways to encourage individual accountability while making thinking visible via a graphic organizer include: students do their own graphic organizer before combining ideas with the group, students are responsible for one section of the graphic organizer, students use a different colour when writing or drawing, and students take turns to explain the group's graphic organizer to visitors from other groups.

Reflection

Have you already tried any of the techniques described above or anything similar? Might any of the other techniques work with your students? If so, how would you use them?

Conclusion

The chapter began with a description of cooperative learning, a research-tested, generic teaching methodology that harnesses peer power to help students learn. The section explained eight cooperative learning principles and linked each to promoting deeper thinking among students. The second section discussed why teachers and students should make their thinking audible and visible, and gave suggestions on how to do this. The chapter's final section described five cooperative learning techniques that encourage students to externalize their thinking. Our ongoing experiences as learners and teachers, as well as our life experiences remind us of the benefits of cooperation. But, cooperation is not easy and has to be learned like other social skills.

Reading and discussing the literature on cooperative learning and related fields is an act of cooperation with our teaching colleagues. In this sharing, we make our thinking audible and visible to others, thus setting an example for them and bringing alive the theme of this chapter.

Further reading

Forest, L. (2001). *Crafting Creative Community: Combining Cooperative Learning, Multiple Intelligences, and Nature's Wisdom.* San Clemente, CA: Kagan Publications.

This innovative book provides lesson plans for primary and secondary school teachers.

Kohn, A. (1992). *No Contest: The Case Against Competition.* (Second edn). Boston, MA: Houghton Miflin.

This wide-ranging book shows the benefits of cooperation rather than competition in many areas of life, including education.

McCafferty, S. G., Jacobs, G. M. and DaSilva Iddings, A. C. (eds). (2006). *Cooperative Learning and Second Language Teaching.* New York: Cambridge University Press.

The first part of the book provides an overview of cooperative learning in terms of theory and implementation. The second part consists of six narratives by teachers about using cooperative learning at primary, secondary and tertiary levels.

Sapon-Shevin, M. (1999). *Because We Can Change the World: A Practical Guide to Building Cooperative, Inclusive Classroom Communities.* Boston: Allyn & Bacon.

Sapon-Shevin is a professor of Inclusive Education and her book is especially strong on ways to make all students feel accepted in cooperative groups.

Tan, I. G. -C., Sharan, S. and Lee, C. K. -E. (2006). *Group Investigation and Student Learning: An Experiment in Singapore Schools.* Singapore: Marshall Cavendish.

A study done in Singapore secondary schools of the use of the Group Investigation method of cooperative learning. The book also contains useful advice on doing research on cooperative learning.

References

Baloche, L. (1998). *The Cooperative Classroom: Empowering Learning.* Upper Saddle River, New Jersey: Prentice Hall.

Cohen, E. G. (1994a). *Designing Groupwork: Strategies for the Heterogeneous Classroom* (Second edn). New York: Teachers College Press.

Cohen, E. G. (1994b). Restructuring the classroom: conditions for productive small groups. *Review of Educational Research,* 64, 1–35.

Ericsson, K. A. and Simon, H. A. (1993). *Protocol Analysis: Verbal Reports as Data* (Revised edn). Cambridge, MA: The MIT Press.

Gardner, H. (2006). *Multiple Intelligences: New Horizons.* New York: Basic Books.

Jacobs, G. M, and Farrell, T. S. C. (2003). Understanding and implementing the CLT (Communicative Language Teaching) paradigm. *RELC Journal*, 34(1), 5–30.

Jacobs, G. M., Power, M. A. and Loh, W. I. (2002). *The Teacher's Sourcebook for Cooperative Learning: Practical Techniques, Basic Principles, and Frequently Asked Questions*. Thousand Oaks, CA: Corwin Press.

Johnson, D. W. and Johnson, R. T. (1999). *Learning Together and Alone: Cooperative, Competitive and Individualistic Learning* (Fifth edn). Boston: Allyn & Bacon.

Johnson, D. W., Johnson, R. T. and Stanne, M. B. (2000). *Cooperative Learning Methods: A Meta-Analysis*. Cooperative Learning Center, University of Minnesota. Retrieved 6 November 2006, from www.cooperation.org/pages/cl-methods.html

Kagan, S. (1994). *Cooperative Learning*. San Juan Capristrano, CA: Kagan Cooperative Learning.

Merriam-Webster Online Dictionary. Retrieved 6 November 2006 from www.m-w.com/cgi-bin/dictionary?book=Dictionary&va=think

Sharan, Y., Gobel, P. and Sim, T. H. (2006). Why do teachers begin at the top? *International Association for the Study of Cooperation in Education (IASCE) Newsletter*, November 25(3), 10–14. Available online at www.iasce.net/newsletters_menu.shtml#previous_newsletters

Slavin, R. E. (1995). *Cooperative Learning: Theory, Research, and Practice* (Second edn). Englewood Cliffs, NJ: Prentice Hall.

Wenger, E. (1999). *Communities of Practice: Learning, Meaning and Identity*. Cambridge: Cambridge University Press.

Wenger, E. *Communities of Practice: A Brief Introduction*. Retrieved 6 November 2006, from www.ewenger.com/theory/index.htm.

Educating values: possibilities and challenges through mathematics teaching

7

Alan J. Bishop and Wee Tiong Seah

Monash University, Australia

Chapter Outline

A modern trend in school education is to instil in students the desired citizenship values. Teaching values through mathematics education is problematic because we know little about what happens with values teaching and learning in mathematics classrooms, or how potentially controllable and effective such values teaching is. Here, three research projects related to 'values through mathematics' are discussed. The case for researching teachers' values will be argued. By perceiving values in mathematics education as being those deep affective qualities which interact with, and are fostered by, mathematics teaching, we suggest 'values through mathematics' is a crucial, ever-present component of the mathematics classroom affective environment. Finally we suggest some teaching activities and strategies to foster and develop values in mathematics classrooms.

Introduction

The chapter picks up themes of affective education from chapters 2 and 6, and applies the insights in a subject-specific context. Citizenship is of concern to educators, as it relates to the nature of the society in which all education, including mathematics education, functions. Citizenship also forces us to think about how mathematics education prepares students for the society in which they will live. A significant aspect of that society and its related culture concerns the values shared, constructed and contested by the diverse members of the society, and among these values are those of democratization and social justice. Thus underpinning any discussion about developing social justice and democratization through mathematics education is the whole issue of values education. In Malaysia, for example, these values desired of students are encapsulated in the '*Budi Bahasa dan Nilai-Nilai Murni*' (Courtesy and Noble Values) and are currently actively being introduced to the country's population. Singapore's 'shared values' and Australia's 'values for Australian schooling' are two other examples. But teachers are not always attuned to values education: many mathematics teachers are not aware that they are teaching any values when they teach mathematics. Changing that perception may prove to be one of the biggest hurdles to be overcome if we are to move to a more socially just and democratic (mathematics) education for all.

> ### Reflection
>
> Can moral, societal and other kinds of desirable values be taught through the teaching and learning of mathematics in schools? Reflect on your experience in the mathematics classroom in your own culture. How are such values teaching being carried out?

Values

Values are part of the deep affective components of a person's mind which influence, and are influenced by, our choices, decisions and beliefs in engaging with life's challenges. These are dialectically related to beliefs and attitudes (see Krathwohl et al. 1964; McLeod 1992; Raths et al. 1987). We argue that values in mathematics education are those deep affective qualities which interact with, and are fostered by, mathematics teaching (Bishop 1991) and as such they are a crucial, ever-present component of the mathematics classroom affective environment. Values are, as educators are nowadays recognizing, a central focus for education (Lewis-Shaw 2001), and becoming more so for subjects such as mathematics (Chin and Lin 2001) and science education. The research challenge we face is that although everyone agrees on the importance of values education, there is little research on the teaching and learning of values in mathematics education in schools.

While our research concern is with the values in mathematics and mathematics education rather than with more general values, the teachers involved in our research talk about valuing *cooperation* in problem-solving, *individual differences*, taking *risks* in finding solutions, being *logical*, showing *creativity*, etc. – all values which are generic.

Bishop et al.'s (1999) assertion that there was relatively little knowledge about what values teachers are teaching in mathematics classes, about how aware teachers are of their own value positions, about how these affect their teaching, and about how their teaching thereby develops certain values in their students still rings true currently. Values are rarely considered in any discussions about mathematics teaching, and a question to teachers about the values they are teaching in mathematics lessons often produces an answer to the effect that they do not believe they are teaching any values at all. It is part of the widespread misunderstanding that mathematics is the most value-free of all school subjects, not just among teachers but also among parents, university mathematicians and employers. In reality, mathematics is just as much human and cultural knowledge as is any other field of knowledge (Bishop 1988/1991); teachers inevitably teach values, and adults ironically express feelings, beliefs and values about mathematics which clearly relate to the mathematics teaching they experienced at school.

Therefore, in this chapter we will present data, ideas and implications from our research projects which we feel at least indicate some directions for both teachers' practices and future research, namely, the 'Values And Mathematics Project (VAMP)' and the 'Values in Mathematics and Science Education' project.

In the light of these two, and other, studies on values in mathematics education, we will also comment on the usefulness and the difficulties of the research procedures used. Finally we will suggest some teaching activities which can foster and develop values in mathematics classrooms.

The VAMP study

This project, in which we collaborated with Gail FitzSimons and Phil Clarkson, relied on researching *with*, rather than on, teachers; that is, the teachers were encouraged to be full participants in the research and not merely the objects of our study. Initially we talked about values with groups of teachers, using video-clips and written classroom incidents as prompts, in professional development settings. A small group of eight volunteer teachers from primary and secondary schools had earlier responded to the study's questionnaire and subsequently indicated their interest in working with us in their classrooms.

The basic approach adopted with each teacher was a cycle of preliminary interview, classroom observation and post-observation debriefing interview. This cycle was repeated for two or three days. The classroom observations were video-taped and the interviews audio-taped. This process not only invited teachers to reflect on their teaching practices and to say what values they were intending to teach, it also asked for authentication of the teacher's analysis by seeking to observe those values being implemented in the classroom situation, with activities devised by the teacher.

Using this strategy we studied the extent to which the teachers were controlling their values teaching. In particular we were interested in whether they could articulate their own intended values, and whether they then implemented these in their classrooms. During the observation lessons we looked specifically for those values being implemented, but also we looked for other values being portrayed by the teacher. Values-related episodes noted in the lessons observed were elaborated and mutually examined with the teachers concerned in the post-lesson discussion sessions, aided by the video-tapes which assisted in the recall of the episodes concerned.

Our research in Victorian school classrooms has indicated a range of scenarios. The teachers were not necessarily aware of possible values arising from the discipline of mathematics nor the field of mathematics education that they portrayed in their classes. When they did make a conscious decision to portray a certain value, it was either addressed explicitly (e.g. 'today we are going to focus on *cooperation . . .*'), or implicitly (e.g. by rewarding cooperative behaviour without mentioning it explicitly). Even when they expressed their intention to portray a nominated value, it sometimes happened that it was not observed by the researcher in the classroom. On the other hand, there were often occasions where the teachers portrayed values which they themselves were unaware of, or which appeared to be unplanned.

Table 7.1 Categories of intended and implemented values observed

		Implemented/Observed		
		Taught explicitly	**Taught implicitly**	**Not observed**
Intended/ Nominated	Nominated explicitly	*Cooperation* (Anna)	*Self-worth and self-esteem* (Ben)	*Creativity* (Colin)
	Not nominated	*Individual differences* (Diane)	*Inclusiveness* (Edward)	–

In analyzing the data collected from the case studies of eight teachers, we were able to categorize whether teachers did, or did not, nominate the values that were subsequently observed (or sometimes not observed). Where teachers were observed to teach the nominated values, we categorized them as explicitly or implicitly taught. These are summarized in Table 7.1 with reference to five of the teachers.

Anna, a primary school teacher, nominated the value of the children *working cooperatively* in small groups, and was observed to implement this value explicitly, discussing it and rewarding cooperative behaviour. In fact, she indicated that this was a value that ran across all her teaching of the Grade 1/2 classes in her suburban Catholic school. Ben, a secondary mathematics teacher, nominated explicitly that he would emphasize the value of student *self-worth/self-esteem*. Over the three lessons observed, it became evident that this value was often emphasized, although its portrayal was implicit in his behaviour; that is, Ben neither introduced nor discussed the value with the students. Rather, he gave his Year 11 male, independent-school, students, plentiful opportunities to demonstrate to themselves (and to the class) that they could 'do it right'.

Colin, another secondary mathematics teacher from a large country town, nominated and personally embraced the value of *creativity* in doing mathematics. However, the promotion of this value was not observed during visits to his Year 7 class. According to Colin, the reality of the class prevented him from portraying the value of *creativity*: few students normally responded to his invitation or stimulation to do so.

At times, values were not nominated by teachers but were subsequently observed. Transcripts of data reveal that sometimes teachers were aware of the underlying values but, to the extent that they had internalized them, they had not considered them worthy of mention. Teachers' strategies for their implementation varied in terms of the prior decisions (if any) made at the lesson planning stage, the timing of the discussion (if any) of the value concerned and the disruption (if any) to the classroom routine established by the teacher.

How should we interpret the failure by teachers to nominate values observed in their classrooms? Are the teachers in control of their values teaching, to the extent that these values are internalized and characterized by the teaching, but taken for granted by the teacher? Or, is this omission an indication of the fact that the teacher concerned had not yet consciously made a commitment to that value, or was even unaware that this value might be classified as such? From our perspective, the self-selected nature of our sample teachers suggests that they are likely to be willing to receive and respond to values not currently considered as part of their teaching repertoire.

Could it be that there was a breakdown in communication between researcher and teacher, due to the lack of a shared discourse for the discussion of values in the mathematics classroom (see Clarkson et al. 2000)? Could it be that the interpretation made by the researcher was actually a *mis*interpretation of the classroom episode? That is, was the issue simply one of lack of shared understanding between teacher and researcher?

Each of the case study teachers was experienced in classroom teaching. As researchers, we wondered whether their failure to nominate particular values may be attributable to their lack of awareness of the values observed. In this case it may be considered that the particular values were not under the teacher's control. On the other hand, it seemed likely that some of these values were so much an integral part of the teacher's repertoire that they were no longer considered to be worthy of mention. Is a failure to nominate a value considered not to be affirming? Diane readily affirmed the value of individual differences once this was pointed out to her. Does it mean that the value is under her control, or not? In fact, Diane was seen, in a class subsequent to the post-lesson interview, to make explicit the nomination and implementation of the value of *individual differences* (FitzSimons et al. 2001).

Reflection

Although we have attempted to explain this phenomenon, what do you think are some of the other possible explanations from the perspective of your own culture? For example, how might the (unequal?) relationship between the researcher(s) and the teacher participants possibly contribute to this?

The cognitive and affective domains of the two related taxonomies of educational objectives constructed by Bloom (ed.) (1956) and by Krathwohl et al. (1964), respectively, may contribute to our understanding of this dilemma. As experienced teachers, their cognitive domain skills of knowledge, comprehension, application, analysis and synthesis, and evaluation, would be well-practised – although still subject to reflection and amelioration as new content and pedagogical knowledges become known and incorporated into their teaching. In the affective domain, the parallel and overlapping categories have been identified taxonomically (Krathwohl et al. 1964) in order of increasing affective levels as namely, receiving, responding, valuing, organisation and conceptualization, and characterization. It is at the highest level of characterization where one 'responds very consistently to value-laden situations with an interrelated set of values, a structure, a view of the world' (p. 35). Ultimately, this characterization by a value or value complex is reflected in an individual's consistent philosophy of life.

As noted by Raths et al. (1987), the process of valuing requires choosing freely, choosing from alternatives, choosing after thoughtful consideration of the consequences of each alternative, cherishing and being happy with the choice enough to be willing to affirm the choice to others and to act upon the choices, repeatedly and persistently. Similarly, at the higher levels of the Krathwohl et al. (1964) taxonomy, the organization of a value system where more than one value is relevant (and may even be in conflict) requires the teacher to internalize the values held and to consciously weigh alternatives.

The episodes above, where observed values were not nominated, may be exemplars of the third level (i.e., valuing) in the affective domain of the taxonomy, where the value is accepted but not yet organized into a coherent system. On the other hand, as in several of the episodes, characterization of a value or value complex tends to render it – at least some of the time – invisible to the teacher. Through the disruption arising from the interview situation, Edward was moved to reassess his values concerning *responsibility* for the homework set; he recognized a teaching strategy previously taken for granted. Similarly, Diane became cognizant of her valuing of *individual differences*. The teachers' conceptualization and subsequent reorganization of value systems by and for themselves is indeed one intended outcome of this project, potentially informing us about how teachers may be supported in the regulating of ongoing evolution of their respective professional and personal value systems.

According to McLeod (1992), much of the research work relating to the affective domain has been conducted from a cognitive perspective – that is, on beliefs, rather than attitudes and emotions. It is recognized that many, if not all, teacher education courses tend to focus exclusively on the cognitive domain: when the term 'Bloom's taxonomy' is used, it is taken as referring only to the educational objectives listed in Bloom (ed.) (1956). In the affective domain, as in the cognitive domain, experienced teachers are likely to have well-developed skills but, because they have never been challenged to interrogate these understandings, they have not developed the language to reflect upon them consciously or to discuss them. Thus, they are likely to remain at the subconscious level. One of the aims of the VAMP project was to raise this level of awareness, through the fostering of an appropriate lexicon.

Reflection

How are the concepts of 'values', 'beliefs' and 'attitudes' represented in your own language? Are these represented by different, similar or identical terms? What are the implications?

Krathwohl (1994) suggests that a future version of the taxonomy should attempt to overcome the division into cognitive, affective and psychomotor domains, and to interrelate them – perhaps even describing objectives in a multi-dimensional space. Following Krathwohl, our assertion is that the development and portrayal of values in the mathematics classroom (as elsewhere) must extend across both cognitive and affective domains, at least, rather than being divided arbitrarily.

Our challenge as researchers is to enable teachers to (re)conceptualize the range of values concerning, *inter alia*, the discipline of mathematics (Bishop 1988/1991) and the field of mathematics education (Seah and Bishop 2000) that they wish to teach explicitly or to portray implicitly – but to do so from a position of maximum understanding within their own particular educational context. That is, to gain control over the particular values that they have decided, consciously, to implement.

The maths and science values studies

This project differed from the previous one in two significant ways. Firstly it involved a comparison between values in mathematics and science. This was

---

1. Epistemology of the Knowledge (Ideological values)

1a *Rationalism*
Reason Explanations Hypothetical Reasoning Abstractions Logical thinking Theories

1b *Objectism*
Atomism Objectivising Materialism Concretising Determinism Symbolising Analogical thinking

2. How individuals relate to the Knowledge (Sentimental values)

2a *Control*
Prediction Mastery over environment Knowing Rules Security Power

2b *Progress*
Growth Questioning Alternativism Cumulative development of knowledge Generalisation

3. Knowledge and Society (Sociological values)

3a *Openness*
Facts Universality Articulation Individual liberty Demonstration Sharing Verification

3b *Mystery*
Abstractness Wonder Unclear origins Mystique Dehumanised knowledge

---

Figure 7.1 Values of Western Mathematical Knowledge (Bishop 1988/1991).

done because of both the similarities between the two subjects and their differences. The second difference in comparison with VAMP was that this project would also involve collecting data from students, and would attempt to explore their values and how these are related to any the teachers might hold. (Thanks are due to our colleagues Debbie Corrigan, Barbara Clarke and Dick Gunstone for their contributions to this project.)

This project used as the basic conceptual framework the six values component model developed by Bishop (1988/1991) through analysis of the activities of mathematicians throughout Western history. In this model six sets of value clusters are structured as three complementary pairs, as shown in Figure 7.1.

The three dimensions are based on the original work of White (1959), a renowned culturologist, who proposed four components to explain cultural growth. White proposed these as technological, ideological, sociological, and sentimental or attitudinal, with the first being the driver of the others. Bishop (1988/1991) had argued that mathematics can be considered as a symbolic technology, representing White's technological component of culture, with the other three being considered as the values components.

Much discussion and analysis of this initial value framework, particularly in relation to whether the same structure could hold for science (see Corrigan et al. 2004), led to a modification of the values of mathematics and science educators (Figure 7.2). In particular, with the value cluster of *objectism*, it

Mathematics	Science
Rationalism	*Rationalism*
Reason Explanations Hypothetical reasoning	Reason Explanations Hypothetical reasoning
Abstractions Logical thinking Theories	Abstractions Logical thinking Theories
Empiricism	*Empiricism*
Atomism Objectivising Materialism	Atomism Objective Materialisation Symbolising
Concretising Determinism Symbolising	Analogical thinking Precise Measurable
Analogical thinking	Accuracy Coherence Fruitfulness
	Parsimony Identifying problems
Control	*Control*
Prediction Mastery over environment Knowing	Prediction Mastery over problems Knowing
Rules Security Power	Rules Paradigms Circumstance of activity
Progress	*Progress*
Growth Questioning Cumulative	Growth Cumulative development of knowledge
Development of knowledge	Generalisation Deepened understanding
Generalisation	Plausible alternatives
Alternativism	
Openness	*Openness*
Facts Universality Articulation	Articulation Sharing Credibility Individual liberty
Individual liberty	Human construction
Demonstration Sharing Verification	
Mystery	*Mystery*
Abstractness Wonder Unclear origins	Intuition Guesses Daydreams
Mystique Dehumanised knowledge	Curiosity Fascination
Intuition	

Figure 7.2 Comparison between values associated with mathematics and science.

was recast as *empiricism* in order to accommodate the scientist's approach. There is still some agreement, but the highly empirical nature of science means that it has many more value aspects there than does mathematics.

We now turn to some of the data collected from primary and secondary teachers by means of specially constructed questionnaires. They are based on the three complementary pairs discussed above, namely, *rationalism* and *empiricism, control* and *progress, openness* and *mystery*. For the purposes of this chapter, only part of the questionnaires will be considered. The statements in these questions are the same for mathematics and science, and 13 primary and 17 secondary teachers volunteered to answer these questionnaires. Primary teachers in the state system in Australia teach both subjects to their classes, and we selected secondary teachers who also taught both subjects to the same classes.

Table 7.2 Rank orders and mean ranks for Questionnaire item 3

Value	Rationalism	Empiricism	Control	Progress	Openness	Mystery
Primary						
Maths rank	2	1	6	4	3	5
(mean rank)	(2.30)	(1.46)	(5.23)	(3.15)	(3.53)	(3.61)
Science rank	2	1	6	4	5	3
(mean rank)	(2.75)	(1.41)	(4.91)	(3.41)	(3.66)	(3.00)
Secondary						
Maths rank	1	2	6	4	3	5
(mean rank)	(1.94)	(2.05)	(4.52)	(3.88)	(3.35)	(4.29)
Science rank	4	1	6	4	3	2
(mean rank)	(3.18)	(1.25)	(5.87)	(3.18)	(3.06)	(2.81)

Questionnaire items 3 and 4 (each of which contained six statements to be ranked by the teachers) produced some particularly interesting data. Each statement relates to one of the values clusters, for example, the statement 'It develops creativity, basing alternative and new ideas on established ones' relates to the value of *progress*. The other statements follow closely the other value descriptors in Figure 7.2 above although their order is different in the two questionnaire items. Note also that the teachers were not made aware of the value structure underlying the two questions and each of the six statements. Tables 7.2 and 7.3 show the results from the two groups of teachers in terms of their rankings and the means of the rankings for the six values clusters.

For item 3, 'Maths/Science is valued in the school curriculum because . . .', the primary teachers showed considerable similarity between the orders for mathematics and science with *empiricism* and *rationalism* being the most important values for both. *Control* was seen as by far the least important value, which is surprising given the findings about *control* that appeared to be valued highly in the local Australian textbook content (Seah 1999). Is this an indication that the intended curriculum which has been interpreted by the textbook writers is then reinterpreted by classroom teachers? For the secondary teachers we can see an important and perhaps predictable difference between the rankings for mathematics and science between *rationalism* and *empiricism*. Once again *control* is a distinct last choice for both. There are also interesting, and once again predictable, differences between the rankings of *mystery* for mathematics and science for both groups of teachers.

Table 7.3 Rank orders and mean ranks for Questionnaire item 4

Value	Rationalism	Empiricism	Control	Progress	Openness	Mystery
Primary						
Maths rank	3	1	5	2	3	6
(mean rank)	(3.66)	(1.33)	(3.75)	(3.00)	(3.66)	(3.83)
Science rank	4	1	6	3	5	2
(mean rank)	(3.41)	(1.41)	(4.75)	(3.33)	(3.83)	(2.58)
Secondary						
Maths rank	1	2	3	4	4	6
(mean rank)	(1.70)	(1.82)	(3.44)	(4.00)	(4.00)	(4.47)
Science rank	3	1	6	2	5	4
(mean rank)	(3.12)	(1.25)	(4.12)	(3.00)	(4.06)	(3.33)

Reflection

If it is indeed true that the intended curriculum is interpreted by textbook writers and classroom teachers in ways which might be different, what does this mean for students in terms of their learning and internalizing of values?

For item 4 'Mathematics/Science is valuable knowledge because . . .', once again the primary teachers put *empiricism* firmly at the top of the list for both subjects, but their second choices are interestingly different. For mathematics they favoured *progress* while for science they favoured *mystery*. Their last choices are also markedly different, with *mystery* being given that place for mathematics and *control* for science. For the secondary teachers, *rationalism* and *empiricism* stand out as the top values for mathematics, while *empiricism* stands very much alone at the top for science. At the bottom, the pattern is the same as for the primary teachers, with *mystery* occupying that place for mathematics and *control* for science.

The comparisons between the values in mathematics and science for the teachers show differences which reflect their concerns with the curriculum and teaching at their respective levels. At the primary level the teachers favour *empiricism* over *rationalism* for both science and mathematics, though both are important. At the primary level of course much mathematical work is empirical in nature. For the sentimental dimension, *control* is much less favoured than *progress* also for both. The main difference between the subjects appears in the sociological dimension where *openness* and *mystery* reverse their positions with the two subjects, the first being more favoured than the second in mathematics and the reverse in science.

For the secondary teachers, the ideological dimension reflects the educators' views, with mathematics favouring *rationalism* and science favouring *empiricism*, disagreeing with the primary teachers. For the sentimental dimension, the secondary teachers largely agree with their primary colleagues and for the sociological dimension, they again agree with their primary colleagues favouring *openness* for mathematics compared with *mystery*, and reversing these for science. Indeed *mystery* for science is ranked 2 and 4 by the secondary teachers and ranked 2 and 3 by the primary teachers, showing how significant they consider that aspect to be.

Reflection

Given that the teacher participants appear to value mystery a great deal in both mathematics and science, would this be the same across all school subjects, or is this phenomenon peculiar to these two disciplines only?

In general, the conceptualization put forward for this project shows interesting and interpretable results. Discussions with the teachers have revealed an interest in the issues of values teaching in all subjects, but also a lack of vocabulary, and conceptual tools to enable them to develop explicitly the values underlying mathematics education. One of the goals of this project was, by contrasting mathematics and science, to help teachers develop those conceptual tools further. As we have seen, and as has been shown above, the contrasts between these two closely related forms of knowledge are provocative, and already reveal worthwhile challenges for mathematics teaching to pursue.

The differences in the views on *progress* are also revealing, with the development of understanding in science contrasting with the construction of new knowledge in mathematics. How can we reconstruct our views of the mathematics curriculum so that progress through that curriculum is not just a matter of acquiring yet more new knowledge or skills, but of ensuring that it

Reflection

The difference between the emphasis on *empiricism* at primary level and on *rationalism* at secondary level implies some important challenges for explicit values development in the teaching of mathematics at those two levels. How should that values development be smoothed across the already problematic primary/secondary divide?

also deepens and broadens learners' understanding of what has been taught before?

Finally could the de-humanized, highly abstract and mystique-laden value of *mystery* of mathematics which appears to be such an obstacle to mathematics learners be made more explicit so that it could be challenged by the more humanized and personal intuitive nature of that value which science appears to enjoy?

Reflection

The assumption here has been that making the valuing of *mystery* more explicit would enable more students to learn mathematics more effectively than they are currently. However, would this risk the subject losing its appeal to some other students, whose interest in and motivation for studying mathematics have been sustained by the very fact that there is much mystery in it?

A case for researching teachers' (versus students') values

We have based our current research on the theoretical notion that values operate, and are revealed, when choices are made. It is interesting to note that the construct of 'beliefs' was not mentioned in the taxonomy constructed by Krathwohl et al. (1964). The essential difference between values and beliefs is that one may hold various beliefs but it is when one must make choices that one's values come into play. Of course, not all that an individual values may be visible through the choices made (Clarkson et al. 2000). From a values research perspective therefore we are interested in teaching and learning situations where choices and decisions are involved. In the case of researching teachers' values, this is a relatively trouble-free criterion, as teachers make choices and decisions all the time in the classroom. When we aim specifically to investigate students' values, however, this criterion of choice becomes more problematic. Under certain kinds of pedagogical practices, for example involving heavily didactic teaching, students may have few choices to make. Meaningful choices for students may evaporate yet values will certainly be taught and learnt. Whether these will be the most desirable values is, however, a topic for another discussion.

Researching values is not, of course, a problem specific to mathematics or science education – values education is a notoriously difficult research area generally. Nevertheless one thing we have learnt from these two small studies is that rather than searching for some kind of mental or emotional linkage between teachers' values and their students' values, it may be more productive to focus on the teachers' actions, behaviours and activities. These may or may not reflect the teachers' value preferences, as these can be affected by other aspects of the situation. However, as far as developing the students' values are concerned, the teachers' actions may be more significant than their preferred values.

This is not to suggest that the teacher need be a model of values and virtues, but rather that by providing mathematical learning situations where their students can make choices, justify them and compare these with others, teachers can enable values to become a legitimate, explicit and overt component of their mathematics teaching (Chin and Lin 2001). They may also, by these means, be leading their students towards a more balanced form of mathematics education. Examples of such worthwhile mathematical learning situations are given in the next section.

Making values teaching more explicit in mathematics lessons

A good way for teachers to explore further some of the values ideas discussed here is to begin looking at their own professional practice and critically reviewing the textbooks they use in terms of the six mathematical values described above. A teacher could tape (sound) some of his or her own lessons and analyze them, or work with a colleague to analyze each other's teaching. A teacher could also discuss these ideas, or related findings, with the parents of their students to help them understand more about mathematical ideas, and the role which mathematics learning plays in educating their children.

The following are some questions to help teachers do the analysis, and perhaps also they might enable more explicit teaching of these values through mathematics teaching and learning:

(1) *Rationalism:* As a teacher, do you encourage your students to argue in your classes? Do you have debates? Do you emphasize mathematical proving? Could you show the students examples of proofs from history (for example, different proofs of Pythagoras' theorem)?

(2) *Objectism:* Do you encourage your students to invent their own symbols and terminology **before** showing them the 'official' ones? Do you use geometric diagrams to illustrate algebraic relationships? Could you show them different numerals used by different cultural groups in history? Could you discuss the need for simplicity and conciseness in choosing symbols? And why that helps with further abstractions?

(3) *Control:* Do you emphasize not just 'right' answers, but also the checking of answers, and the reasons for other answers not being 'right'? Do you encourage the analysis and understanding of why routine calculations and algorithms 'work'? Could you emphasize more the basis of these algorithms? Do you always show examples of how the mathematical ideas you are teaching are used in society?

(4) *Progress:* Do you emphasize alternative, and non-routine, solution strategies together with their reasons? Do you encourage students to extend and generalize ideas from particular examples? Could you stimulate them with stories of mathematical developments in history?

(5) *Openness:* Do you encourage your students to defend and justify their answers publicly to the class? Do you encourage the creation of posters so that the students can display their ideas? Could you create a student math newsletter, or a web page, where they could present their ideas?

(6) *Mystery:* Do you tell them any stories about mathematical puzzles in the past, about, for example the 'search' for negative numbers, or for zero? Do you stimulate their mathematical imagination with pictures, artworks, images of infinity, etc.?

Finally, to what extent do (could) you discuss these values explicitly in your classes? Would it help your students to understand why mathematics is so important today?

Responding to value conflict situations

A greater awareness of one's professional and personal values, and any associated realignment or reprioritizing of one's value system, would perhaps lead to one being more conscious of the process of value conflict and negotiation.

In particular, the potential for a greater consciousness of how one manages competing values provides one with the opportunity to further understand and potentially refine the process of value negotiation. Indeed, if life experiences help us to respond automatically to choice(s) amongst competing values, then the potential for one to be less conscious of why one responds in certain ways in itself provides a compelling reason for one to be in greater control of one's value negotiation. For example, for many teachers, their response to a student's query if there can be less/no homework becomes increasingly automatic with increasing experience in the profession. Unfortunately, the paucity of research into values and their pedagogy in (mathematics) education has also meant that we do not have a comprehensive understanding of how teachers can achieve a more conscious control over their respective valuing processes. The implication here is that there is likely no universally effective way of confronting competing values, whether one operates within or across cultures.

Seah's (2005) study with eight immigrant teachers of mathematics in Australian schools provides a starting point for teachers to reference their valuing efforts and for researchers to explore value negotiation approaches across a bigger sample. In Seah's research, immigrant teachers from a diversity of ethnic and social backgrounds practising in Australia worked with him together to investigate the range of value conflicts involved in the teaching of a supposedly culture- and value-free school subject of mathematics in a cross-cultural context. A range of approaches was documented as a result of following the lives of the eight teachers over a period of six months. These are listed in Table 7.4 below in the original format in order to show the context within which it was constructed. The reader is certainly invited to make interpretations which are relevant to his or her unique professional context.

Reflection

Who are the immigrant teachers of mathematics in your professional workplace? What do they think of the local mathematics curriculum? How have they adapted to practising in a foreign culture?

As Table 7.4 shows, the immigrant teachers' approaches to perceived value conflict situations are mainly regulated by a perceived underlying cultural

Table 7.4 Approaches adopted by immigrant teachers to perceived value differences in mathematics education

Personal value is aligned to . . .	Response	Assumption	Teaching
. . . host culture	Affinity	There is no culture conflict; my value is aligned with the host culture.	The host culture supports my mathematics teaching style.
. . . home culture	Helplessness	There is no apparent way to negotiate the different values satisfactorily.	My mathematics teaching style may not be consistent, and I may not know what to do.
	Status quo	My home culture should be espoused.	I teach mathematics in the same way I did in my home culture.
	Assimilation	The host culture should influence the surface characteristics of my mathematics teaching.	I include the host cultural contexts in my teaching, such as in examples and problem sums.
	Accommodation	The host culture should be espoused.	Planning and classroom decisions portray the host culture.
	Amalgamation	The essence of my home culture and the host culture should guide mathematics teaching.	My teaching reflects a synthesis of teaching styles from my home culture and from Australia.
	Appropriation	My home culture and the host culture should interact to inform my mathematics teaching.	My mathematics teaching style consistently reflects an adaptation of my home culture to local norms and practices.

'pressure' to conform. This point probably remains relevant to all teachers as they research their own valuing processes. There is understandably relatively little conflict if there is a similarity between what the teacher and the cultural context value, which relates to the affinity approach in Table 7.4. If there is a (perceived) clash in these values, however, the teachers' approaches can range from a total rejection of values associated with the context within which the value conflicts take place (be it classroom, school or something wider) – corresponding to the status-quo approach as listed in Table 7.4, to a complete embrace of values associated with such context – corresponding to the accommodation approach.

The most productive approaches, from the cultural reproduction point of view, are the amalgamation and appropriation approaches. In their uniquely different ways (see assumptions listed in Table 7.4), these two approaches harness the most desirable features of host and home cultural values to create negotiated world-views and personalities. It is likely that a well-developed personal capacity to use these approaches will strengthen one's **cultural intelligence (CQ)**.

An important finding from Seah's study is that each of the eight teachers adopted a range of approaches across perceived value conflict situations. It appears that in harmonizing values that come together and needing to be embraced, the dynamism of valuing can facilitate one's cultural border crossing in empowering ways.

Conclusion

Our discussion in this chapter has attempted to show how values are portrayed and taught by teachers in mathematics lessons, with an emphasis on values that are embedded in mathematics pedagogy and in the discipline itself. In so doing, we aim to demonstrate that teachers of mathematics can – and do – contribute to their respective country or culture's aim of inculcating desirable values amongst the young generation. In reporting on three recent research studies on values teaching in mathematics (and science) lessons in Australian primary and secondary schools, we share with readers the teachers' experience, at the same time making explicit barriers (such as a common discourse with which to discuss and consider values) encountered by these teachers. In particular, the studies identify values which tend to be more emphasized by teachers, at the same time noting the implications of differences observed across subjects and across school systems. Some classroom teaching ideas for teachers to research their own values teaching in mathematics lessons have also been given. Possible approaches adopted by teachers to negotiate perceived value differences have also been discussed briefly to support teachers' attempts at exploring values which were hitherto implicit or yet to be embraced. It is certainly hoped that this chapter will stimulate more teachers to research how mathematical values may be taught, in ways which both support meaningful learning in their students, as well as share their professional learnings in the process.

Further reading

Bishop, A. J. (1988/1991). *Mathematical Enculturation: A Cultural Perspective on Mathematics Education*. Dordrecht, The Netherlands: Kluwer Academic Publishers.

This oft-quoted book details the cultural aspect of mathematics pedagogy, and explains the important roles which values play in this perspective.

Bishop, A. J., Seah, W. T. and Chin, C. (2003). Values in mathematics teaching: the hidden persuaders? In A. J. Bishop, K. Clements, C. Keitel, J. Kilpatrick and F. Leong (eds), *International Handbook of Mathematics Education* (second edn, pp. 715–63). Dordrecht, The Netherlands: Kluwer.

This chapter in an internationally acclaimed academic handbook provides a detailed review of most of the research into values in mathematics education that have been conducted around the world.

References

Bishop, A. J. (1988/1991). *Mathematical Enculturation: A Cultural Perspective on Mathematics Education.* Dordrecht, The Netherlands: Kluwer Academic Publishers.

Bishop, A. J. (1991). Mathematical values in the teaching process. In A. J. Bishop, S. Mellin-Olsen and J. van Dormolen (eds), *Mathematical Knowledge: Its Growth Through Teaching* (pp. 195–214). Dordrecht: Kluwer Academic Publishers.

Bishop, A. J., Clarkson, P. C., FitzSimons, G. E. and Seah, W. T. (1999, December). Values in mathematics education: making values teaching explicit in the mathematics classroom. Paper presented at 1999 Australian Association for Research in Education conference. Also available at www.swin.edu.au/aare

Bloom, B. (1956). *Taxonomy of Educational Objectives.* London: Longman.

Chin, C. and Lin, F. L. (2001). Value-loaded activities in mathematics classroom. In M. v. d. Heuvel-Panhuizen (ed.), *Proceedings of the 25th Conference of the International Group for the Psychology of Mathematics Education* (Vol. 2, pp. 249–56). Utrecht, The Netherlands: Freudenthal Institute.

Clarkson, P. C., Seah, W. T., Bishop, A. J. and FitzSimons, G. E. (2000, December). Methodology challenges and constraints in the Values and Mathematics Project. Paper presented at the 26th Australian Association for Research in Education Conference. Also available at www.aare.edu.au/00pap/cla00116.htm

Corrigan, D. J., Gunstone, R. F., Bishop, A. J. and Clarke, B. (2004, August). Values in science and mathematics education: mapping the relationships between pedagogical practices and student outcomes. Paper presented at the Summer School of the European Science Educational Research Association, Mulheim, Germany.

FitzSimons, G., Seah, W. T., Bishop, A. and Clarkson, P. (2001). Beyond numeracy: values in the mathematics classroom. In J. Bobis, B. Perry, and M. Mitchelmore (eds), *Numeracy and Beyond: Proceedings of the Twenty-Fourth Annual Conference of the Mathematics Education Research Group of Australasia Incorporated* (Vol. 1, pp. 202–09). Turramurra, Australia: MERGA.

Krathwohl, D. R. (1994). Reflections on the taxonomy: its past, present and future. In L. W. Anderson and L. A. Sosniak (eds), *Blooms Taxonomy: A Forty-Year Retrospective.* Chicago: National Society for the Study of Education.

Krathwohl, D. R., Bloom, B. S. and Masia, B. B. (1964). *Taxonomy of Educational Objectives: The Classification of Educational Goals (Handbook II: Affective Domain)*. New York: David McKay.

Lewis-Shaw, C. (2001). Measuring values in classroom teaching and learning. In D. Clarke (ed.), *Perspectives on Practice and Meaning in Mathematics and Science Classrooms* (pp. 155–96). Dordrecht, The Netherlands: Kluwer Academic Publishers.

McLeod, D. B. (1992). Research on affect in mathematics education: a reconceptualization. In D. A. Grouws (ed.), *Handbook of Research on Mathematics Teaching and Learning* (pp. 575–96). New York: Macmillan.

Raths, L. E., Harmin, M. and Simon, S. B. (1987). Selections from 'values and teaching'. In J. P. F. Carbone (ed.), *Value Theory and Education* (pp. 198–214). Malabar, Florida: Robert E. Krieger.

Seah, W. T. (1999). Values in Singapore and Victoria lower secondary mathematics textbooks: a preliminary study. In M. A. (Ken) Clements, and Y. P. Leong (eds), *Cultural and Language Aspects of Science, Mathematics, and Technical Education* (pp. 261–70). Brunei: Universiti Brunei Darussalam.

Seah, W. T. (2005). Negotiating about perceived value differences in mathematics teaching: the case of immigrant teachers in Australia. In H. Chick, and J. L. Vincent (eds), *Proceedings of the 29th conference of the International Group for the Psychology of Mathematics Education*, (Vol. 4, pp. 145–52). Melbourne: PME.

Seah, W. T. and Bishop, A. J. (2000, April). Values in mathematics textbooks: a view through two Australasian regions. Paper presented at the 81st Annual Meeting of the American Educational Research Association, New Orleans, Los Angeles.

White L. (1959). *The Evolution of Culture*. New York: McGraw Hill.

Section 3
Teachers and professional development

Valuing knowledge of practice: articulating a pedagogy of teacher education

John Loughran

Monash University, Australia

8

This chapter offers an overview of some issues and ideas in developing and articulating a pedagogy of teacher education. It argues that the nature of teaching, and learning about teaching, is complex, hinging on a recognition that teaching is problematic. Hence, teaching teaching requires skills, knowledge and ability that need to be recognized and acknowledged in the pursuit of quality in teacher education. The chapter examines some of the aspects of teaching, and learning about teaching that influence understandings of a pedagogy of teacher education and argues that making such knowledge public is a crucial element in creating deeper understandings of practice and in better valuing teaching and teacher education.

Introduction

While earlier chapters have dealt with overarching ideas and philosophies about education, and to some extent with methods of teaching/learning, this chapter is the first of a trio which examines the process of teaching teaching, that is, teacher education. In it, I have used the term 'a pedagogy of teacher education', and this needs a definition and some words of explanation.

Pedagogy

In many places (e.g. the United States, Australia, United Kingdom, Canada and New Zealand) pedagogy is sometimes used as a synonym for teaching and carries a range of meanings such as teaching procedures, teaching practice, instruction or classroom activities. Van Manen (1999) offers a restatement of the meaning of pedagogy based on European traditions (e.g. The Netherlands, Belgium, Germany and Scandinavia): pedagogy as the art and science of educating children. These meanings focus on the relationship between teaching and learning such that one does not exist as separate and distinct from the other; this is critical to a deeper understanding of the term and implications for its application and use. Pedagogy becomes, if you will, 'the theory of teaching and learning', a theory explicitly linking the two functions.

In this way, it becomes possible to see how, through closer examination of pedagogy, powerful ways of tapping into the professional knowledge of practice immediately emerge. But there is a further connection that must be made. Korthagen (2001b) draws attention to relationships in better understanding pedagogy. He suggests that 'many durable learning experiences are rooted in the . . . relationship between teacher and student . . . in which both are . . . in contact with their inner selves' (p. 264). Therefore, personal relationships between teachers and students influence identity formation, which means that personal growth inherently emerges from the nature of pedagogy; for both teacher and student. Pedagogy is, then, the theory of teaching/learning and of the relationships necessary to underpin them.

Pedagogy and teacher education

So we can move to what comprises a pedagogy of teacher education. Given the definition of pedagogy, above, it follows that the pedagogy of teacher education means something like: a theory of how educators might convey and student-teachers might learn, about the theory of teaching/learning in classrooms and the complex relations that underpin them. As student-teachers struggle to understand this they might take note of Korthagen's (2001) caveat:

> Being a teacher educator is often difficult . . . in most places, there is no culture in which it is common for teacher education staff to collaboratively work on the question of how to improve the pedagogy of teacher education. (p. 8)

In teacher education, pedagogy matters. Students of teaching embark on their quest to become teachers – to learn about teaching – and teacher educators are responsible for teaching them about teaching. Teacher education therefore has two important foci: learning about teaching; and, teaching about teaching, each of which involves complex skills, knowledge, abilities and competences (Koster et al. 2005).

A pedagogy of teacher education revolves around a focus on the relationship between teaching and learning in the programs and practices of learning *and* teaching about teaching to better explicate what teaching looks like and how it influences learning. Developing a pedagogy of teacher education means that these practices are purposefully examined, described, articulated and portrayed in ways that are intended to better inform our understanding of this complex interplay. If that is the case, then the resultant knowledge will not only offer insights into teaching and learning but also be influential in shaping the way that they might be developed and practised in schools and teacher education programs more generally. This rest of this chapter explores these ideas.

Learning about teaching

> Preservice teachers . . . should be encouraged to be metacognitive and become more aware of how they learn in teacher education courses with the intention of informing their decision-making as they construct their personal pedagogies. (Hoban 1997, p. 135)

Hoban's suggestion means, for students of teaching, that there is a need for them to be learning *that which* is being taught while at the same time questioning, examining and learning about *the way in which* it is actually being taught. They should be encouraged to ask questions about the nature of the teaching they are experiencing, the influence of that practice on their subsequent learning, the manner in which the teaching they experience has been constructed and so on. Therefore, for learners of teaching, there should be a real expectation of a need to consistently pay attention to learning about the particular content that is being taught as well as learning about teaching through that which they experience. This is clearly a difficult task as responding to both simultaneously is demanding; hence Hoban's suggestion about meta-cognition.

A difficulty for learners of teaching is that it is easy to pay attention to the content that is being taught and to gloss over the manner of the teaching being employed. For most students of teaching, that is what 13 years of formal schooling has encouraged. It is also what traditional university teaching often reinforces. Therefore, for students of teaching to begin to question the taken-for-granted in their learning about teaching requires energy. It also requires an expectation that in so doing, there will be genuine learning rewards.

In learning about teaching, there is a need to focus on one's own learning so that an understanding of the teaching practices being experienced are thoughtfully linked to the manner in which learning in a given situation is understood in relation to the nature of that teaching. Therefore, for students of teaching, their learning agenda includes: learning about the specific content being taught, learning about learning, and learning about teaching. All of these inevitably shape their developing understanding of the complexity of teaching and learning, but may not be fully appreciated if not explicitly linked to their learning agenda. Therefore, teacher educators need to overtly encourage meta-cognition in learning about teaching as one important aspect of the learning about teaching agenda for students of teaching, not least because:

> Student teachers' expectations of their preservice programs are strongly influenced by their prior experiences as learners, together with popular stereotypes about teachers' work. Student teachers commonly enter their teacher education with a view of teaching as simple and transmissive. They believe that teaching involved the uncomplicated act of telling students what to learn. (Berry 2004, pp. 1301–02)

Clearly, for Berry's points to be seriously addressed, students of teaching then must see into teaching in new ways.

Teaching about teaching

[B]ecoming a teacher educator (or teacher of teachers) has the potential (not always realized) to generate a second level of thought about teaching, one that focuses not on content but on how we teach . . . This new perspective constitutes making the 'pedagogical turn', thinking long and hard about how we teach and the messages conveyed by how we teach . . . I have come to believe that learning to teach is far more complex than we have ever acknowledged. (Russell 1997, p. 44)

Teachers of teaching are confronted by a similar situation to that of students of teaching. The need to teach the given content is obvious but, unfortunately, it is all too often the only focus of attention. However, if students of teaching are to genuinely 'see into teaching', then they require access to the thoughts and actions that shape such practice; they need to be able to see and hear the pedagogical reasoning that underpins the teaching that they are experiencing (Loughran 1996).

Teaching about teaching should not be confused with simply modelling a range of teaching procedures. Teaching about teaching must be more. It should involve unpacking teaching in ways that give students of teaching access to the pedagogical reasoning, uncertainties and dilemmas of practice that are inherent in understanding teaching as being problematic. It involves making clear through practice that the teaching approach being used purposely encourages learning. It should also offer insights into how learning influences teaching such that that very act may be critiqued as part of the teaching about teaching agenda because 'teacher educators, whether intentionally or not, teach their students as well as teach about teaching' (Korthagen et al. 2005, p. 111).

One way of considering the nature of teaching *and* learning about teaching in order to better articulate and portray a pedagogy of teacher education is through the concepts of episteme and phronesis (Korthagen et al. 2005).

Knowledge of practice

Most teacher educators will recognize the example: A student teacher formulates a problem from practical experiences, which leads the other students or the teacher educator to come up with possible solutions . . . Sometimes such a sharing of thoughts seems to help . . . But sometimes – more often than we wish – it does not seem to help . . . What to us seems directly applicable in practice appears

> to be too abstract, too theoretical, and too far-off to someone else . . . No matter
> how carefully we consider the problem, we do not find a way into it . . . there is
> an unbridgeable gap between our words and the student's experiences. (Kessels
> and Korthagen 2001, pp. 21–22)

Korthagen et al. (2001) outline episteme as propositional knowledge. It consists of assertions of a general nature that apply to many different situations and problems. It is that which might be described as traditional, scientifically derived knowledge and is often considered to be objective and timeless. Phronesis is a form of practical wisdom derived through understanding specific situations and cases. It tends to be developed through experience but is not normally immediately generalizable; it is often context specific. In better understanding teaching and learning about teaching, the distinction between episteme and phronesis can help to explain some of the ongoing difficulties confronted by teacher educators and students of teaching.

For example, for students of teaching, epistemic knowledge may not be helpful in addressing their immediate problems of practice because in the absence of teaching experience, generalizable knowledge about practice does not necessarily help neophytes see into their teaching behaviours in ways that might lead to constructive solutions. Therefore, telling student teachers about the solution to their problems of practice is more likely to be interpreted as the transmission of propositional knowledge and, generally, fails to help. Teacher educators need to be challenged about the 'why' of practice not just the 'how' of practice in order to articulate their own understandings. Through articulation, problem and solution become clearer and the practical knowledge of phronesis stands out as useable in practice. Recognizing it in oneself is part way to helping teach others how to recognize it in their own practice.

In many ways then, phronesis may be a conduit to episteme so that in developing a pedagogy of teacher education, the difference between theory and practice need not be a chasm, rather a bridge for approaching the development of knowledge as learning through experience. In so doing, such learning may better inform future experience:

> A coherent pedagogy of teacher education . . . requires considering how teachers
> learn about teaching and what it means to know and understand teaching and
> learning [about teaching]. (Northfield and Gunstone 1997, p. 55)

The distinction between teacher educators' teaching about teaching, and students of teaching learning about teaching is then shaped by the manner in which the underlying frames of episteme and phronesis might be understood and interpreted in terms of the nature of knowledge that influences teaching and learning. They impact the way in which knowledge might be identified, portrayed, applied and shared in teaching and learning about teaching, and therefore dramatically impact what it means to develop a pedagogy of teacher education.

Reflection

How does thinking about pedagogy in the way described above influence your thinking about teaching *and* learning about teaching? What knowledge of your practice would you describe as influenced by episteme? What knowledge of your practice would you describe as influenced by phronesis? How do you teach teaching in ways that respond to these different forms of knowledge?

Teaching is problematic

Teaching is 'a complex and messy terrain, often difficult to [map and] describe' (Berry 2004, p. 1312). One difficulty with conceptualizing teaching as being problematic is that, for novices, the messiness, the apparent lack of a clear path and the reliance on individuals to accept responsibility for directing their own learning about teaching can be impediments and create a yearning for a much simpler solution.

Seeing teaching as problematic means that mapping the terrain of practice needs to be intellectually challenging and practically engaging so that it is concurrently professionally rewarding. It is a process through which teachers learn to adapt, adjust and construct approaches to teaching and learning in the ongoing quest to be better informed about practice. For the novice, such a view of practice may be far from comforting.

Recognizing and building on that which is problematic in practice can be enhanced through noticing (Mason 2002). An important aspect of noticing is the realization that a situation may not really be seen until it is seen differently, and so noticing is important in helping to see into practice in different ways. However, with so many different things able to be 'noticed' in teaching, it can be very difficult to narrow one's focus to just one or two things that might be more easily seen and appreciated; especially for students of teaching.

Just as the novice teacher needs to be sensitive to the complexity of teaching, so too teacher educators need to illustrate that they also embrace the creativity, experimentation and risk-taking that so shapes understandings of pedagogy. Teaching about teaching therefore hinges on supporting students of teaching as they learn to be comfortable with managing the dilemmas, issues and concerns in pedagogic situations for there is not necessarily one 'right way' of doing teaching. Dealing with such uncertainty is part of learning to deal with teaching as being problematic. The following vignette from a teacher education class illustrates one way that teaching as being problematic might be examined and how such an approach can shape a pedagogy of teacher education.

Making the problematic explicit

We were doing the initial 'modeling' of teaching with the class and my role was to do the de-brief in such a way as to bring out as much as possible about the teaching, learning and pedagogical reasoning. I wasn't too concerned as we'd decided to use the same teaching approach as last year – John would do a POE (a Prediction, Observation, Explanation teaching procedure based on exploring the nature of air pressure) and that usually engaged the students quite well.

As the session progressed, things seemed fine, then for some reason which was not clear to me, a student question led John into some ideas on static electricity.

This certainly didn't happen last year and although it was interesting, I couldn't quite see how it was linked to the air pressure topic he was doing, nor why he was spending so much time on it.

As the session came to an end, I moved into the de-briefing mode. After asking John about his purpose in the session and the manner in which he had conducted it, I asked if there was anything in the session that surprised him. He spoke about the level of student engagement and how the POE seemed to work well but he didn't mention the static electricity bit that had caught my attention.

I thought it was worth the risk so I said, 'Well, what happened with that static electricity bit? You spent ages playing with the balloon trying to get it to "stick" to the wall and I wasn't sure why you got so caught up with that. What was happening there?'

John then explained how at first, he was simply responding to a student's suggestion about static electricity. He said he did not want to be seen to be discounting a 'wrong response' and so took the suggestion seriously and pushed it further. However, at every step of that, he told us that he felt himself getting further and further away from the 'real' topic and that he couldn't find a way out of his dilemma and back to the task. He said he felt like he just didn't know how to resolve the situation without making the student's idea seem (now) more unrelated, or how to 'force' a way of making a link back to the topic. Eventually he said he just made a joke of his inability to create static electricity and abruptly went back to the air pressure topic.

However, in so doing, he felt as though he'd lost the impetus of the session and from then on things were less than satisfactory – from his perspective.

The students all had a lot to say at this point.

Many were surprised that John thought he had made the situation worse than it was. Others didn't think the static electricity was a side-track at all and that things were going 'as intended'. The student who put the static electricity idea forward said she was pleased that her idea had so much impact on the teacher.

As the de-brief came to a close, I drew the class' attention back to the static electricity one more time. I asked what they made of the examination of the episode and how it might influence their own teaching.

Jacinta said, 'Well what you think you are doing as the teacher is not always what the class think you're doing, and it's good to see that happening with our lecturers because it sure as heck happens to us. I think it's good that we see you struggle in ways just like us. But maybe your experience covers it up so that we just don't see the reality often enough. I liked having a chance to talk about it. It's good to see the thinking behind the teaching that we experience.' (Berry and Loughran 2004, pp. 17–18)

Opening up teaching in the manner portrayed through the vignette (above) highlights the value of teaching about teaching being embedded in the unfolding practices of teaching and learning within the relative safety of a teacher education setting. In so doing, students of teaching begin to appreciate the varying perspectives crucial to shaping understandings of that which may be interpreted as problematic in practice.

Through our students' eyes: seeing our practice anew

Of all the pedagogic tasks teachers face, getting inside students' heads is one of the trickiest. It is also one of the most crucial . . . If we know something about the symbolic meanings that our actions have for students, we are better able to shape our behaviour so that desired effects are achieved. (Brookfield 1995, p. 92)

As learners, we see such practice differently from the way we come to see it when we are the teacher. There are many ways of seeing our practice through our students' eyes (Brookfield 1995; Bullough and Gitlin 2001; Dinkleman 1999; Hoban 1997; Nicol 1997; Northfield and Gunstone 1997; Peterman 1997). However, fundamental to all is the importance of communicating the 'why' of our practice so that students of teaching can make informed decisions about what they need to learn about their teaching in order to enhance the learning of their students. The implicit messages and intentions of teaching must be challenged, students of teaching need to know what we think are the intended learning outcomes from our practice and, as teacher educators, we need to be able to articulate not only what we are doing, but why we are doing it and how we are communicating that through our practice. Consider for example what the following anecdote[1] suggests about that which is communicated by a teacher educator and the way it is interpreted by his students of teaching.

A lesson on policy

The tutorial room was quiet. Only the professor's voice broke the silence. I had to say something. I disagreed with what he was saying. I spoke up. That's what I thought we were supposed to be learning to do. To be actively engaged in our learning. To question our understanding. We're certainly expected to be doing that with our students in school.

'I don't think that policy has to be about change!' I said, and I gave some examples to support my point of view. With that, others in the class also started to contribute.

'This is what the definition is! Reputed researchers agree!' was his rather forceful response.

Faced with that, what else could I say? He was the expert. He would take it as a personal insult if I again raised issues, so I kept my mouth shut. As the rest of the monologue surged forth, the class returned to its earlier silence. I opened my note book and wrote furiously, 'I disagree, I disagree.'

We had just been talking about including people in discussions, accepting others' point of view, inclusion, understanding. I don't think that classrooms should be lecture theatres. Teaching is not a one-way process. (Loughran 1997, pp. 5–6)

If teaching is to be regarded as more than achieving competence in the delivery of tips, tricks and procedures, if it is to go beyond the simple transmission of information about teaching, then the professional knowledge of teaching must be made clear to students of teaching. As the anecdote above illustrates, all that is done in teacher education models something about teaching. Therefore, it is crucial that teacher educators constantly work to illustrate that practice is problematic and to explicitly draw the links between teaching and learning so that views of teaching are not reduced to those associated with a search for technical competence alone. In so doing, a pedagogy of teacher education may not only be developed but purposefully enacted.

Reflection

How does seeing your practice through your students' eyes influence your ideas about a pedagogy of teacher education? Can you think of instances when your teaching sent different messages to your students than those you intended? If so, what did you do about it?

Articulating principles for practice

An important aspect of a pedagogy of teacher education is in the ability to articulate the principles that underpin one's practice. Kroll (2004; Kroll et al. 2005) and her colleagues purposefully work to ensure that the principles on which their program is based are explicitly used to shape their teaching. In so doing, Kroll has also used them to inquire into her own practice in an attempt to better link what she does with outcomes in terms of her students' learning. The six principles are:

1. Teaching is a moral act invoking an ethic of care.
2. Teaching is reflective and requires an inquiry stance.
3. Learning is a developmental/constructivist process.
4. Subject matter matters.
5. There is a need to develop strong collegial bonds.
6. Teaching is a political act.

Kroll explains that these principles are intended to help students of teaching see into teaching. The principles help to challenge participants' assumptions of teaching and learning by creating contexts in which such challenges might be enacted and built upon. The importance of program principles being translated into practice is significant. It suggests that knowledge of practice is being used not only to shape practice but to also inform that which occurs in the way that teaching is planned, conducted and reviewed. If that is the case, then insights into teaching surely become clearer and more obvious to teacher educators and students of teaching alike, and is an illustration of a pedagogy of teacher education in action. But what does that mean for how students of teaching might be challenged to think about their learning of teaching through a pedagogy of teacher education?

Shaping an identity: challenging the learning for students of teaching

Bullough (1991) has illustrated well how identity influences the development of practice in students of teaching. He has shown that the nature of self-image and issues of identity formation matter in learning about teaching. Therefore, how teacher educators help students of teaching see into their own behaviours and practice is crucial in helping them develop as teachers.

Knowing oneself is crucial in coming to understand how one acts in given situations. In the anecdote below, Dana, found herself in a situation that she had not envisaged and she responded in ways that disappointed her and undermined her original teaching purpose. She wanted her students to appreciate a second language and not to experience the type of teaching she had endured as a student. She knew what she did not want to do but it happened anyway.

Dear Diary,

I had the worst class ever today. Year nine, double Indonesian on a Friday afternoon. The year nines had been on camp so I had no experience of what they were like or capable of! I walked in fairly confident. I had planned this lesson thoroughly as it was my first year nine class and my first ever double. I had created communicative activities: pair work, surveys, everything any beginning teacher would need to engage a bunch of apathetic year nines. I would surely catch their attention and help them see the value of being able to speak another language; as opposed to what I had experienced as a student!

My supervising teacher walked in and the noisy year nines straggled in behind him. I walked to the front of the class and introduced myself.

'Good afternoon, year 9. I am Miss Soultan and I will be teaching you for the next few weeks.' I said sounding like I'd done it all a hundred times before.

Mr. Cool who reeked of a 'couldn't careless attitude' despite needing to have his cap sit 'just so' on his head called out, 'Are you a real teacher or a student teacher?'

I tried to ignore his question and carried on with some (pathetic) spiel about how we could all learn from each other and how the next few weeks would just fly.

I then launched into my lesson plan. I introduced myself in Indonesian and then asked each student to do the same. I said we would go around the room and hear something about each student. I emphasized that it didn't matter how simple it was, as long as it was said in Indonesian.

The first student stood up and hesitantly said, 'Nama saya Ben. Saya tinggi.'

I could hear some of the boys around him saying how stupid they thought all of this was because they already knew each other but I ignored them as I attempted to reward Ben's effort.

'Very good Ben.' I responded.

I was all for positive comments even though I really didn't mean it because I was disappointed with his too simple, 'My name is Ben. I'm tall.'

I looked along to Josh, the next student. He slowly stood and said,

'Nama saya Josh. Saya tinggi.'

The class erupted into laughter. Josh was maybe half the size of Ben. My heart was sinking fast as I could feel these year nines slipping away from me.

I battled on, but things got no better. It was hard to get their attention so I waited. I waited a bit longer.

Waiting, waiting, hoping.

I couldn't stand it anymore so I mustered up the angriest face I could and told them all how rude they were and that I would not tolerate calling out and talking over one another.

'Miss, your face is going red,' came out of nowhere; but more than likely from under that cap, although they were all starting to look a bit more painful now.

I started sinking ever deeper.

I stormed over to the rubbish bin and threw in the worksheets and surveys I had spent so much time and care preparing then turned and told them all (well maybe I yelled) to begin copying a large slab of writing from their out-of-date textbook.

I never wanted to be that sort of teacher. But there I was doing boring work, punishing them and making them do irrelevant work that would make them like the subject even less.

What have I become? Why did this have to happen to me?

(Dana) (Loughran 2006, pp. 110–11)

What she did, what she wanted to do and what she will do next time are all influenced by how well she knows herself. The image she carries of herself and the professional identity she is gradually developing are important in shaping her teaching. Seeing the possibilities for growth and accepting that learning about teaching involves learning from dissonance in practice is important – but is not necessarily understood by being told about it, it needs to be felt through experience. Therefore, students of teaching need opportunities to learn about themselves and how they react in situations so that they might genuinely see how they teach; that can be a powerful catalyst for change. Dissonance offers possibilities for seeing that which might normally be overlooked and is one way of actively seeking out instances of being a living contradiction (Whitehead 1993) and taking responsibility for determining how to act in response – and that is at the heart of learning about teaching. Coming to know oneself matters in learning about teaching, and should be an outcome of teacher education practices based on a meaningful pedagogy of teacher education.

Reflection in shaping learning about teaching

Enacting a pedagogy of teacher education requires students of teaching to be encouraged to search for, and respond to, their own problems of practice. Dewey's (1933) conceptualization of reflection as described by Zeichner and Liston (1996, p. 9) involves: 'a holistic way of meeting and responding to problems, a way of being as a teacher . . . [it] . . . involves intuition, emotion, and passion and is not something that can be neatly packaged as a set of techniques for teachers.' Therefore, in teaching *and* learning about teaching, reflection is a cornerstone to seeing oneself and one's problems in ways that invite a response. Again, how teacher educators help students of teaching reflect on their practice and learn through that experience is central to a pedagogy of teacher education. Consider how that has been achieved for Brad in the following anecdote.

What you hear in silence

This was the first time I taught this particular year 10 class. The topic was melody writing and I was more than prepared for the lesson with every word scripted and carefully emblazoned on the pages in front of me in my lesson plan.

'O.K., melody writing is a fairy simple concept.' I started, 'As long as you follow the seven rules.'

'Rule number one is . . .' and so I started blurting out the rules as the class frantically raced to write them down in their note books.

'And rule number seven, are you with me now James?' my confidence growing with every word as I pushed them to keep up, 'You must always end on the tonic.'

It was as easy as that!

I knew that now all they had to do was follow the rules and they would all be melody writers extraordinaire.

'And for homework tonight I want you to follow those rules and write your own melody. Any questions?' I asked as I scanned the room quite pleased with my delivery.

The silence beckoned so I asked again, 'O.K., quite simple really. Any questions?'

Not a sound.

'Great, they all understand.' I said to myself in a congratulatory tone.

The bell sounded right on cue and as the students filed out of the room I started to pack up my things to follow them out.

I was pleased with today's lesson and was quietly rewarding myself on a job well done as I strode to the door.

'Did you understand any of that?' Ben asked Jeff as they spilled out into the corridor.
'Nup, not one bit.' Jeff said.
'Me either.'
(Brad) (Loughran 2006, p. 130)

Placing the experiences of students of teaching at the centre of learning to teach is fundamental to developing deeper understandings of teaching. Reflection as a meaningful action offers genuine ways of helping students of teaching to value their developing knowledge of practice. Students need to learn to be able to recognize what they know and to be able to articulate how they know it so that they can be active builders of their professional learning in their practice. A pedagogy of teacher education demands practices of teacher educators that foster such growth.

Conclusion

The basis for the need to develop and articulate a pedagogy of teacher education is deeply rooted in understandings of teaching as complex and dynamic. Therefore, there is an ongoing need for knowledge of practice to be better articulated and communicated in order to illustrate that teaching is about the development of sophisticated knowledge of practice in action. Teacher education is where such processes should prosper. A pedagogy of teacher education is vital in making that possible.

Note

1 Anecdotes in this use of the term are a tool developed by Max van Manen (1999) for gaining insights into students' thinking about a situation. Students are asked to think about a critical event in their learning and to construct an anecdote (using simple guidelines) to portray that for others. The anecdotes in this paper have been written by students of teaching.

Further reading

Berry, A. (2007). *Tensions in Teaching About Teaching: Understanding Practice as a Teacher Educator.* Dordrecht: Springer.

This is an outstanding book that illustrates how knowledge of teaching about teaching can be developed and is crucial to enhancing the nature of teacher education programs and practices.

Brandenburg, R. (2004). Roundtable reflections: (re-)defining the role of the teacher educator and the pre-service teacher as 'co-learners'. *Australian Journal of Education*, 48(2), 166–81.

This paper introduces excellent research into how to create a strong learning about teaching environment for student teachers.

Hoban, G. F. (ed.). (2005). *The Missing Links in Teacher Education Design: Developing a Multi-Linked Conceptual Framework*. Berlin: Springer.

An excellent book explaining fundamental features necessary to a quality teacher education program.

Loughran, J. J., Hamilton, M. L., LaBoskey, V. K. and Russell, T. (eds). (2004). *International Handbook of Self-Study of Teaching and Teacher Education Practices*. Dordrecht: Kluwer Academic Publishers.

The most authoritative text on self-study of teaching and teacher education practices, a must-read for anyone interested in self-study.

Russell, T. and Bullock, S. (1999). Discovering our professional knowledge as teachers: critical dialogues about learning from experience. In J. Loughran (ed.), *Researching Teaching: Methodologies and Practices for Understanding Pedagogy* (pp. 132 –51). London: Falmer Press.

An excellent chapter regarding how to bring student teachers into the learning about the teaching process in new and engaging ways.

References

Berry, A. (2004). Self-study in teaching about teaching. In J. Loughran, M. L. Hamilton, V. LaBoskey and T. Russell (eds), *International Handbook of Self-Study of Teaching and Teacher Education Practices* (Vol. 2, pp. 1295–332). Dordrecht: Kluwer Academic Publishers.

Berry, A. and Loughran, J. J. (2004, April). *Modeling in Teacher Education: Making the Unseen Clear*. Paper presented at the American Educational Research Association, San Diego.

Brookfield, S. D. (1995). *Becoming a Critically Reflective Teacher*. San Francisco: Jossey-Bass Publishers.

Bullough, R. V. Jr. (1991). Exploring personal teaching metaphors in pre-service teacher education. *Journal of Teacher Education*, 42(1), 43–51.

Bullough, R. V. J. and Gitlin, A. (2001). *Becoming a Student of Teaching: Linking Knowledge Production and Practice* (Second edn). London: RoutledgeFalmer.

Dewey, J. (1933). *How We Think*. Lexington, Massachusetts: D.C. Heath and Company.

Dinkleman, T. (1999, April). *Self-study in Teacher Education: A Means and Ends Tool for Promoting Reflective Teaching*. Paper presented at the Annual Meeting of the American Educational Research Association, Montreal, Quebec.

Hoban, G. (1997). Learning about learning in the context of a science methods course. In J. Loughran and T. Russell (eds), *Teaching About Teaching: Purpose, Passion and Pedagogy in Teacher Education* (pp. 133–49). London: Falmer Press.

Kessels, J. and Korthagen, F. A. J. (2001). The relation between theory and practice: Back to the classics. In F. A. J. Korthagen, with, J. Kessels, B. Koster, B. Langerwarf and T. Wubbels (eds), *Linking Practice and Theory: The Pedagogy of Realistic Teacher Education* (pp. 20–31). Mahwah, New Jersey: Lawrence Erlbaum Associations, Publishers.

Korthagen, F. A. J. (2001a). Teacher education: a problematic enterprise. In K. F. A. J., with, J. Kessels, B. Koster, B. Langerwarf and T. Wubbels (eds), *Linking Practice and Theory: the Pedagogy of Realistic Teacher Education* (pp. 1–19). Mahwah, New Jersey: Lawrence Erlbaum Associates, Publishers.

Korthagen, F. A. J. (2001b). Building a realistic teacher education program. In F. A. J. Korthagen, with, J. Kessels, B. Koster, B. Langerwarf and T. Wubbels (eds), *Linking Practice and Theory: The Pedagogy of Realistic Teacher Education* (pp. 69–87). Mahwah, New Jersey: Lawrence Erlbaum Associates.

Korthagen, F. A. J., Loughran, J. J. and Lunenberg, M. (2005). Teaching teachers: studies into the expertise of teacher educators. *Teaching and Teacher Education*, 21(2), 107–15.

Koster, B., Brekelmans, M., Korthagen, F. and Wubbels, T. (2005). Quality requirements for teacher educators. *Teaching and Teacher Education*, 21(2), 157–76.

Kroll, L. R. (2004). Constructing constructivism: how student-teachers construct ideas of development, knowledge, learning and teaching. *Teachers and Teaching: Theory and Practice*, 10(2), 199–221.

Kroll, L. R., Crossey, R., Donahue, D. M., Galguera, T., LaBoskey, V. K., Richert, A., et al. (2005). *Teaching as Principled Practice: Managing Complexity for Social Justice.* Thousand Oaks: SAGE.

Loughran, J. J. (1996). *Developing Reflective Practice: Learning About Teaching and Learning Through Modelling.* London: Falmer Press.

Loughran, J. J. (1997). An introduction to purpose, passion and pedagogy. In J. Loughran and T. Russell (eds), *Teaching About Teaching: Purpose, Passion and Pedagogy in Teacher Education* (pp. 3–8). London: Falmer Press.

Loughran, J. J. (2006). *Developing a Pedagogy of Teacher Education: Understanding Teaching and Learning About Teaching.* London: Routledge.

Mason, J. (2002). *Researching Your Own Practice: The Discipline of Noticing.* London: RoutledgeFalmer.

Nicol, C. (1997). Learning to teach prospective teachers to teach mathematics: struggles of a beginning teacher educator. In J. Loughran and T. Russell (eds), *Teaching About Teaching: Purpose, Passion and Pedagogy in Teacher Education* (pp. 95–116). London: Falmer Press.

Northfield, J. R. and Gunstone, R. F. (1997). Teacher education as a process of developing teacher knowledge. In J. Loughran and T. Russell (eds), *Teaching About Teaching: Purpose, Passion and Pedagogy in Teacher Education* (pp. 48–56). London: Falmer Press.

Peterman, F. (1997). The lived curriculum of constructivist teacher education. In V. Richardson (ed.), *Constructivist Teacher Education: Building a World of New Understandings* (pp. 154–63). London: Falmer Press.

Russell, T. (1997). Teaching teachers: how I teach IS the message. In J. Loughran and T. Russell (eds), *Teaching About Teaching: Purpose, Passion and Pedagogy in Teacher Education* (pp. 32–47). London: Falmer Press.

Van Manen, M. (1999). The language of pedagogy and primacy of student experience. In J. Loughran (ed.), *Researching Teaching: Methodologies and Practices for Understanding Pedagogy* (pp. 13–27). London: Falmer Press.

Whitehead, J. (1993). *The Growth of Educational Knowledge: Creating Your Own Living Educational Theories*. Bournemouth: Hyde publications.

Zeichner, K. M. and Liston, D. P. (1996). *Reflective Teaching: An Introduction*. Mahwah, New Jersey: Lawrence Erlbaum Associates.

Practising an ethic of caring in teaching: challenges and possibilities

Michalinos Zembylas

Open University of Cyprus

9

Chapter Outline

This chapter aims to provide an overview of conversations regarding caring in education, and to draw implications from these particularly in terms of the emotional labour involved when an ethic of caring teaching is practicsed. Given the competing perspectives of care in education, the goal is not to create a list of principles and practices of caring teaching, but to outline a number of possibilities that are opened when school cultures are organized in ways that engage caring relationships. The chapter addresses the question: In what ways can teachers and learners formulate and sustain caring cultures in schools?

Introduction

Recent attention to caring (Noddings 1984, 1992; Gilligan 1988; Thompson 1998; Katz 1999; Valenzuela 1999; Rauner 2000; Dance 2002) emphasizes its importance in teaching, learning and the student/teacher relationship (see Chapter 8). Caring, writes Noddings, 'is the very bedrock of all successful education' (1992, p. 27) and caring can transform schooling if it becomes an integral part of the curriculum. As opposed to an ethic of justice, an ethic of caring, she asserts, emphasizes receptivity, relatedness and responsiveness rather than rights and rules (Noddings 1984). Caring for children, for example, involves much more than assuring that children's rights are upheld and that no discrimination occurs.

Caring requires teachers to elicit, and listen to, how students are feeling, to evaluate their purposes, to help them to engage in self-evaluation, and to help them grow as participants in caring relations (Noddings 1992). This orientation suggests that teachers have to shift their perspectives in teaching, become more receptive and learn new skills. 'As teachers,' writes Noddings, 'we may have to learn new subject matter to maintain the growth of our best students, and we may have to change our methods entirely to work effectively with students who have great difficulty learning. In a fundamental, essential way, caring implies a quest for competence' (1996, p. 162). When this stance becomes a professional practice in the classroom, caring takes the shape of encouraging dialogue, showing sensitivity to students' needs and talents, and providing engaging materials and activities for students (Rogers and Webb 1991). In other words, it is argued that the whole orientation of schooling has to change to develop a system that nurtures people in becoming caring human beings (Noddings 1995). This notion implies choosing and organizing themes of care in the curriculum, nurturing pre-service and in-service teachers in developing a caring ethic, and generally providing the supporting structures for creating a school environment of caring ethic.

However, McKamey (2004) argues, caring means different things to different theorists whose perspectives may ignore the social, cultural, racial and gender context in which caring is enacted. Thus caring 'is a symbolic concept charged with multiple political, social and cultural meanings' (p. 6). Hamovitch rejects assumptions about uniformity in the interpretations of caring, raising the question: 'Who is going to be doing the caring, within what context, based on what assumptions about why it is that students are in need of caring?' (1995, p. 3).

This chapter has three purposes: to clarify some theoretical conversations regarding caring in education, to outline some implications particularly in terms of the emotional labour involved when an ethic of caring teaching is practised and to consider ways with which practitioners may begin to formulate and sustain school cultures of care that exemplify the multiple meanings of caring.

An overview of conversations regarding caring in education

Caring remains an ambiguous term implying a variety of different meanings for different scholars. Chaskin and Rauner (1995) explain that caring is 'an umbrella concept that encompasses and connects a range of discrete subjects, such as empathy, altruism, prosocial behaviour, and efficacy' (p. 670). This accessibility of caring, however, may create confusion, as Noddings says: 'People do all sorts of things in the name of caring' (1999, p. 13). Even in reading Nodding's work, points out McKamey (2004), her meanings of caring shift: sometimes she refers to caring as a moral orientation to teaching and sometimes she writes about caring as a curriculum that addresses social inequities (see Noddings 1984, 1992).

In order to disentangle the meanings that scholars attribute to the term 'caring' and their underlying assumptions, McKamey proposes three theories of caring. First, the *caring teacher behaviour theory* locates caring in teacher behaviours, asserting that there may be causal relationships between teacher caring behaviours and student outcomes. The underlying assumptions of this theory emphasize that there are a finite number of caring teacher behaviours, that is, if teachers do certain things (e.g. increasing student-teacher interactions, tutoring after school, listening to students, asking questions about personal life, recognizing that each student is unique) then academic outcomes (increased student motivation, resiliency, engagement and increased attendance) will be improved (cf. Ferreira and Bosworth 2001; Teven 2001; Wentzel 1997).

Second, *the caring capacity theory* locates caring within the capacities of people and communities; this theory assumes that schools and/or communities have the capacity and the obligation to provide caring contexts for students who lack caring experiences in their lives. This theory (McKamey 2004) is based on the notion that caring capacity is something that students can develop over time, and that it is something which belongs to students/communities and thus can be transferred. The implications for school reforms include explicit development of students' caring capacities through modelling, dialogue, practice and cooperation (Noddings 1984, 1992). An instructional arrangement based on this theory requires that teachers and students spend time together to develop communities of learning and contexts for moral experiences (cf. Freeman et al. 1999).

Finally, the *caring difference theory* locates caring within different social groups and explores the differences in the ways that social, ethnic, class and gender groups express caring. The underlying assumption of this theory is that an '(authentic) caring orientation is (cultural) and informed by race, class, or gender. Denying someone's orientation is denying someone's identity' (McKamey 2004, p. 9). This theory addresses issues of power relations and seeks to empower students by attending to their personal lives, their cultural traditions, their gendered orientations and their communities (e.g. see Rauner 2000; Thompson 1998; Valenzuela 1999). The implications of this theory for school reform include the idea that schools must reorganize their curricula and teaching practices in order to recognize people's different caring orientations.

Each caring theory has important limitations that need to be acknowledged; these limitations reiterate the notion about the multiplicities in the meaning of caring. The caring teacher behaviour theory is somewhat deterministic in its assertion that students will benefit from conforming to universal, caring norms. In other words, this theory does not account for diverse (cultural) conceptions of caring. There is evidence, for example, that teacher caring based on white, middle class conceptions of caring can oppress students of colour or diverse cultural background and thus caring might not always be beneficial (Hamovitch 1995; Valenzuela 1999). Rather than questioning the meanings of different interpretations of caring, studies that are based on caring teacher behaviour theory may view different elements of caring as variations of a universal theme (McKamey 2004).

The caring capacity theory has limitations in terms of relying on a deficiency model: people and communities are considered deficient in caring and thus their caring capacity has to be cultivated. Implicit in this assumption that something is missing from students' lives is the notion that some interpretations of caring (i.e., those expressed by teachers and the institutions) are superior to those that students carry with them. 'While well intentioned,' writes McKamey, 'this assumption of deficiency serves to pathologize students who do not fit into the norms and might have difference in expectations of idealized and re-visioned educational, racial, or gendered institutions, and seeks to change students to fit into idealized norms' (2004, p. 20). In an effort to 'develop' the habits of caring norms for these children, this account devalues the capacities and qualities of caring that exist within children. This theory also ignores issues of power relations: who decides the social values that students should learn to care about.

Finally, the caring difference theory falls into the dichotomy that generally challenges theories of multi-culturalism, that is, in focusing on differences, dichotomies between 'us' and 'them' (e.g. black/white, male/female) may be perpetuated and the prospects for unity may be unsettled. In other words, while this theory celebrates differences, it re-establishes cultural and social divisions. Thus, despite the considerable contribution of relational feminists (e.g. Noddings and Gilligan) these writers have been criticized for assuming that women naturally have such values and ways of thinking (although British literature on caring has taken a different direction from that of relational feminists, see Acker 1995). At the same time that women's ways of knowing are legitimized, the meanings of being a 'woman' are limited. In other words, such a conceptualization risks stereotyping women.

However, in the light of critiques of white feminist conceptions of caring, the theory of caring difference prompts further exploration about the relationships between identity formation, school context, and acts and interpretations of caring. Thus, McKamey suggests a fourth theory, which she calls a *process theory* of caring; this theory raises 'questions about the tensions, relationships, and interconnections between identit(ies), context, and expressions of caring' (2004, p. 43). Along similar lines, Antrop-González and De Jesús call this a theory of *critical care*, 'a term that captures the ways in which communities of colour may care about and educate their own, and their intentions in doing so' (2006, p. 413). While other theories of caring focus on what teachers and schools need to do in terms of caring to improve academic outcomes for students, this theory engages in a deeper exploration of the complexities in the meanings of caring and its role in education.

Critical care theory acknowledges the 'politics of caring' (Valenzuela 1999) in the ways that caring has been defined within particular socio-cultural, gendered and economic contexts. Caring is not understood as something necessarily beneficial or something that teachers do largely voluntarily, but caring can produce tensions and conflicts because of the expectations attached to different students. For example, Thompson (1998) criticizes the colour-blind assumption of white feminist perceptions on caring that are characterized by low expectations for disenfranchised students, resulting from the pity felt for students' social circumstances. The critical care theory examines the tensions relating to competing conceptions of caring and advocates that caring has to be understood within particular situations and for particular people. Thompson in exploring the differences between caring in white and black tradition, writes:

> Whereas caring in the White tradition is largely voluntary emotional labour performed in an intimate setting or else underpaid work in a pink-collar profession like teaching or nursing, caring in the Black community is as much a public undertaking as it is a private or semi-private concern. It is not surprising, therefore, that caring in the Black community is not understood as compensatory work meant to remedy the shortcomings of justice, as in the 'heaven in a heartless world' model. (1998, p. 9)

These different expectations about caring inevitably fuel conflict and power struggles between teachers and students who see each other as not caring (Antrop-González and De Jesús 2006). As a result, conceptualizations of caring must explicitly challenge the idea that assimilation to dominant notions of caring is a neutral process; instead, educators need to question the ways in which particular socio-cultural contexts shape identities and thus influence expressions and interpretations of caring.

In the next two sections, I will build on the notion that scholars and teachers need to acknowledge how different communities understand caring within their socio-cultural context, and I argue that we need to move away from the idea that teachers need to be told what they should do to be caring in schools. Instead, we need to acquire a deeper understanding of the ways that social and cultural resources shape a learner's, a teacher's and a community's expressions and interpretations of caring. In the following section, I am particularly interested in the implications of practising an ethic of caring in teaching, and focus on the interpretations of the emotional labour involved.

Reflection

Do we all mean the same thing when we talk about caring? What are the assumptions of different theories of caring? How do particular social and cultural contexts shape interpretations and expressions of caring in education? Is there a universal concept of caring? How can teachers account for different understandings of caring in their teaching?

Implications of practising an ethic of caring: the emotional labour of caring teaching

Current discussions about caring teaching focus on the notion that caring is integral to teaching (Goldstein 1997, 2002; Lipsitz 1996), and the growing literature on caring in teaching acknowledges the association between caring and good teaching (Collinson et al. 1999; Heath 1994; Noddings 1992, 1994; Rogers and Webb 1991). Also, research studies have asserted relationships between caring and positive learning environments, especially for students of colour (Nieto 1998; Valenzuela 1999; Walker 1996). Other studies claim that caring learning environments help students develop into caring individuals (Freeman et al. 1999; Rauner 2000).

However, the implications of practising an ethic of caring in teaching are not limited to the positive learning outcomes or the constructive learning environment; there are important implications in terms of the *emotional labour* demanded by teachers to enact caring. The emotional labour of caring teaching (rarely so called) is generally marginal or at best regarded as a side-effect, rather than as a significant factor in teachers' acts or lives. Analysis of caring teaching has tended to focus either on pre-conceived conceptions of what caring is (Goldstein 2002) or on atheoretical discussions of the importance of 'a teacher being nurturing, supportive, nice, inclusive, responsive, and kind' (Goldstein 2002, p. 2).

Arguments that caring teaching and caring teacher education have three cornerstones – commitment, intimacy and passion (Goldstein 2002) – fail to recognize that performing caring teaching also involves different perceptions about the nature and the amount of emotional labour; such perceptions become a principal site for the formation of how a 'caring teacher' or a 'caring school culture' are perceived. For example, emotional labour may be perceived as a voluntary performance of a teacher changing how she feels or what emotions she expresses when interacting with a student (in order to hide her anger or disappointment) and instead demonstrate that she cares by smiling or making humorous comments. Or emotional labour may be interpreted as a conscious, public and private commitment to create competent youth. In either case, however, caring is an emotion-laden practice in which emotions may be underplayed, overplayed, neutralized or changed (Zembylas 2002, 2003b) in order to advance particular educational goals (Hargreaves 1999).

In my own work, I explore the emotional labour associated with caring teaching as a source of conflict about the nature of a caring teacher/culture and of attempts to shape and reshape the social, professional and intellectual stance of a caring teacher (Isenbarger and Zembylas 2006). A 'genealogy' of caring teaching (Zembylas 2005) addresses the meanings and practices that act upon teachers within particular social, historical and cultural contexts, and define how teachers understand and experience the emotional labour involved. Consequently, the issue is not whether 'the teacher's ability to engage in genuine caring encounters is decreased [. . .] when the working environment is structured in a way that turns caring into demanding and unrewarding "emotional labour"' (Goldstein 1999, p. 660). My research experience so far has shown that the relationship between emotional labour and caring teaching is much more complex than Goldstein's description.

Although caring relationships in teaching may be a source of professional satisfaction for teachers (van den Berg 2002), teaching can also become a source of emotional strain, anxiety, anger and disappointment (Vandenberghe and Huberman 1999). These emotions become emotional labour when teachers engage in efforts to modify and control negative emotions for the purpose of expressing only those emotions that are socially acceptable. Taking the time to listen to students' problems or worries, giving advice or guidance to them and showing warmth and love are all examples of emotional labour associated with some functions of caring. Thus, emotional labour is clearly one of the ways through which interpretations and expressions of caring are built. But emotional labour involves many emotional costs, and is often invisible, unacknowledged or devalued. Conceptualizing emotional labour as a complex process, challenges assumptions of care as natural, voluntary or effortless.

Caring teaching, then, may be associated with both *negative* and *positive* emotional labour. Thus, caring in teaching may force teachers into a type of emotional dissonance in which what one feels (or wants to feel) does not match with the emotions displayed (Shuler and Sypher 2000); suppressing the self in this way can lead to such consequences as stress and burnout (Troman 2000). By contrast, there might be positive aspects of the emotional labour demanded in caring teaching: for example how teachers can and do enjoy their emotional work as carers despite the fact they have to display ingenuine positive emotions. So the relationship between emotional labour and caring teaching does not necessarily have to be harmful in terms of 'decreasing' one's ability to care, as Goldstein (1999) assumes. Caring teaching as an intellectual and professional stance may be immensely enjoyable.

My previous research into the emotional labour of caring teaching (Isenbarger and Zembylas 2006) has shown that a teacher's emotional labour is related to her professional and philosophical stance about the role of caring in teaching and learning; in other words, her goals (beliefs, values and purposes) as well as her actions (customs, habits, ways of behaving) attempt to use 'care' as a social and intellectual stance. This research demonstrates that emotional labour – both positive and negative – is an important aspect of the reality of caring teaching. It is also shown that this understanding of caring teaching takes a different direction from that of Noddings (1984, 1992) and Goldstein (1997, 2002) in terms of the assumptions that are implied in the conceptualization of caring. Thus, I agree with Acker (1995) who argues that caring can be seen both as an approach and as an emotion, and as such, it requires not only 'love' but also 'labour'. Consequently, the social and institutional contexts in which caring teaching takes place need to be scrutinized, and the implications of the social expectations that teachers' caring work should blur the distinction between labour and love needs to be problematized (Zembylas and Isenbarger 2002).

Three interpretations

Another angle for understanding the relationship between caring and emotional labour, my research suggests, directs attention to the following three interpretations of caring teaching: *pedagogical* caring as caring about children's academic expectations; *moral* caring as caring about the values communicated in learning communities; and *cultural* caring as caring that communicates or challenges the norms of the culture of which the school or classroom is part (Isenbarger and Zembylas 2006). Again, as a teacher engages in the emotional labour of caring there is not one kind of caring encompassing all her actions and beliefs; there are several kinds as a result of the nature of emotional labour involved and the context in which it takes place.

Finally, a teacher's caring approach has a lot to do with the school culture in which she or he teaches and especially the fact that in Western cultures most teachers do not make a distinction between labour and caring. In practical terms it is often difficult to tell caring and emotional labour apart: either or both may be adopted as part of a teacher's sense of personal, social and intellectual stance, and so her emotions are likely to remain unquestioned as long as children appear to benefit. Yet the lack of distinction between caring and labour has important implications for teachers abandoning or remaining in the profession, because the emotional demands of caring teaching may often go unrealized. Unrealized also remain the tensions and complexities relating to competing notions of the relationship between emotional labour and caring teaching – again as a result of the particular socio-cultural context of schooling.

Reflection

In what ways do you consider that you perform emotional labour in your teaching? How are those ways related to your conceptions about caring teaching? How are those conceptions formed? What kinds of changes could you make to your own teaching to change the nature of the emotional labour performed?

Ways with which practitioners may begin to formulate and sustain school cultures of care

In the last part of this chapter, I identify some ways with which practitioners may begin to formulate and sustain school cultures of care. The argument put forward here is not that a set of normative practices will deterministically lead to caring teaching. Rather, the challenge is much more complex and therefore attention has to be directed at the important task of trying to establish a *culture of care* (Nias 1999). A culture of care is not a simple set of caring activities but a sustained effort to create a community that enacts beliefs and values of caring and ethical thinking. This effort is essentially an ongoing *process* that constantly problematizes the tensions and interrelationships between community practices and expressions of caring. The notion of culture of care, then, captures the ways in which school communities care about children. Here, I describe three such ways which provide some general directions but do not constitute principles or practices of caring teaching in any way.

First, to establish cultures of care, teachers have to understand that caring works as an *affective economy* (Ahmed 2004). Ahmed's (2004) notion of 'affective economy' is another way of arguing that caring is an affect that does not reside 'inside' an individual but rather it circulates involving relations of difference, whereby what is 'moved' and what 'moves' individuals and meanings is the effect of affective intensities and energies. In other words, Ahmed acknowledges the significance of the ways in which emotions (e.g. caring, empathy, love) become attached to objects, bodies and signs – a process that is crucial in the constitution of each individual and each community. What characterizes caring, then, is that it functions as an economy; it connects us to others, a process that is never over.

Teaching can readily embody an ethic of caring, as Nias (1999) points out, if teachers accept that they are affectively involved with learners, and thus establish ethical practices that emphasize *responsibility* – responsibility for learners and responsibility for affective connections throughout the school community. Viewed this way caring teaching is a culture that nurtures activities worthwhile to learners, in that teachers regard their responsibility as ethical rather than a bureaucratic one. In their consideration of an ethic of caring, teachers need to create, maintain and enhance affective connections with learners.

Affective connections with learners call attention to individuals' demands for respect and recognition. The task at hand for teachers who struggle to create and sustain cultures of care is to find new ways that 'can form a strong, wondrous sense of vitality, potentiality, and creation' (Albrecht-Crane 2003, p. 587). Caring as an affective economy operates as a force that exceeds and escapes each individual and 'allows for (communal) connections at a level within and yet outside of social organization' (p. 588). This analysis then puts emphasis on caring affective relations, not on caring individuals (teachers); such an account provides an opening for community-building and offers critical tools for responding to the political implications of caring in education (Valenzuela 1999). The critical task of caring cultures implies inventing strategies of subverting the disempowering ways that function in schools.

A second way with which practitioners may begin to establish school cultures of care is the promotion of interactions that embody values such as trust, vigilance, tolerance and *collective witnessing* (Boler 1999; Boler and Zembylas 2003). Collective witnessing is a collectivized engagement in learning to see, feel and act differently. In other words, in school cultures of care, teachers and/or learners make a conscious ethical choice to care about others through becoming 'witnesses' and not simply 'spectators' (Zembylas and Boler 2002). 'Witnessing' is different from 'spectating' in that witnessing assumes a collectivized engagement in learning to see differently (Boler 1999). Caring as witnessing is a call to action – action hopefully as a result of learning to see differently. This does not assure any change; however, it represents the first step towards that direction.

Therefore, it matters a great deal how teachers, for example, invite learners to care for one another by engaging in collective witnessing (e.g. cultivate altruism, empathy, tolerance). Once again, it is emphasized that caring is not simply an individual practice but a collective one. As teachers and learners become willing to see things differently and understand how their lives are intertwined with others, they can begin to determine 'for themselves what kinds of actions make sense for them to take given their own ethical vision' (Boler 1999, p. 198). Some might choose to express alternative perspectives in the classroom or in the public arena; others might choose to participate in groups that reformulate education.

Caring cultures, therefore, encourage *listening* to each and every other. Caring as an ethic is born and reborn – not in terms of normative rules but in the sense of community members who listen *actively* to others (Garrison 1996). To listen actively, says Garrison, one must be 'vulnerable' to the other. That means suspending those beliefs that constitute a static identity. The rewards of listening are that each member of a caring school culture can teach everyone else to see and tell the story of one's life in new ways, and thereby, grow, as Garrison says. But there are enormous emotional costs for individuals and groups engaged in caring as witnessing, as the discussion on the emotional labour of caring has shown earlier.

Finally, the third way with which practitioners may begin to establish school cultures of care is investing in an orientation bound up with a sense of *empathy* and *social justice*. Empathy as an activity in the world (not in the mind) is an important aspect of responding ethically to others. This kind of empathy includes a critical effort to accept the other as a distinct individual and thus challenges the process of dehumanizing him or her (Halpern 2001). Halpern and Weinstein (2004) suggest that there are three important qualities in empathy that are significant for disrupting the normalizing rules of a caring ethic and establishing a caring ethic culture that constantly questions itself. First, empathy entails actively seeking the individual perspective of another; this can serve as an important step to begin caring for the other by placing one's self in another's circumstances and accepting that he or she possesses the same rights. Second, empathy involves a genuine effort to get to know the other and his or her perspectives; in this way, teachers and learners within a community can open their mind towards the other's experiences. Third, empathy involves the toleration of ambivalence; this ambivalence entails viewing differences as an enriching part of creating caring relationships with others.

The outcome of such an approach should work by defining the new uncovered perspectives as challenging the present uncaring realities through the shaping of new social relationships and affective connections (asking for example: What types of transformations do we need in our values and behaviour to establish caring school cultures? How can schools really care and make a difference in the lives of the poor or underprivileged?) Bearing witness to the politics of caring – as Valenzuela (1999) argues – signifies the demand for new affective connections. It is precisely in the possibility of such connections that teachers and learners are called into being witnesses of one another.

Reflection

Are there any principles and practices of caring teaching that teachers can use to establish caring cultures in their classroom? Justify your answer.

Conclusion

This chapter has put forward the argument that it is very deterministic to outline a number of principles and practices for caring teaching; instead, my analysis here has identified some general ways with which practitioners may begin to formulate and sustain school cultures of care. Such an approach could avoid reducing caring teaching to maternal nurturance and reproducing the tyranny of deterministic pedagogical models, and at the same time avoid slipping into the trap of an uncritical celebration of rampant caring.

Further reading

Katz, M. S., Noddings, N. and Strike, K. A. (eds). (1999). *Justice and Caring: The Search for Common Ground in Education.* New York: Teachers College Press.

An interesting collection of essays about care and justice as moral orientations in education.

Rauner, D. M. (2000). *They Still Pick Me Up When I Fall: The Role of Caring in Youth Development and Community Life.* New York: Columbia University Press.

Rauner's work is a good example of showing the impact of caring on youth life; it is representative of the difference theory of caring.

Valenzuela, A. (1999). *Subtractive Schooling: U.S. Mexican Youth and the Politics of Caring.* Albany: SUNY Press.

A powerful ethnographic account of multi-cultural secondary schooling that shows the political aspects of caring in American schools.

References

Acker, S. (1995). Carry on caring: the work of women teachers. *British Journal of Sociology of Education*, 16, 21–36.

Ahmed, S. (2004). *The Cultural Politics of Emotion*. Edinburgh, United Kingdom: Edinburgh University Press.

Albrecht-Crane, C. (2003). An affirmative theory of desire. *JAC*, 23, 563–98.

Antrop-González, R. and De Jesús, A. (2006). Toward a theory of critical care in urban school reform: examining structures and pedagogies of caring in two Latino community-based schools. *International Journal of Qualitative Studies in Education*, 19, 409–33.

Boler, M. (1999). *Feeling Power: Emotions and Education*. New York: Routledge.

Boler, M. and Zembylas, M. (2003). Discomforting truths: the emotional terrain of understanding difference. In P. Tryfonas (ed.), *Pedagogies of Difference: Rethinking Education for Social Change* (pp. 110–36). New York and London: Routledge.

Chaskin, R. J. and Rauner, D. M. (1995). Youth and caring: an introduction. *Phi Delta Kappan*, 76, 686–92.

Collinson, V., Killeavy, M. and Stephenson, H. (1999). Exemplary teachers: practising an ethic of care in England, Ireland, and the United States. *Journal for a Just and Caring Education*, 5, 349–66.

Dance, L. J. (2002). *Tough Fronts: The Impact of Street Culture on Schooling*. London: Falmer.

Ferreira, M. M. and Bosworth, K. (2001). Defining caring teachers: adolescents' perspectives. *Journal of Classroom Interaction*, 36(1), 24–30.

Freeman, N., Swick, K. and Brown, M. (1999). A caring curriculum within an early childhood teacher education program. *Education*, 120, 161–67.

Garrison, J. (1996). A Deweyan theory of democratic listening. *Educational Theory*, 46, 429–52.

Gilligan, C. (ed.). (1988). *Mapping the Moral Domain*. Cambridge, MA: Center for the Study of Gender, Education and Human Development.

Goldstein, L. (1997). *Teaching with Love: A Feminist Approach to Early Childhood Education*. New York: Peter Lang.

Goldstein. L. (1999). The relational zone: the role of caring relationships in the co-construction of mind. *American Educational Research Journal*, 36, 647–73.

Goldstein. L. (2002). *Reclaiming Caring in Teaching and Teacher Education*. New York: Peter Lang.

Halpern, J. (2001). *From Detached Concern to Empathy: Humanizing Medical Practice*. Oxford, United Kingdom: Oxford University Press.

Halpern, J. and Weinstein, H. (2004). Rehumanizing the other: empathy and reconciliation. *Human Rights Quarterly*, 26, 561–83.

Hamovitch, B. A. (1995). Caring in an institutional context: can it really occur? *Educational Foundations*, 8(4), 25–39.

Hargreaves, A. (1999). The psychic rewards (and annoyances) of classroom teaching. In M. Hammersley (ed.), *Researching School Experience: Ethnographic Studies of Teaching and Learning* (pp. 87–106). London: Falmer Press.

Heath, D. H. (1994). *Schools of Hope: Developing Mind and Character in Today's Youth.* San Francisco: Jossey-Bass.

Isenbarger, L. and Zembylas, M. (2006). The Emotional Labor of Caring in Teaching. *Teaching and Teacher Education*, 22, 120–34.

Katz, S. (1999). Teaching in tensions: Latino immigrant youth, their teachers, and the structures of schooling. *Teachers College Record*, 100, 809–40.

Lipsitz, J. (1996). Prologue: why we should care about caring. *Phi Delta Kappan*, 76, 665–66.

McKamey, C. (2004, April). *Competing Theories of Care in Education: A Critical Review and Analysis of the Literature.* Paper presented at the annual meeting of the American Educational Research Association, San Diego, CA.

Nias, J. (1999). Teaching as a culture of care. In J. Prosser (ed.), *School Culture* (pp. 66–81). London: Paul Chapman Pub.

Nieto, S. (1998). Fact and fiction: stories of Puerto Ricans in U.S. schools. *Harvard Educational Review*, 68, 133–63.

Noddings, N. (1984). *Caring: A Feminine Approach to Ethics and Moral Education.* Berkeley: University of California Press.

Noddings, N. (1992). *The Challenge to Care in Schools.* New York: Teachers College Press.

Noddings, N. (1994). Foreword. In L. G. Beck (ed.), *Reclaiming Educational Administration as a Caring Profession* (pp. ix–x). New York: Teachers College Press.

Noddings, N. (1995). Teaching themes of care. *Phi Delta Kappan*, 76, 675–79.

Noddings, N. (1996). The caring professional. In S. Gordon, P. Benner and N. Noddings (eds), *Caregiving: Readings in Knowledge, Practice, Ethics and Politics* (pp. 160–72). Philadelphia: University of Pennsylvania Press.

Noddings, N. (1999). Care, justice, and equity. In M. S. Katz, N. Noddings and K. A. Strike (eds), *Justice and Caring: The Search for Common Ground in Education* (pp. 7–20). New York: Teachers College Press.

Rauner, D. M. (2000). *They Still Pick Me Up When I Fall: The Role of Caring in Youth Development and Community Life.* New York: Columbia University Press.

Rogers, D. and Webb, J. (1991). The ethics of caring in teacher education. *Journal of Teacher Education*, 42, 173–81.

Shuler, S. and Sypher, B. D. (2000). Seeking emotional labour: when managing the heart enhances the work experience. *Management Communication Quarterly*, 14, 50–89.

Teven, J. J. (2001). The relationships among teacher characteristics and perceived caring. *Communication Education*, 50, 159–69.

Thompson, A. (1998). Not the colour purple: Black feminist lessons for educational caring. *Harvard Educational Review*, 68, 522–34.

Troman, G. (2000). Teacher stress in the low-trust society. *British Journal of Sociology of Education*, 21, 331–53.

Valenzuela, A. (1999). *Subtractive Schooling: U.S. Mexican Youth and the Politics of Caring*. Albany: SUNY Press.

van den Berg, R. (2002). Teachers' meanings regarding educational practice. *Review of Educational Research*, 72, 577–625.

Vandenberghe, R. and Huberman, A. M. (1999). *Understanding and Preventing Teacher Burnout*. Cambridge, England: Cambridge University Press.

Walker, E. S. (1996). Interpersonal caring in the 'good' segregated schooling of African-American children: evidence from the case of Caswell County Training School. In D. Eaker-Rich, and J. Van Galen (eds), *Caring in an Unjust World: Negotiating Borders and Barriers in Schools* (pp. 129–46). Albany: SUNY Press.

Wentzel, K. R. (1997). Student motivation in middle school: the role of perceived pedagogical caring. *Journal of Educational Psychology*, 89, 411–19.

Zembylas, M. (2002). 'Structures of feeling' in curriculum and teaching: theorizing the emotional rules. *Educational Theory*, 52, 187–208.

Zembylas, M. (2003a). Caring for teacher emotion: reflections on teacher self-development. *Studies in Philosophy and Education*, 22, 103–25.

Zembylas, M. (2003b). Interrogating 'teacher identity': emotion, resistance, and self-formation. *Educational Theory*, 53, 107–27.

Zembylas, M. (2004). The emotional characteristics of teaching: an ethnographic study of one teacher. *Teaching and Teacher Education*, 20, 185–201.

Zembylas, M. (2005). *Teaching with Emotion: A Postmodern Enactment*. Greenwich, CT: Information Age Publishing.

Zembylas, M. and Boler, M. (2002). On the spirit of patriotism: challenges of a 'pedagogy of discomfort.' Special issue for 'Education and September 11', Teachers College Record Online. Retrieved 10 January 2007, from www.tcrecord.org

Zembylas, M. and Isenbarger, L. (2002). Teaching science to students with learning disabilities: subverting the myths of labelling through teachers' caring and enthusiasm. *Research in Science Education*, 32, 55–79.

Too busy teaching to find time for learning?

John MacBeath

University of Cambridge, United Kingdom

10

Chapter Outline

This chapter reports on studies commissioned by the National Union of Teachers to assess the impact of government initiatives on the professional lives of teachers in primary, secondary and special schools in England. It takes as its specific focus the secondary study in order to draw out some of the key themes and raises the questions of how these may be common or different in differing cultural contexts. A number of recurrent issues worked together to diminish opportunities for spontaneous and creative teaching.

Introduction

In exploring the debates about teaching in this book, the title of this final chapter has proved surprisingly prophetic even if the outcomes are slightly depressing; for the picture it paints represents a crucial conflict between the professional educator and government policy-makers.

Teaching is not what it used to be, not in England anyway, where teachers entering the profession have to adjust rapidly to a changed world. The classrooms may look very like the ones they attended as pupils but the dynamics of what happens within are fundamentally different. What has changed in the last generation, in England and elsewhere, is a complex mix of a tired curriculum, intensified testing (Wilhelm, Dewhurst-Savellis and Parker 2000), a changing profile of the profession (Johnson 2004), a reconfiguration of family life and, for young people themselves, a changed context of growing up (Normore 2004). Teaching is having to rise to the challenge of a world in which the pace, nature and contexts of learning have been radically transformed (Castells 2000).

The same holds true in varying degrees in other countries of the world. We are living in the global village that McLuhan (1988) foresaw three decades ago, a world in which information travels instantaneously and in which policy-makers cherry-pick from places which appear to offer solutions to the perceived crisis in their own countries. In England, politicians and their advisors have played an active role in scouring the world for exemplars of 'good' and 'best' practice, sending emissaries to Taiwan or Finland, or wherever the latest OECD reports point to as exemplifying high standards. It is this race to raise the attainment bar through increased testing, performance monitoring and prescriptive teaching that explains much of the disillusionment of teachers and a steady flow of teachers leaving the profession (Ingersoll 2003).

The NUT studies

Between 2002 and 2005 the National Union of Teachers (NUT) in England commissioned three studies (Galton and MacBeath 2003; MacBeath and Galton 2005; MacBeath and Galton 2006) to shed light on the quality of professional life for teachers in an era of successive reform initiatives and increasing demands on schools. The purpose of those studies was to gauge the impact of present and previous government's policies on the working lives of teachers. The first report, *A Life in Teaching,* setting out the views of a representative sample of primary teachers, showed that government initiatives had produced dramatic changes in the working lives of teachers when compared to earlier surveys going back as far as the 1970s (Galton 1987).

The issues which emerged from this study may or may not apply directly in other countries of the world but they raise questions which are worth asking in any country in which teachers find themselves as intermediaries between prescriptive government policies and the desires and expectations of school pupils and their families.

Time for teaching?

One of the central findings of the NUT study was that the amount of time available for teaching each day did not allow for a broad and balanced curriculum with subjects such as Art, Drama and Music being marginalized into lunchtime and after-school clubs. Some schools had responded by extending the teaching day, starting school 15 minutes earlier in the morning, reducing lunchtime and cutting out the afternoon break in an effort to create more teaching time. One consequence was that teachers spent more time at home marking, planning and preparing work. In a typical week a classroom teacher would spend 4 to 6 evening hours marking, 11.8 hours planning and preparing lessons, and a further 5.4 hours on school work during weekends. The rigid structure of the National Curriculum, particularly the pressure to meet curriculum targets and excessive levels of testing, served to compound the dissatisfaction. Not feeling in control of their work was a major cause of teacher stress.

In the light of the findings from the primary survey it was an obvious next step to replicate the study with a sample of teachers drawn from secondary schools. In both primary and secondary studies, a leading concern had been the government's policy of inclusion (children with special educational needs taught alongside other children in mainstream schools and classes), raising concerns which led to a third inquiry focusing specifically on the impact of this policy shift and its effects on staff in special, primary and secondary schools.

In this chapter the focus is on the secondary study which picks up the key themes of the primary study and anticipates findings of the third study into how schools accommodate special needs.

Reflection

To what extent do these issues raised in English primary schools resonate with primary/elementary school practice in your own country? How does the nature of the teachers; working day compare? To what extent do teachers, in your experience, feel 'in control' of their work?

The secondary study

The purpose of the secondary survey was similar to its predecessor – to assess the impact of recent and present government polices on the working lives of teachers. It followed a similar pattern to the primary version: a survey followed by interviews with teachers. A key difference lay in the range of subjects and different forms of pressure and support for secondary teachers. Identifying a 'typical' day or week was problematic given the range of conventions and working practices in different subject disciplines.

The survey instrument consisted of six sections. The first gathered demographic information about teachers (gender, age, years of teaching, responsibility, position, subject specialism and type of school). The second explored the amount of time teachers spent on timetabled and non-timetabled work and the nature of that work. Section Three asked about the amount of support teachers received in the class and who provided it and how much opportunity teachers have to work with colleagues through peer observation, mentoring and formal appraisal. Section Four explored curriculum coverage and opportunities for cross-curricular activities. Section Five probed the amount of time in a week on record-keeping, assessing pupils' work, formally testing pupils in class and in lead up to statutory external examinations. Section Six sought teachers' opinions on eight educational initiatives, on the positive or negative impact they have had on their own working conditions and how they thought they had impacted on pupils' educational experience and opportunities. The final page of the questionnaire provided space for open-ended comments.

For interviewing purposes we followed up on the data from the survey, asking teachers about their working day, about work done in evenings and weekends, and about how various **National Initiatives** and **Workload Agreements** were impacting their professional and personal lives. In interviews lasting around an hour each, we asked about matters such as job satisfaction, future career intentions and the effects of current government policies on their working and personal lives. We were also interested in pupils' perspectives and their understanding of what was involved in 'being a teacher'. We also took the opportunity to ask about their daily experiences as pupils and whether they thought that their school differed from others in any way.

What follows uses survey data illuminated by 216 surveys, nearly 50 hours of taped interviews involving some 40 teachers and approximately 60 pupils. Schools represented urban, suburban and rural settings, the smallest having 500 pupils the largest over 1,500.

The findings

While teachers frequently commented on a rise in standards this was seen as bought at a heavy price. The following quotations from respondents reveal in their own colloquial expressions, without editorial 'smoothing', their responses to the policy context within which they were working.

> Exam results have improved dramatically but nonetheless we are squashing them through and we are more and more successful and we look carefully at lessons to try and share good practice but we ask ourselves why? Why are doing this? Do these pupils really need to know these things we labour so hard to teach them?
>
> (Head of Humanities, 10 years' experience)

Teachers were quick to acknowledge some of the good ideas within the Government's **National Curriculum** and **Key Stage Strategies** but their enthusiasm was tempered by the reduction of freedom to teach inventively.

> There used to be much more freedom but having come as young member in just those years freedom to teach, opportunities to have that freedom, to make more exciting lessons have been cut and cut and cut as more and more prescription. I just don't feel that the lessons I am planning or the lesson I am planning for other teachers are necessarily the best, not the best for me not the best for the pupils.
>
> (Head of Humanities, 12 years' experience)

The most positive responses tended to come from less experienced teachers who welcomed the strategies that gave them direction and practical guidance and helped them survive in a challenging climate. Headteachers and teachers with longer experience expressed concern that newly qualified teachers had embraced the strategies 'like a security blanket', and found it difficult to conceive of teaching in which they might be required to think for themselves and devise their own strategies. The more experienced teachers, however, were more inclined to look beyond the immediate advantages of having a ready supply of material for lessons to consider the effects on pupils' motivation. Here, the research evidence supports their judgments in that pupils' attitudes towards the core subjects and liking for school has declined since the introduction of the Key Stage Strategies in the first two years of secondary school, Years 7 and 8 (Galton et al. 2003).

Target setting at national level also tended to be viewed negatively as constraining teachers' freedom, increasing pressure and reinforcing a dependency culture. On the other hand, helping pupils to set their own targets and take more responsibility for their own learning was welcomed as the 'upside' of the target setting regime.

> Well, the upside of it is getting the kids themselves to have some vision or ambition about their own learning rather than just meandering along waiting for the teacher to teach. Real target setting, rather than just working to someone else's target is what it's all about.
>
> (Mathematics teacher, 10 years' experience)

Three other interconnected issues also emerged from the survey as initiatives that were broadly positive but with caveats. Initial teacher education and mentoring of newly qualified teachers was seen as an important step forward. But, while generally applauded, these were seen as yet another set of pressures.

> In this school we try and protect young teachers, take the pressure off them, give them a lighter load, offer support where we can, take time out to observe and coach them. In a more ideal world that is precisely what they need, what we need, what the kids need. But in this world of non-stop hassle we don't feel we are doing justice to them or to the scheme. I'm afraid we may have to start turning down students too. It's a time issue. Nothing else.
>
> (Head of Science, 12 years' experience)

Reflection

To what extent do teachers, in your experience, feel constrained by the policy directives within which they carry out their practice? What is the nature of support given to newly qualified teachers in your country and how important is that as an issue?

Factors that inhibit teaching

What do teachers consider to be the most serious obstacles affecting their work? We asked teachers to choose the five issues that they regarded as most seriously inhibiting of their ability to teach well, and to rank these issues in order of seriousness. Limiting teachers to only five options gave us a clear priority order but did not imply that other factors with lower rankings were not also important. So, in reading Table 10.1 it is important to bear in mind that in the final column entitled 'missing or not in top 5', these responses do not

Table 10.1 Teachers' ranking of obstacles to teaching (n = 216)

	Rank	Missing (or not in top 5 issues)
Poor pupil behaviour	1	175
Lack of time for discussion and reflection	2	104
Large class sizes	3	127
Too many national initiatives	4	114
Overloaded curriculum content in own subject	5	146
Pressure to meet assessment targets	5	135
Poor resources, materials and equipment	7	145
Inclusion	8	156
Lack of parental support	9	156
Inadequate pay	10	173
Preparation for appraisal/inspection	11	174
Poorly maintained buildings	12	200
Prescribed methods of teaching	13	198
Limited professional opportunities	14	198
Insufficient pastoral support	15	210

indicate a lack of concern for those issues but rather that they were of lesser priority than the headline items.

In one way or another the leading issues are reflections of government policy – an interrelated combination of too many national initiatives, overloaded curriculum, assessment targets, inhibited by large class sizes and inadequate resources, of which poor pupil behaviour is a related outcome.

Examining these perceived obstacles whether by role and status of staff, or by years of experience produced similar findings. Teachers with 25 years plus experience, in common with teachers of less than five years experience, each ranked poor pupil behaviour as the most serious obstacle to teaching.

Coping with pupil behaviour

Most of the teachers interviewed mentioned classroom disruption as their biggest problem. It was, as one teacher claimed, echoing views of her colleagues:

[A] constant battle just to be allowed to teach.

(Science AST, 15 years' experience)

However much time was invested in planning there was always the possibility of the unforeseen, and often trivial, incident or irritant that could sabotage a lesson. Typical was this response from one interviewee when asked the least satisfactory aspect of her job:

> It's the abuse you get really. I don't think anyone else, like when you're with friends and no one else would go to work in an office and be told to f... off and be expected to put up with it. It's what really drags you down. But I do like working in this school. The pupils can be funny and challenging at times and I do enjoy that but at the same time the other: it's disheartening sometimes.
>
> (Head of History, 4 years' experience)

Most of the teachers we spoke to received an additional allocation of two or three extra free periods but the non-teaching time allocated for subject matters such as planning, preparation and marking was now mainly being used to deal with disciplinary matters and subject relevant activity had to be dealt with outside school hours. Dealing with the underlying causes of indiscipline rather than the immediate symptoms takes time. Problems are often deeply rooted and not amenable to a quick fix. But time is the commodity most lacking. Because teachers are under so much pressure, issues are left unresolved and problems then resurface in other places. Teachers' frustrations arose from the growth in the number of such incidents, preventing them from fulfilling their main role as a subject specialist, and from the increased administrative burden that such incidents imposed.

Behaviour: a matter of context

Poor pupil behaviour, ranked as the number one issue does not, as we have seen, exist in a vacuum. It is not to be remedied by being tougher, by better counselling, by new packages or magic potions. What was plainly evident from our fieldwork in schools was the intrinsic relationship of behaviour to class size, inappropriate curriculum, pressure to meet targets and having to keep up with initiatives, with a consequent lack of time for professional sharing and reflection.

Where there were opportunities for professional development they often failed to address the issues most important to teachers or to provide the kind of accompanying support that would allow initiatives to take root. The 'unpredictable factor' of pupil behaviour and lack of time for planning militated against the most rational planning. A Year 11, sixteen-year-old pupil commented:

> Teachers' attitudes are changing because nothing seems to stay the same for long. It's like there's a lot less time for you because there's lots of changes in one term

or half term, new teachers and teachers leaving, so that causes its own problems, discipline problems and learning because it is your relationship with the teacher that matters and you have to start building that all over again.

(Female student, Year 11)

Another pupil pointed out the ramifications of teachers' need to keep on top of things, and strictness generating a blanket approach which ended in overreaction and unfair treatment.

If they've got a really disruptive pupil they have to be really stern to just to keep one bad behaving pupil in line but not all pupils need that level of stern and then they suffer and they sometimes get it and get treated as if they're the problem pupil.

(Female student, Year 10)

Inclusion

Although ranked in eighth place **inclusion** was closely related to the first seven items. Young people with complex learning needs often expressed themselves in highly disruptive behaviour, which had a ripple effect through the rest of the class and gave licence to others to make mischief. For teachers the problem was to discriminate between 'bad' behaviour and behaviour that was integral to a medical, physiological or psychological condition. Teachers professed an inability to respond adequately to challenging behaviour without the requisite resources, expertise and class size.

We also found a systemic relationship with neighbouring schools' selective policies, parental choice and performance tables. Schools willing to take those rejected elsewhere ended up with a critical imbalance in their intake and then paid the price for what they saw as an ethical decision to accept 'unwanted' children. This had the knock-on effect of lowering the school's overall attainment scores, discouraging some parents from sending their children to that school and so creating a vicious circle or lowering morale. Constant disciplinary intervention, lack of appropriate resourcing and support, pressure on targets together with the overloaded curriculum, all conspired against achieving a genuinely inclusive approach

Lack of parental support

Although ranked ninth in order of priority, parental support was widely seen during interviews as a matter of concern. It was most acutely felt in relation to pupil attitudes and behaviour. Parents were, it was felt, more likely to take umbrage, to support the pupil's version of events rather than side with the teachers, as would have been more common in the past. The nuclear and extended family were fast becoming a historical relic. Children and young people, it was said, were growing up in a new and challenging world, often bewildering to their teachers but it was they 'who bear the brunt', 'who are at the sharp end' – two of the metaphors among many which describe the impact 'in here' of the society 'out there'.

> Parents do come in upset, angry, expressing a sense of injustice. If you take the time to listen, to be calm and hear them out they eventually confess that they are struggling with discipline. Their children are out of control. Their partners have left. They can't pay the bills. They are fragile, volatile.
>
> (English teacher, 10 years' experience)

It's a matter of time

Poor pupil behaviour tended not to be framed by school staff in terms of 'bad' pupils or inadequate teaching but in terms of a set of systemic factors, the most serious of which was lack of time – lack of time to plan adequately, to tailor work, to follow up on behavioural issues, to find appropriate support to deal with learning and behavioural difficulties, or deal with students on an individual basis. We were able to gain a deeper and more rounded understanding of this by asking teachers to take us through a typical school day.

For teachers the school day comprising timetabled and non-timetabled work was, on average, of 6 hours and 48 minutes duration. This represented the period from when school officially started to when it officially finished. On the face of it this is a reasonable working day and comparable with teaching days 10 or 20 years ago. These figures do, however, conceal more than they reveal. The story to be told has three key elements all of which return us to the issue of time.

- The teachers' extended day and extended week.
- The changing nature and quality of the teachers' work.
- The impact of these changes on the professional and personal lives of teachers and on their pupils.

The 'day' began for teachers before school started and ended beyond the time pupils left. The day might begin with briefings, planning and preparation, breakfast clubs or *ad hoc* meetings. It then extended beyond school hours encompassing a wide rage of activities – meeting with pupils, counselling, preparation, marking, meetings, extra-curricular activities, study support, professional development activities.

The first hour in the morning was not a time for quiet preparation and planning. It was described as 'tense' because of unpredictable and unforeseeable crises:

> The first hour is very tense. It's very filled. And then we find out there's staff not in so we have to cover register and sometimes, if it's Monday there's an assembly to do. If I'm not doing that I'm seeing miscreants or I might even be doing good things (laughs) like handing out good conduct certificates.
>
> (Head of Upper School, 32 years' experience)

On average, each week, teachers reported spending 2.5 hours before the official start of school and nearly 5 hours a week after school. This added 7.5 hours to the 35-hour working week, to which may be added a further 10 hours per week (again as an average figure) devoted to school work at home in evenings and weekends. On average the working week then becomes 52.5 hours. A recent study in England (Futurelab: teachers as innovators, 2007) ranked teachers above doctors in the number of hours worked in a typical week.

Teaching, learning and an overloaded curriculum

The overloaded curriculum ranked fifth in order of priority among obstacles to teaching. It reflects a view that there is too much content to be 'covered', too little time for following up pupils' interest and too driven by targets, tests and other external pressures. How teachers teach was, until a decade or so ago, left mainly to the discretion of the individual teacher. Although some of that discretion remains, teaching methods have increasingly been the subject of government policy and intervention. The three, four and five part lesson is now more commonplace and a focus of inspection. The picture we get of teaching in 2004 shows only around a quarter of classroom time given to teacher whole-class talk without about 60 per cent of the lesson spent in group or individual work. Teachers were asked to estimate the amount of time given to the following five categories:

- Talking to the class as a whole.
- Pupils working together cooperatively in groups or pairs, on work given by the teacher.
- Pupils working individually, at their own pace, on work given by the teacher.
- Pupils working on topics of their own choice.
- Other; please specify.

The distribution of mean times for teaching at Key Stage 3 (13–14 year-olds) is shown in Figure 10.1.

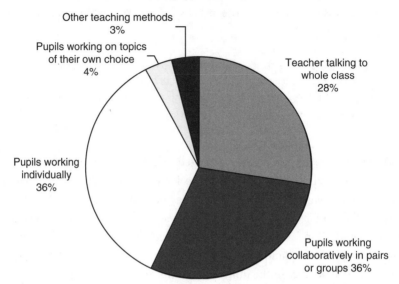

Figure 10.1 Teaching approaches at Key Stage 3 (Year 8 of secondary school).

The approaches illustrated in Figure 10.1 inevitably conceal wide variations in teaching approaches among teachers, even within the same subject area, although we may be noticing a trend for greater convergence as government strategies become increasingly prescriptive. The 'other' category produced a list of 30 approaches including the following:

- Aural Work
- Class discussion/question/answer sessions/speaking and listening activities
- Games
- Thinking skills routines
- Independent research (out of the class)
- Independent thinking, through starter activities
- Long term project research
- One-to-one work with pupils on a rota
- Pupils listening to tapes
- Pupils presenting ideas to the class
- Pupils teaching class
- Role play, investigative/problem-solving, exam technique
- Teamwork
- Video and audio presentations by the teacher
- Whole-class interactive whiteboard

Cross-curricular activities appeared to be relatively rare. This is indicated by the very low response to this question – numbers of respondents in the high-twenties and thirties out of a possible 216. Of those who did answer this question the majority replied 'none'.

Examples of cross-curricular activity that were cited did, nonetheless, illustrate some of the potential scope of this work. 82 examples were given, including cross-curricular themes such as numeracy, literacy, data handling and citizenship. There were examples of integration with the timetable being suspended for activity weeks, a 'One World Week', one-off days such as a 'Flexi Friday', a 'Zulu Day' integrating Music/Art/Dance and Y6 to 7 transition schemes integrating English, Maths, Science and ICT, in addition to mainstream initiatives such vocational education, work experience and Careers Days.

Reflection

We may view teachers personal and professional lives as caught in a force field of factors, incentives and disincentives, pushing and pulling in opposite directions. What are the things, in your experience, most likely to make teachers stay or leave the profession?

A sense of satisfaction in teaching?

Interviewees were unanimous as to what it was that gave them greatest satisfaction. In their different ways, everyone said it was the pupils on a good day:

> The buzz you get when that little light goes on and it could be an understanding or it could be a piece of work that you think twice, 'Wow!' I think the biggest buzz I get is the learning.
>
> (AST English Teacher, 23 years' experience)

These positive feelings had to be set against certain disadvantages such as excessive paperwork and the feeling that attitudes in society have changed in ways that make the job of teaching more difficult. Essentially, it was the pupils on a bad day, coupled with the excessive paperwork and lack of time '*to finish anything properly*', that constituted the less attractive side of the job. Positive feelings were also undermined, to some extent, by the fact that few of those interviewed felt that the general public appreciated their work.

> I don't broadcast it (that I'm a teacher). I think the status of teaching has dropped. They see us as 9 to 4s who get lovely, long holidays. 'Oh! You're on holiday again

> Jim.' My neighbour says and I reply, 'Yeah! Yeah! I can't help it you know but I will go into work if you like – only there's nobody there.' That kind of attitude is still there. It's an undervalued profession, both in remuneration and the way other people think about it.
>
> (Mathematics teacher, 33 years' experience)

Observing and being observed

Classroom teaching is now more transparent than it has ever been. Gone are the days when teachers closed their doors and no one but their pupils ever saw them teaching. Resentment from teachers came not because they wished to maintain the secret garden of their practice but because of the intrusive nature of monitoring, not only from Ofsted (the inspection régime) but the internal monitoring of performance management.

> We are also much more observed and kept an eye on by senior staff and we in turn have to keep an eye on other people. Ever since Ofsted we are doing much more monitoring.
>
> (Curriculum manager, 10 years' experience)

This comment from a curriculum manager in one school describes a climate in which what teachers do has become much more open to scrutiny. But how much and how often are teachers typically observed? Answers to this question suggest on average 3 to 4 hours per term for different kinds of observation. This is no more than a rough estimate, hiding a considerable differential and including observation of quite different kinds – collegial or peer-observation, mentoring and formal appraisal. Teachers reported overall about 1.5 hours of formal appraisal per term, a similar amount for peer-observation and about 1.2 hours a term of mentoring. Even though senior management claimed they attempted to build positive elements into the appraisal process they found it difficult to overcome the negative feelings of self-worth that the competitive nature of the present system generates among teachers. A feeling of inadequacy can translate into a lowering of morale.

Support for teaching

In what was generally described as an oppressive climate, teachers frequently mentioned a need for support. 'Support' is, however, a broad and ambiguous notion. While most teachers clearly welcomed support they were discriminating about what form it might take. Many talked about the desirability of 'an extra pair of hands' but when asked how they would use an extra member of

Table 10.2 Teachers citing the need for various forms of support (n = 215)

	No. of teachers	%
Help with assessment and recording	35	15.8
Teach small groups more intensively	118	53.4
Give you non-contact time for preparation	37	16.7
Free you to work alongside colleagues in class	16	7.2
Other	15	6.8

Table 10.3 Non-teaching support available (Senior management excluded) (n = 203)

Type of support	No. of teachers	% of teachers
Reprographic support	176	86.7
Technician support	88	43.3
Librarian support	144	70.9
Secretarial support	147	72.4
Data inputting	69	34.0
Media resources	48	23.6

staff they overwhelmingly opted for more intensive help with small groups. The distribution of answers to this last question is shown in Table 10.2.

Among other forms of support seen as desirable teachers cited:

- Assistance with lower ability groups
- Behavioural support
- Time to plan together with other staff
- Support with special needs and/or able and talented
- Planning courses
- Assistance with ICT usage in class
- Help in developing new teaching materials
- Help in preparing resources and organizing fieldwork
- Smaller classes
- Varying approaches and working with different learning styles

What teachers did get by way of support was rarely another qualified teacher, or an expert in special needs, for example, but help from teaching assistants (unqualified) or qualified technicians. Table 10.3 shows the nature of support available to teachers. While 'secretarial support' suggests a very high figure, this tended to refer to the office staff of half-a-dozen at most serving the whole school.

Other forms of support cited were:

- Chasing pupils about attendance or coursework
- Help with registers and attendance
- Report writing
- Covering classes to allow teachers to deal with pastoral issues
- Help with marking

Collegial and moral support

To discuss support simply in terms of technical or classroom assistance is, however, to miss the essential point. Support in its most profound sense refers to what teachers need emotionally, physically and intellectually to do the job and to gain the satisfaction and fulfilment that teaching can inspire. This is the kind of support for which the need is most acutely felt by newly qualified and less experienced teachers in their first years of practice. The need to be seen as strong, to keep on top of things, to convey an image of competence and control means a reluctance to admit to problems and ask for help. Teachers with long experience were no less likely than newly-qualified staff to talk about need for support in order to cope with the range of tasks they were expected to undertake in a climate of greater pressure, deteriorating pupil behaviour and constant teacher turnover. In one case study school there was a turnover of 24 staff in the year, rendering the existing support structure unsustainable.

Three comments written by teachers on their questionnaire forms have a poignant resonance and tell their own story of the effects of perceptions of a thankless task, overworked and undervalued.

> I have lived/taught through a period where we were respected as professionals and if asked we would do whatever was requested. Now heavy accountability has replaced this. I have excellent examination results, the pupils love my lessons and write to me after leaving describing what they ended up doing and thank me but I now hate the job and am considering leaving for a career in entomology.
>
> (Science teacher, 21 years' experience)

> I would be happy to give up teaching. It is dominating my term time, non-school time. I achieve less in a classroom because the system is placing a stronghold on all available time. By a teacher marked 'Excellent' in 2 recent Ofsted inspections.
>
> (Economics teacher, 16 years' experience)

I'm leaving the profession I love because I want my life back. It will break my heart to leave those kids but my family miss me!

(Science KS3 Coordinator, 7 years' experience)

Reflection

We may view teachers personal and professional lives as caught in a force field of factors, incentives and disincentives, pushing and pulling in opposite directions. What are the things, in your experience, most likely to make teachers stay or leave the profession?

What have we learned?

This study was set in England at a particular time and place and in the context of a particular set of policies. Many of these findings are, therefore, peculiar to that context. However, in a global context, we have found strong resonances with these findings in Asia-Pacific countries (cf. MacBeath 2006a) as well as in Australia and in North America (Thomson et al. 2003). Teachers in almost all developed countries are under pressure to deal with a growing set of demands that emanate not simply from policy-makers but from a changing society and a changing world. In Japan, Shimahara (2003, p. 3) characterizes schools as experiencing 'the troubled relationship between the children who are the main actors in the educational process and the system itself' and describes intensification as a 'loss of autonomy, caused by prescribed programs, mandated curricula, step-by-step methods of instruction combined with pressure to respond to various innovations and diversification of students' academic and social needs'. However, those common global forces play out differently in different cultural contexts. In Japan, intensification is seen as coming from within, as teachers adhere to the collectively defined ethos of teaching, accepting what is termed *shukumei,* an acceptance of your lot, a situation not to be challenged.

In these circumstances and with an understanding of the cultural embeddedness of thinking and practice, what are the lessons for teachers and those who lead them?

The first and most powerful counsel is for teachers to recognize their own responsibility and their own 'agency'. Blaming others diminishes their authority, while internalizing blame is even more destructive. Compliance to something which runs counter to one's deepest educational values is unethical. Education is a subversive activity (Postman and Weingartner 1971) because it is committed to values which often run counter to mainstream society and sometimes to current government policy. It is 'educational' because it challenges common sense or 'conventional wisdom', which, in its original meaning carried the implication of 'convenient truth' rather than a primary goal of education as revealing truth to be inconvenient and disturbing. Teachers are, above all, models for their pupils, and if they wish to cultivate critical thinking and risk-taking in their pupils they have to lead by inspiration and example. This is not a lonely individual activity but a collective responsibility in which teachers collaborate to achieve a common purpose and a united stand for what is good and good for their pupils. That is why strong leading edge schools in England, and elsewhere in the world, are characterized by a confident moral centre nurtured by critical inquiry, self-evaluation, collaborative planning, peer observation and by moral leadership (Starrat 1998; MacBeath 2006b).

From time to time, under the weight of government policies, we need to be reminded about the purposes and process of education, respect for the professionalism of teachers, and collaborative inquiry – which is the oxygen of professional development. Only then is there time to do a good job, to learn with and from colleagues and strengthen the community of practice. It means framing and reframing the nature of learning and teaching in ways so that young people can genuinely engage with what is worthwhile. The best teachers, the best leaders and the best schools in our study believed that together, with a sense of agency and common purpose, they could resist pressure to simply conform and could, in concert, change things for the better.

Further reading

Labaree D. F. (1997). *How to Succeed in School Without Really Learning: The Credentials Race in American Education*. New Haven: Yale University Press.

Lieberman, A. and Miller, L. (2004). *Teacher Leadership*. San Francisco: John Wiley.

MacBeath, J., Gray, J., Cullen, J., Frost, D., Steward, S. and Swaffield, S. (2006). *Schools on the Edge: Responding to Challenging Circumstances*. London: Sage.

Stoll, L., Earle, L. and Fink, D. (2004). *It's About Learning: What's in it for Schools?* London: Routledge.

References

Castells, M. (2000). *End of Millennium*. Oxford: Blackwell.

Futurelab. (2007). *Teachers as Innovators.* Retrieved 5 February 2007, from www.futurelab.org.uk/teachersasinnovators.

Galton, M. (1987). Change and continuity in the primary school: the research evidence. *Oxford Review of Education*, 13(1), 81–93.

Galton, M., Gray, J. and Rudduck, J. (2003). *Transfer and Transitions in the Middle Years of Schooling (7–14): Continuities and Discontinuities in Learning.* Research Report RR 443. Nottingham: Department for Education and Skills.

Galton, M. and MacBeath, J. with Steward, S. and Page, C. (2003). *A Life in Teaching?* London: University of Cambridge, National Union of Teachers.

Ingersoll, R. M. (2003). Is there really a teacher shortage? Center of the Study of Teaching and Policy, University of Washington, Seattle. Retrieved 3 July 2005 from www.ied.edu.hk/principal conference

Johnson, S. M. (2004). *Finders and Keepers: Helping New Teachers Survive and Thrive in our Schools.* San Francisco: Jossey-Bass.

MacBeath, J. (2006a). *Leadership as a Subversive Activity.* ACEL Monograph 39, Australian Council for Educational Leaders, Winmalee, New South Wales.

MacBeath, J. (2006b). New relationships for old: inspection and self evaluation in England and Hong Kong. *International Studies in Educational Administration*, 34(2), 2–18.

MacBeath, J. and Galton, M. (2005). *A Life in Secondary Teaching?* London: University of Cambridge, National Union of Teachers.

MacBeath, J. and Galton, M. with Steward, S., MacBeath, A. and Page, C. (2006). *The Costs of Inclusion.* London: University of Cambridge, National Union of Teachers.

McLuhan, M. and Powers, P. (1988). *The Global Village: Transformations in World Life and Media in the 21st century.* Oxford: Oxford University Press.

Normore, A. H. (2004). Recruitment and selection: meeting the leadership shortage in one large Canadian school district. *Canadian Journal of Educational Administration and Policy*, 30: 2–16.

Postman, N. and Weingartner, G. (1971). *Teaching as a Subversive Activity.* Harmondsworth: Penguin Books.

Shimahara, N. (2003). *Teaching in Japan: A Cultural Perspective.* New York: Routledge.

Starratt, R. J. (1998). Grounding moral educational leadership in the morality of teaching and learning. *Leading and Managing*, 4 (4), 243–55.

Thomson, P., Blackmore, J., Sachs, J. and Tregenza, K. (2003). High stakes principalship – sleepless nights, heart attacks and sudden death accountabilities: reading media representations of the United States principal shortage. *Australian Journal of Education*, 47(2), 118–32.

Wilhelm, K., Dewhurst-Savellis, J. and Parker, G. (2000). *Teacher Stress? An Analysis of Why Teachers Leave and Why They Stay.* School of Psychiatry, University of New South Wales, Sydney, NSW, Australia.

Glossary

Cultural intelligence (CQ): A term first coined by Christopher Earley and Elaine Mosakowski in 2004 to describe a dimension additional to intelligence quotient (IQ) and emotional quotient (EQ), a measurement of which describes the extent to which an individual is able to function effectively across social and cultural settings.

Department for Education and Employment (DfEE): See DfES.

Department for Education and Skills (DfES): Government department overseeing educational provision in England at the time of writing. It has been through various transformations in recent decades and also appears in the text under a previous name – Department for Education and Employment (DfEE). Now relabelled Department for Children, Schools and Families (DCSF).

Differentiated instruction: An approach to teaching in which teachers modify curricula, teaching methods, resources, learning activities and student products to address the diverse needs of individual students and to maximize the learning opportunities for each student – so defined by its guru Carol Ann Tomlinson.

General Certificate of Education (GCE): Examination offered in a wide range of subjects taken by students aged about 18 years who stay at school beyond the statutory school leaving age of 16 years; these 'advanced level' examinations are used to determine entry to university.

General Certificate of Secondary Education (GCSE): Examination offered in a wide range of subjects and taken by almost all school students at age 16 years (sometimes earlier for able students). Schools are expected to ensure that students gain passes in at least five subjects (including mathematics and English) within the grade range A* to C, where A* is an enhanced A grade.

Inclusion: A term used to describe government policy which brings children with special needs into mainstream classrooms to be taught beside their same age peers. It does not necessarily bring with it any further resources, support or professional expertise.

Individualized education: A general term for all educational methods focusing on the individual student's needs and aptitudes; see *personalized learning, differentiated instruction.*

Key Stages and Key Stage Strategies: In England primary and secondary education are distinguished by Key Stages (abbreviated as KS 1–5), at the ages of 7, 11, 14, 16 and 18. The Key Stage Strategies are government interventions to guide curriculum and assessment at, and in between, these landmarks in pupils' progress.

League tables: Examination results from SATs, GCE and GCSE exams (*quo vide*) for each school are required to be published; these published results are formed into comparative tables of school performance nationally and locally.

Local Education Authorities (LEAs): The more than 100 councils in the United Kingdom who are charged with the task of delivering education services to local communities.

The National Curriculum: A framework used by all maintained schools to ensure that teaching and learning is balanced and consistent. It sets out the subjects taught; the knowledge, skills and understanding required in each subject standards; or attainment targets in each subject that teachers can use to measure pupils' progress and plan their future learning.

National Initiatives: A term used for a diverse number of programmes by government covering the whole range of a school's operations.

National Standards for Qualified Teacher Status (QTS): Minimum standards for QTS laid down by the UK government agency in charge of training (see TTA).

National Vocational Qualifications (NVQs): A range of examinations designed to provide tests of skills in the vocational, as opposed to the academic, areas.

Personalized learning: A method aimed at nurturing the unique talent of each student and respecting his or her autonomy – backed by the UK government as part of its educational policy.

Plowden Report: Issued in 1967, this was a seminal government-sponsored report into primary education which has an enormous influence on the philosophy of education across the age spectrum; the panel that produced it was chaired by Lady Bridget Plowden.

Public Private Funding Initiative (PPI): A scheme devised by the New Labour government in the United Kingdom whereby private commercial companies finance the building of new schools in return for access to some government monies and the right to run the services to the schools at a discretionary cost for a period of time; the scheme has been fiercely criticized for transferring money from the public to the private purse.

Self-concept: One's beliefs and feelings about, or relating to, one's self.

Self-confidence: One's belief in one's capacity to succeed at a given task.

Self-esteem: One's level of satisfaction with the global ratio of one's achievements to aspirations.

Self-respect: The extent to which one follows a moral code and is disposed to avoid behaving in a manner unworthy of oneself.

Standard Attainment Tests (SATs): Compulsory tests set to school students at ages 7, 11 and 14 from which the DfES (see above) draws national statistics.

Target setting: It occurs at a number of levels within the system. The government sets targets for schools as measured by tests of pupils' achievement in each National Curriculum subject. Schools are expected to set their own targets and involve pupils themselves in the process of individual target setting.

Teacher Training Agency (TTA): Government agency charged with responsibility for training UK teachers.

Workload Agreements: In Easter 2001, the government agreed to an independent assessment of how many hours teachers worked to be conducted by independent management consultants, prompted by industrial action from the two main teachers' unions. The government promised to recruit 10,000 more teachers and 50,000 more support staff.

Author index

[Where sources have been jointly authored only the first author has been included in the index]

Subject index